Ultra Versus U-Boats

Ultra Versus U-Boats

Enigma Decrypts
in the National Archives

Roy Conyers Nesbit

Foreword by John Cruickshank VC

Pen & Sword
MILITARY

First published in Great Britain in 2008 by
Pen & Sword Military
An imprint of Pen & Sword Books Ltd
47 Church Street
Barnsley
South Yorkshire
S70 2AS

ISBN 978 1 84415 786 0

Typeset in 10pt Palatino by Mac Style, Beverley, East Yorkshire
Printed and bound in the UK
By CPI

Pen & Sword Books Ltd incorporates the Imprints of Pen & Sword Aviation, Pen &
Sword Maritime, Pen & Sword Military, Wharncliffe Local History, Pen & Sword Select,
Pen & Sword Military Classics, Leo Cooper, Remember When, Seaforth Publishing and
Frontline Publishing

For a complete list of Pen & Sword titles please contact
PEN & SWORD BOOKS LIMITED
47 Church Street, Barnsley, South Yorkshire, S70 2AS, England
E-mail: enquiries@pen-and-sword.co.uk
Website: www.pen-and-sword.co.uk

Contents

Foreword

By John A. Cruickshank VC

Those of us who flew in Coastal Command or its overseas equivalents during the Second World War had no knowledge of the decryption of enemy signals achieved by experts at the Government Code and Cipher School at Bletchley Park. Even after the war, this process remained secret for many years, although the equipment developed led to the introduction of the modern computer.

Aircrew who flew in maritime aircraft assumed that our intelligence officers must have gained knowledge of U-boat locations and movements via secret agents operating in enemy territory or from prisoners of war. Pre-flight briefing required aircrews in operational aircraft to hunt over certain areas of the sea, in order to locate U-boats either visually or with our 'Air to Surface Vessel' radar, and if possible to attack them.

These operational flights were long and often fruitless, with only occasional bursts of intense action, but the interceptions and attacks became far more frequent from 1943 onwards. We now know that the Ultra decryption of Enigma signals was one of the main aids in the eventual destruction of the U-boat Arm of the Kriegsmarine.

The author of this book was given special access to the National Archives (formerly the Public Record Office), which holds the original teleprinted translations of intercepted German U-boat communications. He has worked through over 100,000 decrypts and selected almost 200 examples. These have been captioned and arranged chronologically to represent the war against U-boats. He has also picked out about 200 photographs to illustrate this vital aspect of the war at sea. This is the first time that such a combination has been made available to air and naval historians as well as to the general public.

Preface

Work on this book began several years ago, during a period when I was invited by the Public Record Office (as the National Archives was then named) to help promote the unique collection of photographs available in its Image Library. This holds a huge number of images from the past, such as maps and plans, advertisements, designs, posters, prison records, state papers, and photographs which include both world wars. My specialism concerned the RAF in the Second World War, and I wrote several illustrated books based on the numerous photographs available and occasionally gave illustrated talks to the public in the lecture hall.

Towards the end of this period, Paul Johnson of the Image Library pointed out that Ultra decrypts of German Naval Signals relating to U-boats, which had been released to the PRO from 1977 onwards, had received little publicity. There are thousands of these in fifty-four files, and I gradually worked through all of them, and eventually selected about 200 to represent the huge collection. These examples were captioned after carrying out much further research, although it must be said that some details are uncertain, since the precise evidence was taken to the bottom of the sea. About 200 photographs were added, partly from my own collection.

The decrypts in each file are arranged in chronological order, according to the German dates of origin. They were decoded by cryptanalysts at the Government Code and Cipher School at Bletchley Park in Buckinghamshire, translated into English and then passed to the Operational Intelligence Centre of the Admiralty. The signals sent back to base by the U-boats often gave their grid positions, thus enabling the Allies to instruct their escort vessels and air forces to concentrate on hunting in the correct locations.

The signals usually gave the number of the U-boat but sometimes only the name of the commander, so that the present-day researcher needs to establish that U-boat number from published books of reference. There is no separate index of either U-boats or commanders in the files, so anyone researching a particular boat might face quite a lengthy hunt.

The German war machine's U-boat Arm was regarded by the Allies as a major menace and the destruction of one was always greeted with grim satisfaction. Nevertheless, in retrospect it is clear that the German crews displayed exceptional courage and fortitude. A single war cruise usually lasted about two months without respite, or sometimes even longer. During that period the men were cooped up in foul and damp conditions, eating tinned food, with little chance of breathing fresh air on deck, and with the ever-present prospect of a terrifying death. Their casualty rate was appalling, steadily increasing as the war progressed. It is estimated that 28,000 of the 37,000 men who served in U-boats were killed, a proportion of over 75 per cent. In addition, about 5,000 were taken prisoner.

The decryption of enemy signals proved a major factor in the defeat of the U-boats, the others being the increased naval and air strength of the Allies, together with ingenious tracking devices, plus the skill and courage of servicemen. The scientists and specialists at Bletchley Park who created the 'Colossus' machine which achieved this miraculous result were technically in advance of their time. German cryptanalysts were incredulous when the information was disclosed many years later. The method was considered so secret that after the war Winston Churchill ordered all ten of these machines to be destroyed. However, one has now been rebuilt and is on display to the public at Bletchley Park.

Acknowledgements

I am extremely grateful to Paul Johnson and Hugh Alexander of the Image Library, the National Archives, for initiating this book and providing facilities for the lengthy research required, as well as help and advice during its progress. Two ex-RAF friends from wartime days have provided further help by checking the manuscript and captions, and also making suggestions for improvement; they are Sqn Ldr Dudley Cowderoy and Warr Off Jack Eggleston. More help was provided by others with specialist knowledge. They are Mrs Maureen Annetts of the Commonwealth War Graves Commission; J. Sebastian Cox of the Air Historical Branch (RAF); Chris Davies of the Oscar Parkes Society: Fregattenkapitän a.D. Günther Heinrich in Germany; Flt Lt A.H. Hilliard; Wg Cdr Mike D. Mockford OBE of the Medmenham Collection; Air Comm Graham L. Pitchfork MBE, air historian and author.

Roy C. Nesbit
Swindon, 2008

CHAPTER ONE

Opening Rounds

At the outbreak of the Second World War the Kriegsmarine (German Navy) faced enemies at sea which seemed vastly superior in strength and experience to the vessels and personnel it could muster. These were the combined forces of the British and French Navies. The outlook seemed so gloomy that Grossadmiral Dr Erich Raeder, the Commander-in-Chief of the Kriegsmarine, told Adolf Hitler that all his force could do was to show the world how to 'die with dignity'. This force consisted of the fast battleships *Scharnhorst* and *Gneisenau*, the 'pocket battleships' *Deutschland*, *Admiral Graf Spee* and *Admiral Scheer*, the ancient and obsolete battleships *Schlesien* and *Schleswig-Holstein*, five cruisers and seventeen destroyers. There were also fifty-six U-boats, of which thirty-five were immediately operational; of the total, twenty-five were ocean-going types while the remaining thirty-one had been designed for coastal work, primarily in the Baltic Sea.

In contrast, the Royal Navy alone possessed sixteen battleships, plus five more of the King George V class nearing completion, sixty-one cruisers and ten aircraft carriers. Some of these were outdated, but the Royal Navy stood to be victorious in encounters between heavy warships. If the war could have been deferred for about three years, the Kriegsmarine would have become far more powerful. In May 1935 Hitler had announced that he was deliberately breaching the conditions of the Treaty of Versailles imposed on his country after the First World War. The Luftwaffe was already being re-formed, conscription into the armed forces was being reintroduced, and a vast new programme for rebuilding the Kriegsmarine was under way. There were to be six new battleships, two or three new aircraft carriers, eighteen new cruisers, about thirty new destroyers and about 17,500 tons of new U-boats. All these were intended to be completed by 1942. Hitler had undertaken to restrict this growth so that the ultimate strength of the Kriegsmarine would be no more than 35 per cent of that of the Royal Navy, although of course guarantees from this individual were worthless. The international community was intent on a desire to avoid another ruinous armed conflict and did nothing to impede this programme.

Raeder's words were prophetic, but there would be years of unremitting struggle in a harsh and unforgiving environment before they became a reality. His prognosis underestimated the enormous successes that would be achieved by his small U-boat Arm from the early months of the war and the dismay, coupled with fury, which it would cause in Britain.

It was only a few hours after Britain and France declared war on 3 September 1939, in response to Germany's invasion of Poland two days earlier, that the British public received a foretaste of the conflict at sea. The Type VIIA *U-30* under the command of Leutnant Zur See Fritz-Julius Lemp was already out in the Atlantic in preparation for war, about 250 miles north-west of Ireland, when a lookout spotted a large vessel steaming in a westerly direction. At 2100 hours Lemp ordered two torpedoes to be fired. Both hit the vessel, which sank. She was the liner *Athenia* of 13,581 tons, carrying over 1,100 passengers to America, including child evacuees. Of those on board, 112 lives were lost, including 28 Americans.

According to Hague Conferences relating to the humanisation of war, which had taken place between 1899 and 1907, unarmed vessels sailing outside the convoy system were exempt from attack, although they could be stopped and searched. Although this convention was not sanctioned by international law, it was generally accepted in the London Submarine Agreement which Germany had signed on 8 November 1936. Of course, Lemp asserted that his target appeared to be an auxiliary cruiser or a troopship, although it is more likely that he was frustrated since there were no convoys to be found and he was eager for a victory to impress his superiors.

Anxious not to inflame public opinion in America, the German Propaganda Ministry denied that the liner had been sunk by a U-boat; instead it must have been sunk by a mine or a British submarine. But Hitler issued an order to the effect that U-boats must conform with the conditions laid down in the London Submarine Agreement – although this order would soon fall into oblivion.

Of course, a great wave of revulsion swept through the English-speaking world. Henceforth the U-boat was an example of German perfidy and cruelty – a vicious enemy to be crushed without mercy. But neither the Royal Navy nor the Royal Air Force possessed adequate means to do so, for the whole of their country's armed forces had been starved of new resources in the interwar years, partly in the mistaken belief that the First World War had been so terrible that it was truly the 'war to end wars'.

The Royal Navy placed much reliance on the sonar device known as Asdic after the Allied Submarine Detection Committee, which had been developed to locate U-boats at the end of the First World War. This consisted of a transmitter/receiver which sent out impulses in a sound wave ahead of a patrol craft. These produced a distinctive 'ping' when an underwater object was detected and thus enabled an attack with depth charges to take place. Partly because of Asdic's known effectiveness, as late as 1937 the Naval Staff had expressed the opinion that the submarine no longer presented the problems experienced in that earlier war. The main threat was perceived as coming from surface raiders, particularly from the German 'pocket battleships' which could wipe out an entire convoy and its escorts if allowed to operate in the Atlantic. There was certainly much justification for this belief, but the threat from U-boats was being significantly underestimated.

In 1939 the British merchant fleet consisted of about three thousand deep-sea vessels, including tankers, plus about a thousand coasters. These totalled some 21 million tons and the country was dependent on their safety in times of war. The majority of the merchant vessels would be formed into convoys to sail at the speed of the slowest, usually about 7 knots. The Royal Navy possessed about one hundred and fifty destroyers fitted with Asdic as potential escorts but half of them dated back to the First World War. There were also twenty-four sloops and some coastal patrol vessels. Only about half these warships were available as convoy escorts, for the rest had to perform other duties such as screening capital ships and cruisers. By August 1939 fifty-six new escort vessels in the form of corvettes and frigates were being built, but the first of these would not begin entering service until the following May.

The support provided by the RAF to these slow-moving convoys was also extremely limited at the beginning of the war. An attempt on 4 September 1939 by fifteen Bristol Blenheims and fourteen Vickers Wellingtons of Bomber Command to destroy German warships in Wilhelmshaven and Brunsbüttel during daylight ended in failure, in spite of the determination of the crews. Five aircraft from each force failed to find the targets in the overcast weather conditions. Of those which attacked, five Blenheims and two Wellingtons were shot down, and the only result was minor damage to the cruiser *Emden*.

Coastal Command consisted of only nineteen squadrons, of which thirteen were capable of providing some cover to convoys. Ten of these squadrons were equipped with the Avro Anson I, a reliable twin-engined monoplane but with a meagre radius of action of no more than 390 miles. Some of these Anson squadrons were necessarily engaged on other duties, such as reconnaissance over the North Sea in case surface raiders ventured out of their ports. There was justification for these duties, since the pocket battleships *Admiral Graf Spee* and *Deutschland* had slipped out of Wilhelmshaven in late August and taken advantage of foggy conditions to pass unobserved through the North Sea. They had not been detected before reaching the South Atlantic and the North Atlantic respectively.

Three other Coastal Command squadrons were equipped with the modern Short Sunderland I flying boat, with a radius of action of 1,490 miles. But aircraft ranges were severely curtailed by the need to patrol for as long as possible around convoys, so that cover was available only on short stretches during outward or inward bound passages near British ports. When the Royal Navy tried to improve air cover by employing the aircraft carrier HMS *Courageous* on longer stretches of their passages, she was sunk south-west of Ireland on 17 September 1939 by the Type VIIA *U-29* under the command of Leutnant zur See Otto Schuhart. This resulted in the loss of 518 lives as well as the Fairey Swordfish Is of the Fleet Air Arm's 811 and 822 Squadrons which were on board the carrier.

Moreover, none of these air escorts possessed special equipment designed to spot U-boats, while the anti-submarine bombs they carried proved to be almost ineffective since they required a direct hit on a small target. Aerial depth charges were being developed but had not yet come into service. The best that the aircrews could hope to achieve was to spot periscopes cutting through the sea and then to call destroyers into the attack. But the new tactic of the U-boats was to attack convoys only at night and on the surface, when aircraft were not operating. In any event, the U-boat commanders preferred whenever possible to attack the faster vessels, known as 'runners' or 'independents', which did not sail in convoys.

The ocean-going U-boat Arm, consisting of the Types VII and IX, was commanded without restriction by Admiral Karl Dönitz, reporting directly to the Naval Staff. He also commanded the coastal Type II U-boats, but for these he came under the direction of Naval Group West. He was a fervent adherent to the creed of National Socialism but possessed immense drive and enterprise. His Chief of Staff was Fregattenkapitän Eberhardt Godt, a man with an immense capacity for clear-headed and precise organisation. Based at the beginning of the war at Wilhelmshaven, these two men would be largely responsible for causing immense losses to the Allies. The destruction would have been even greater if Dönitz had had his way before the war, for he fumed at the neglect of the ocean-going shipbuilding programme in favour of the concentration on surface warships.

It was normally possible to maintain at sea only a third of these ocean-going U-boats at any one time. But in anticipation of the forthcoming conflict, seventeen of the twenty-five available had sailed during August 1939. These and the others that followed them into the Atlantic achieved initial successes, sinking 420,000 tons of shipping before the end of 1939. About 330,000 tons were sunk by other means, including surface raiders, air attacks and magnetic mines laid by U-boats or dropped from aircraft.

During this period Dönitz intended to begin concentrated 'wolf pack attacks' on convoys, with several U-boats working in unison. This followed experiments which had begun in 1936. The German B-Dienst, or Radio Monitoring Service, was able to decode most of the messages sent by the Royal Navy, which increased the possibility of making interceptions. An early attempt at forming a wolf pack was made in October 1939 but had to be abandoned after three U-boats were sunk on the outward journey and three others were withdrawn with mechanical faults. Another attempt was made in the following month, but four U-boats had to be withdrawn for other duties.

One remarkable achievement took place on 14 October 1939 when Kapitänleutnant Gunther Prien penetrated the major naval base of Scapa Flow with his Type VIIB *U-47* and sank the battleship HMS *Royal Oak* at anchor. This audacious and unexpected move resulted in the loss of 786 men. On the following day Dönitz was appointed the commander of all U-boats. Meanwhile, the Kriegsmarine crushed the small Polish Navy, while the land forces of that country were soon overrun by the Wehrmacht, and all organised resistance ceased at the end of September.

The Kriegsmarine did not escape unscathed during this period. The pocket battleship *Admiral Graf Spee* was damaged by gunfire by the cruisers HMS *Ajax, Exeter* and *Achilles* off the river Plate on 13 December and forced to take refuge in Montevideo; she emerged four days later and was scuttled. Meanwhile her sister-ship *Deutschland* found few targets in the North Atlantic, ran out of her allotted time and returned to Wilhelmshaven at the end of November; she was then renamed *Lützow,* to avoid the national humiliation that would result if a warship bearing the country's name went to the bottom of the sea. Nine ocean-going U-boats were also sunk in the Atlantic before the end of 1939 and many others had to be withdrawn for servicing after their intensive use. But the rebuilding programme had made good these losses and increased the total number to thirty-eight. Morale was at a peak among the crews, consisting mostly of highly motivated sailors who had volunteered for the service and been thoroughly trained before the war.

On the British side, on the first day of war Prime Minister Neville Chamberlain appointed Winston Churchill as First Lord of the Admiralty, a post he had occupied from 1911 to 1915. He brought his usual dynamism and forcefulness to his old role, but senior naval officers and naval historians were unanimous in criticising his first proposal for combating U-boats. He advocated an independent flotilla which would search the western approaches for these menaces, operating 'like a cavalry division' and destroying them. In fact, the U-boats were almost immune to detection by such a method with the facilities available at the time. The 'independent flotilla' would have simply wasted limited resources and effort.

The true requirements at this early stage were more escort vessels, improved depth charges with the means of delivering them, air cover with longer ranges and electronic 'air to surface vessel (ASV)' equipment, escort carriers with shorter-range aircraft and ASV equipment, and accurate intelligence of enemy movements. The latter could be obtained by two main methods, long-range air reconnaissance and decryption of enemy signals which disclosed the whereabouts of U-boats.

Progress in air reconnaissance over Germany had been made by Sidney Cotton, an entrepreneur who had served as a pilot in the Royal Naval Air Service during the First World War and subsequently specialised in air photography. In September 1938 he had been approached by Alfred J. Miranda Jr of the American Armaments Corporation, who was associated with Squadron Leader Fred W. Winterbotham of RAF Intelligence in the Air Ministry. At the time, the Deuxième Bureau de l'Armée de l'Air was collaborating with MI6 of the British Intelligence Service in developing espionage systems in the western part of Germany. Cotton and Miranda flew to Paris and agreed that a civil aircraft should be used for this air reconnaissance. On their return to Britain they met Winterbotham and decided to use a Lockheed Model 12A, fitted with extra fuel tanks and a French air camera.

Cotton chose Flying Officer Robert H. Niven, a Canadian serving in the RAF, as his co-pilot. Under the cover of a newly formed company named Aeronautical Sales & Research Corporation, they successfully photographed numerous targets in Germany in late March and early April 1939, including Ludwigshafen. This first aircraft was handed over to the French and two more were ordered, one for each country. The British aircraft was fitted with three F24 cameras from the RAF, concealed by sliding panels.

The next trip began with a flight to Malta in June 1939, after which they photographed bases in Sicily, the Italian Dodecanese, Libya and Eritrea. On its return to Britain the Lockheed was equipped with two Leica cameras in the wings and they flew on a 'business trip' to Frankfurt on 28 July. More photographs were taken, including the Siegfried Line on the return flight. Several other flights were made, over Wilhelmshaven, Sylt and the Frisian islands. The final flight in a civilian aircraft was made on 1 September 1939, the day Germany invaded Poland, when Niven flew a single-engined Beech 17 over Wilhelmshaven. All these aerial photographs were interpreted in secrecy by skilled employees of two civilian companies based at Wembley, Aircraft Operating Company and Aerofilms Ltd, with which Cotton was associated.

On 23 September 1939 a new RAF unit named the Heston Flight was formed under Cotton, who was given the rank of Squadron Leader, acting Wing Commander. The only aircraft at the outset were the Lockheed 12A and the Beech, plus two Bristol Blenheim IVs. However, Cotton managed to persuade Air Chief Marshal Sir Hugh Dowding, Commander-in-Chief of Fighter Command, to relinquish some of his precious Supermarine Spitfires. The first two arrived on 30 October. These were stripped of all armament and fitted with extra fuel tanks and F24 cameras, being labelled Spitfire PR1As. More Spitfires followed, and the unit was renamed No. 2 Camouflage Unit on 1 November. This was the nucleus of the famous photo-reconnaissance squadrons that were eventually formed and made a vital contribution to Allied intelligence, including the war at sea. Some of the Spitfires were flown to Seclin in France from 4 November and this detachment was named the Special Survey Flight.

The other essential need was the decryption of enemy signals. All the German armed forces had adopted the Enigma coding machine by the outbreak of the Second World War. The basic machine was not new, for a civilian version had been invented in 1918 by a German electrical engineer, Arthur Scherbius, primarily for security in inter-bank communications. The military Enigma system had been adopted by the Kriegsmarine in 1926 and other branches of the armed forces had followed some years later. The operator could code message quite simply, by typing the message on a keyboard of a machine arranged with the settings of the day. There were three wheels in the original machine used by the Kriegsmarine, one of which rotated each time a key was pressed. This continued until the end of all the letters of the alphabet, when the next wheel began working. The internal arrangements in the machine were such that unauthorised decryption was considered impossible, even if the receiver had possession of an Enigma machine, unless he had access to the relevant code books.

The Germans were quite confident that messages sent on their Enigma machines could not be broken, and they remained so throughout the war and for many years afterwards. The Kriegsmarine was even more careful than other branches of the armed services. Its version was named *Schlüsselmaschine M* (Coding Machine Marine). Several codes were used for different purposes, being given names of mythical gods and goddesses such as Freya, Thetis, Medusa, Hermes, Hydra and Triton. Some messages sent 'For Officer Only' were typed and coded twice. Messages sent or received at sea were printed with soluble ink, so that they would become illegible if divers recovered them after a U-boat was sunk. The U-boats always closed down their wireless rooms when in port and kept them securely locked.

The Kriegsmarine also developed its own wireless system by building powerful transmitting stations, the largest of which could reach anywhere in the world. Signals were repeated at intervals and could be picked up by U-boats, other than in exceptional weather conditions. The operators in U-boats were selected for special hearing aptitude and then carefully trained. Their transmissions were kept to a minimum for security reasons, since enemy listening stations might be able to pinpoint positions. Of course, such transmissions were weaker than those from land, but aerials were fixed to the boats and additional rod aerials could be raised. The whole system was extremely effective and considered to be the most proficient in the world.

The British were well aware of the need to break into the German Enigma coding system. The site chosen for this was the mansion of Bletchley Park in Buckinghamshire, built in the late 1870s and the former residence of Sir Herbert Leon, who had died in 1926. He had enlarged the mansion considerably during his lifetime and it remained the residence of his wife until her death in 1937. The Air Ministry took it over during the following year as the new headquarters of the Government Code and Cipher School (GC and CS) and named

Bletchley Park in Buckinghamshire, which was taken over by the Air Ministry in 1938 as the headquarters of the Government Code and Cipher School, named 'Station X'. The photograph was taken in 2001.
Author's collection

it 'Station X'. Among its advantages were the grounds of about 55 acres and a convenient situation roughly halfway between Oxford and Cambridge, with easy access to London.

The early use of Bletchley Park was simply as a wireless receiving station but by 1939 this was discontinued since the mansion might become a target for German bombers. The GC and CS controlled several other listening stations in the country, operated mainly by the army and known as the 'Y' Service. A number of wooden huts were built in the grounds of Bletchley Park and these became a base for cryptanalysts. These were mainly mathematicians recruited from universities on the outbreak of war. Among them were three brilliant young men, Harry Hinsley, Alan Turing and Gordon Welchman, all from Cambridge University. In 1939 about 200 staff in various categories worked at Station X and all were sworn to absolute secrecy.

Fortunately for the young British mathematicians, they did not have to start with a completely blank sheet. Between 1932 and 1938 a poorly paid cipher clerk in German military service, Hans-Thilo Schmidt, had been improving his financial position by selling copies of secret documents concerning the German Enigma system to the cipher section of the Deuxième Bureau. Copies of these were passed to Polish Intelligence, in accordance

The 'Enigma' coding machine, as used by the German armed forces at the beginning of the Second World War.

Author's collection

with the Franco-Polish Treaty of collaboration, and handed to the mathematician Marian Rejewski, who led a small section of code-breakers consisting of two other mathematicians plus cipher clerks. Using these German documents the Poles were able to build replicas of the military Enigma machine, which was more advanced than the original civilian version. They also recorded wireless messages sent by the Wehrmacht. Before long, Rejewski was able to use the 'group theory' of higher algebra to decode German signals.

This was indeed a magnificent accomplishment, but it was not all. In the year after their rearmament programme of 1935, the Germans changed the wheels in their Enigma machines more often, from quarterly to monthly and then daily. The little Polish Cipher Bureau kept pace with these changes by using perforated sheets passed over each other, to pick out positions where holes corresponded. These were wired up to six Enigma machines so that an electric circuit closed when this happened. The Poles called this system a 'Bomba', and it would be later developed further by Bletchley Park. But in December 1938 the Polish decryption system no longer worked, for the Germans increased the number of wheels available from a choice of three to a choice of five. A far more elaborate 'Bomba' was required to solve this problem and the facilities needed were beyond the resources of the small section.

One outcome of this was that British and French experts were invited to a meeting in Warsaw on 24 July 1939, at a time when great war clouds were gathering ominously. The British party consisted of Commander Alistair G. Denniston and Dillwyn Knox from GC and CS, with Commander Humphrey Sandwich from Naval Interception and Direction-finding. These three men were astonished at the accomplishment of the small section of Polish code-breakers and delighted when they were presented with an Enigma machine and copies of the stolen German documents. These were made available to the young British mathematicians at Bletchley Park, with orders to 'achieve the impossible' by breaking into the latest Enigma coding system.

The winter of 1939/40 was particularly harsh and bitter. British and French armies faced the Wehrmacht, with the British Expeditionary Force on the left covering the Belgian border and the French armies behind their fortified Maginot Line opposite the German

Siegfried Line. There was almost no activity on the ground and the British Press dubbed these circumstances 'The Phoney War'. But these conditions did not apply to the war in the air or at sea, although both side refrained from air attacks on enemy soil which might kill or injure civilians. Air reconnaissance over Germany continued, with No. 2 Camouflage Unit at Heston growing in importance and being renamed the Photographic Development Unit (PDU) on 17 January 1940. The Special Survey Flight in France also grew and was renamed 212 Squadron on 10 February 1940.

At sea, the U-boat Arm continued to operate in the Atlantic, sinking about 111,250 tons of shipping in January, 169,500 tons in February and 62,500 tons in March, for the loss of nine U-boats. It is probable that even more merchant ships would have been sunk had problems not been experienced with the German torpedoes. One of the U-boats sunk was the Type VIIA *U-31* commanded by Kapitänleutnant Johannes Habekost, which was undergoing post-refit trials in daylight off Borkum on 11 March. It was spotted from 4,000 feet by the crew of Blenheim serial P4852 of 82 Squadron, Bomber Command, which was on patrol in the area. The pilot, Squadron Leader Miles V. Delap dropped a salvo of four bombs, which sank the U-boat immediately with the loss of all crew members. This was the first U-boat sunk by the RAF, and the circumstances were unexpected.

The Phoney War ended when the Wehrmacht invaded Denmark and Norway on 9 April 1940, under Operation Weserübung. Danish forces were unable to resist their mighty neighbour and the country had no option but to capitulate. The Norwegians had not mobilised their forces but were intent on resistance and the subsequent campaign resulted in a stiff and bloody fight. One of Hitler's objectives in the occupation of their country was to secure the essential flow of high-grade iron ore from Sweden which supplied about two-thirds of his wartime requirements. The ore from the northern fields was transported by sea from the Norwegian port of Narvik. Hitler assumed, quite correctly, that the British intended to land forces to block this supply route.

The Luftwaffe supplied over 400 fighter and bomber aircraft for the operation, plus over 500 transports which dropped parachutists on Norwegian airfields. Warships of the Kriegsmarine had left port in the evening of 6 April, over two days earlier. These included the battleships *Scharnhorst* and *Gneisenau*, with the cruiser *Admiral Hipper* and an escort of destroyers. They had been spotted by the RAF but air attacks by Bomber Command had ended in failure, partly because of very poor weather conditions and limited visibility. The Kriegsmarine had an additional objective in this operation, for with the occupation of Norway its warships and ocean-going U-boats would be able to use Norwegian ports, thus shortening their voyages into the Atlantic.

The U-boat Arm provided thirty-one boats for the invasion, including six from the Training School. These included eighteen coastal Type IIs, one coastal Type I and eight ocean-going Type VIIs. There were also three of the latest Type IXs, which had even longer ranges than the Type VIIs. The main task for all of them was to intercept the warships and transports of the Royal Navy, for the British had anticipated the invasion and gathered an expeditionary force.

Although the Royal Navy had made preparations by laying mines in Norwegian waters, the first element in the British expeditionary force did not sail until 12 April. This was led

A convoy of twenty-four merchant vessels, mostly colliers, steaming in line in the North Sea during the early days of the war. They were escorted by warships of the Royal Navy, steaming up and down the line while keeping a lookout for U-boats and enemy aircraft.

Author's collection

by the battleship HMS *Valiant*, with nine destroyers escorting three liners which carried the 24th Guards Brigade to land at the small port at Harstad, near Narvik, three days later. These were followed by other contingents which included French Alpine troops, Foreign Legionnaires and Polish troops. The Royal Navy sent more warships, including aircraft carriers, and there were other landings in central Norway.

The main defect was insufficient air cover. The Fleet Air Arm did its best against the superior strength of the Luftwaffe, but all eighteen Gloster Gladiators of RAF Fighter Command's 263 Squadron from the carrier HMS *Glorious*, which landed on 24 April on a frozen lake near Aandalsnes in the central region, were lost to air attack after shooting down several enemy aircraft. By this time it was clear that military operations in the central region would have to be abandoned, but fighting continued in the northern Narvik region, where there was far more hope of success.

On 26 May more Gladiators of 263 Squadron from the carrier HMS *Furious* landed at Bardufoss in the northern region, where they were soon to be joined by Hurricanes of 46 Squadron from the same carrier. Progress was made on the ground and at one stage the Allies seemed to be gaining the upper hand. But catastrophic events in Holland, Belgium and France were affecting the entire conduct of the war and eventually it became obvious that the campaign in Norway could not be sustained without major reinforcements from the RAF. Complete withdrawal from the country became essential and this was begun in early June.

There were heavy losses at sea during the campaign. The small Norwegian Navy was either sunk at sea or captured in harbour. The Kreigsmarine lost the heavy cruiser *Blücher* in Oslofjord to shore batteries on the first day of the German landings, as well as a torpedo boat. The battleship *Gneisenau* was seriously damaged on the same day by the battle-cruiser HMS *Renown*, but managed to outstrip her enthusiastic pursuer in the subsequent chase. The light cruiser *Karlsruhe* was sunk by the submarine HMS *Truant*. Another light cruiser, the *Königsberg*, was sunk by a combination of fire from shore batteries and FAA Skuas flown from the Orkney Islands. Nine German destroyers were sunk in actions with the Royal Navy, or so badly damaged that they had to be scuttled. A German minelayer was sunk by the submarine HMS *Starlet*.

The Royal Navy lost four destroyers, while a French destroyer and a Polish destroyer were also sunk. The cruiser HMS *Effingham* struck rocks in the Narvik area and had to be abandoned and then destroyed. But the worst loss took place during the evacuation on 8 June, when the aircraft carrier HMS *Glorious*, carrying the aircraft and personnel from 46 and 263 Squadrons, was sunk off Narvik by the battleships *Scharnhorst* and *Gneisenau*. Two RN destroyers were sunk in the same action, but not before the *Gneisenau* had been damaged by a torpedo hit.

One of the curiosities of the Norwegian campaign was the failure of the U-boat Arm to achieve a single success. In fact, it lost four boats in the campaign. Two of these were Type IIs, probably as a result of striking mines. One Type VII was sunk by a Swordfish of the FAA and another by depth charges from a destroyer. The defect lay in their main weapon, the torpedo, which failed to explode when striking a target. This was the case with warheads armed with either a contact or a magnetic pistol. For instance, two hits were claimed on the battleship HMS *Warspite,* but there were no results. The failures were so complete that Dönitz ordered the withdrawal of all U-boats on 17 April.

Later tests showed that the torpedo needed to strike a hull at almost a right angle before it would explode. If the angle was acute, it would fail. Thus there had been successes against slow-moving targets such as merchant vessels, but the effectiveness was limited against fast-moving and manoeuvrable warships. In some cases it appeared that the magnetic warhead exploded prematurely as a result of local conditions in the earth's magnetism. There also seemed to be failures with depth-setting mechanisms, for the torpedo dived on occasions and passed underneath the target. This knowledge had a seriously adverse affect on the morale of the U-boat Arm, but the men did not know that the most successful phase of their war at sea was about to begin.

Above: Destroyers of the Royal Navy steaming at full speed on escort duties round the coast of England in the early days of the war.

Author's collection

Opposite Top: The Avro Anson I entered service with Coastal Command in 1936 and equipped ten of its squadrons on the outbreak of the Second World War. By this time it was already obsolescent, with a radius of action of no more than 390 miles, capable of carrying only 330 lb of bombs and armed with a single machine-gun firing forward plus another in a manually operated turret. Nevertheless, the Anson was highly reliable and gave a good account of itself before being replaced by more modern aircraft such as the Lockheed Hudson. It remained in RAF service as a trainer and communications aircraft until June 1968. This photograph shows the prototype, serial K4771, which first flew on 24 March 1935.

Ref: AIR 2/1511

Opposite Bottom: The Lockheed Hudson, built in the USA, first entered service with Coastal Command in May 1939, gradually replacing the Avro Anson and eventually equipping thirteen squadrons. The Mark I could carry a bomb-load of 750 lb and had a maximum radius of action of 1,080 miles. It was armed with up to seven machine-guns. This example, Hudson III serial T9465 of 269 Squadron, was built by employees of Lockheed-Vega in their spare time from material provided by the company and donated to the RAF. It was photographed over Iceland against the background of a glacier and lava slopes.

Ref: AIR 15/470

Bristol Blenheim IVs were introduced into Coastal Command in January 1940 and employed on reconnaissance, anti-shipping attacks and as short-range escorts for convoys or fishing vessels. The aircraft had a crew of three and was armed with a single machine-gun firing forward and another in a power-operated turret. It could carry 1,000 lb of bombs. Some were fitted with four-gun packs under the nose and were known as Blenheim IVFs. This Blenheim IV serial N6212 was one of the first to be built.

Ref: SUPP 9/1

The Short Sunderland flying boat first entered service with Coastal Command in June 1938 for long-range work on general reconnaissance and anti-submarine patrols. This prototype, serial K4774, was photographed while loaded to its all-up weight of 56,000 lb. Heavily armed with four machine-guns on each of the nose and tail turrets, plus two more in beam positions, it became known as the 'Flying Porcupine' by the Luftwaffe. Only two squadrons were equipped with the Sunderland I at the outbreak of the Second World War, while another was partially equipped. More aircraft arrived, including new variants, until sixteen squadrons were equipped. The Sunderland gave excellent service throughout the war and beyond.

Ref: AIR 2/2928

Top: The Type VIIB *U-55* was built by Germaniawerft of Kiel and commissioned on 21 November 1939. It left Kiel on 16 January 1940 for its first war cruise, under the command of Kapitänleutnant Werner Heidel, and sank three merchant vessels. In the early afternoon of 30 January 1940, when about 90 miles south-west of the Scilly Isles, it was spotted on the surface by the crew of Sunderland I serial N9025 of 228 Squadron flown from Pembroke Dock by Flying Officer Edward J. Brooks, which had been called

to the assistance of Convoy OA80G. Brooks attacked with one anti-submarine bomb, which missed narrowly, and then exchanged fire with the U-boat. It was evident that the U-boat was unable to dive, and indeed it had already been depth-charged to the surface by the sloop HMS *Fowey*. The Sunderland flew to the destroyers about 5 miles away, and flashed a signal asking them to follow it. When the destroyer HMS *Whitshed* and the French destroyer *Valmy* approached and opened fire, the U-boat was scuttled. Forty-one of the crew were rescued, but the commander did not survive. This was the first sinking of a U-boat in which Coastal Command participated.

Ref: AIR 15/473

Right: A Vickers 0.5 inch quad gun on a destroyer, with the crew ready to fire its solid ammunition against low-flying aircraft.

Author's collection

Top: Germany's fortified naval base on Heligoland, a small island forming part of the North Frisian Islands, was photographed from the air before the outbreak of the Second World War.

Author's collection

Left: A torpedo boat of the Kriegsmarine loading a torpedo from her mother ship. These warships operated mainly in coastal waters along the enemy's lengthy coastline in north-west Europe.

Author's collection

Top: A German publicity photograph of a minesweeper squadron steaming at full speed while flak gunners and other crewmen watch for the approach of RAF aircraft.
Author's collection

Right: A U-boat with decks awash in the North Atlantic.
Author's collection

Top: A U-boat ploughing through heavy seas in the Atlantic.

Author's collection

Left: The engine room of a U-boat.

Author's collection

The first U-boat sunk by the Royal Navy in the Second World War was the Type IXA *U-39*, built by A.G. Weser of Bremen and commissioned on 10 September 1938. It left Wilhelmshaven on 19 August 1939, under the command of Oberleutnant zur See Gerhard Glattes, and attempted unsuccessfully to torpedo the escort carrier HMS *Ark Royal* west of the Iberian peninsula on 14 September 1939. It was depth-charged and damaged by the destroyers HMS *Faulkner, Foxhound* and *Firedrake*. After surfacing, the crew of forty-four abandoned the stricken U-boat. In this photograph whalers are engaged in rescuing survivors.

Author's collection

All forty-four crew members of the *U-39* were rescued by the Royal Navy, including the commander. They were photographed, looking extremely cheerful, by a seaman of one of the destroyers which sank their U-boat. Two of them were shot later in the war while making an attempt to escape.

Author's collection

Destroyers of the French Navy on convoy patrol in the early months of the war.

Author's collection

The Type VIIA *U-31*, commanded by Kapitänleutnant Johannes Habekost, was the first U-boat to be sunk by the RAF in the Second World War. It was built by A.G. Weser of Bremen, commissioned on 28 December 1936, and achieved considerable success by sinking eleven Allied ships in three months of active service. At midday on 11 March 1940 Blenheim IV serial P4852 of Bomber Command's 82 Squadron from Watton in Norfolk was on patrol off Borkum, with Squadron Leader Miles V. Delap at the controls, when the U-boat was spotted, as shown here. Delap dropped all four bombs in a salvo from low level, two of which hit the target. The force of the explosions damaged the Blenheim but it returned safely. The U-boat sank, leaving black oil on the surface, and all fifty-eight crew members lost their lives. (See also p. 42.)

Ref: ADM 199/2057

CHAPTER TWO

Survival after Defeat

By May 1940 the Royal Navy had escorted vessels carrying almost 500,000 men and 89,000 vehicles across the Channel to France, without loss. Warships of the Kriegsmarine had been unable to interfere with this massive deployment of British forces, while its U-boat Arm had been ineffective in these confined waters. The British Expeditionary Force formed part of the Allied Northern Army Group, with the French First, Second and Ninth Armies as the other forces. These troops had remained in static positions for over six months. It was anticipated that they would form the main resistance to any assault, for the obvious reason that the Wehrmacht would eventually sweep through the Netherlands, Belgium and Luxembourg instead of attempting a frontal attack on the strongly fortified Maginot Line further south. Plan 'Dyle' proposed that the British would advance to that river in Belgium. It was believed that retreating Belgian forces would also form part of the resistance in this crucial sector.

The British Air Force in France (BAFF), consisting of the RAF's Air Component and its Advanced Air Striking Force (AASF), supported the British Expeditionary Force (BEF). By May 1940 the Air Component included four squadrons of Westland Lysanders, two squadrons of Bristol Blenheims for reconnaissance and two squadrons of Hawker Hurricanes. There was also the tiny detachment of Spitfire photo-reconnaissance aircraft from 212 Squadron. The AASF consisted of eight squadrons of the obsolescent Fairey Battle light bomber, two squadrons of the more modern Bristol Blenheim light bomber, and two squadrons of Hurricanes.

Apart from these aircraft on airfields in France, the BAFF could also call upon six more squadrons of Blenheims from Bomber Command and it was expected that more squadrons of Hurricanes could be made available from Fighter Command. The Armée de l'Air could muster about a hundred bombers, of which only twenty-five were modern. This weakness in the air would prove a fatal defect in the Allied front. The Allied air forces were puny compared with the three huge fleets of the Luftwaffe which opposed them.

The storm which burst on these Allied forces on 10 May 1940 came as an unwelcome surprise. Although the direction of the attack had been anticipated, the date of its launch was not known. Also the method of attack, which soon became known as the 'Blitzkrieg', was unprecedented. Swarms of Junkers Ju87 dive-bombers screamed down on Allied positions, acting as airborne artillery and delivering their bombs with pinpoint accuracy. These were immediately followed by columns of Panzers and mobile troops, fast-moving and with superior weaponry, punching holes in the Allied lines and then attacking positions from the rear. Airborne troops from gliders and parachutists dropped from Junkers Ju52 carriers caused confusion behind Allied lines. German bombers delivered devastating raids on Allied airfields, particularly on the French. All these attacks from the air were heavily protected by masses of Messerschmitt Bf109 and Bf110 fighters.

On the day after this attack began, a new National Government was formed in Britain, with Winston Churchill as Prime Minister. He retained his office as First Lord of the Admiralty and also occupied the position of Minister of Defence. From this moment it was clear that under his leadership Britain would fight the war with the utmost resolution. However, it would be years before all the defects in the equipment of the armed forces could be made good.

The Allied troops in France were ill-equipped with anti-aircraft guns, possessed inferior weapons, and had inadequate cover from their air force. The Battle squadrons of the AASF suffered heavy losses in daylight attempts to bomb bridges in Belgium and hinder the German advances. By 15 May they were ordered to operate only at night. A Blenheim squadron sent from England lost eleven of the twelve aircraft dispatched, while the remaining survivor crash-landed near its base. Other attacks by Bomber Command behind the enemy lines were carried out but were far too small in scale to be effective.

The Netherlands had always refused to coordinate military plans with the Allies, for fear of antagonising Germany. Its air force was soon destroyed and the ground forces could not withstand an overwhelming attack. By 13 May the military situation had become desperate and Queen Wilhelmina and the Crown Princess left on a British destroyer. On the following day Ju87 dive-bombers delivered a mass attack on the unprotected port of Rotterdam, destroying 20,000 buildings and killing almost 1,000 citizens. This was the first example of the ruthless slaughter of civilians by air attack in the war. The country capitulated during the following morning. The Belgians resisted fiercely but attempts by the Allies to support them petered out. Their armed forces were ordered to capitulate on 17 May by King Leopold III, who remained in his country and was placed under house arrest. His Cabinet managed to escape and some of its members eventually reached Britain.

On 19 May the commander of the BEF, Field-Marshal Lord Gort, was ordered by the War Cabinet to fight his way south. At the same time the remnants of the BAFF were ordered to begin withdrawing to the south of England, from where they could continue to fight from far more secure bases. Most of the stores and equipment had to be left behind. Fighter Command had dispatched squadrons of Hurricanes to stiffen the defences but they faced fearful odds. From these and those already with the BAFF, only 66 pilots managed to fly their aircraft to England. Of the 261 aircraft which had operated from France, 75 had been destroyed in combat while 120 other machines were either damaged or had become unserviceable. The loss of these 195 Hurricanes represented about a quarter of Fighter Command's front-line strength.

The War Office and the Admiralty began to discuss the possibility of a mass evacuation from France under the code name of operation Dynamo. Meanwhile, the seven Panzer divisions of the German Army Group B had smashed through the French front on the Meuse and were heading west for the Channel coast. They reached it at Abbeville on 22

May, thus cutting off the Allied Northern Army Group from the majority of the French Army. At the same time the German Army Group A continued a frontal attack on the Allied Northern Army Group. The whole situation had become truly desperate for the BEF, which could only retreat towards Boulogne, Calais and Dunkirk, leaving rearguards to delay the enemy.

On 26 May the Admiralty ordered the Flag Officer Commanding Dover, Vice-Admiral Bertram H. Ramsay, to put operation Dynamo into effect. It was expected that about 45,000 men might be evacuated within two days before the great majority were overwhelmed by the Wehrmacht. Boulogne and Calais had been strengthened by troops from England, who had fought off the Panzers for as long as possible to prevent them from driving up the coast to Dunkirk, the main port chosen for the evacuation. The troops in these two ports were being withdrawn by sea when Ramsay received his orders. He was allocated thirty-nine destroyers for the main evacuation, as well as an anti-aircraft cruiser, ninety-nine minesweeping craft, eighteen anti-submarine trawlers, six corvettes, a sloop, two gunboats and seventy-six miscellaneous small craft. The French Navy provided nineteen destroyers or torpedo boats. A major contribution came from the Merchant Marine in the form of thirty-six passenger ferries. It also supplied hospital carriers, stores ships, tugs, trawlers, dredgers, fishing boats, lifeboats and cockle boats, as well as other miscellaneous small craft.

Apart from these, there was a multitude of small craft manned by civilian volunteers, many of which had never ventured beyond rivers and coastlines. To these were added 'schuyts' (fast motor boats) from the Netherlands, trawlers and tugs from Belgium, plus other small craft from France. These were all gathered at Ramsgate, where the Navy gave the skippers route instructions to Dunkirk. In total, about 850 of these 'little ships' saw service with the Royal Navy and the Merchant Marine in operation Dynamo.

The next few days were among the most momentous of the war for Britain. Fortunately the weather favoured the operation, remaining calm and without the heavy seas which could have been disastrous for small craft. The sandy beaches of Dunkirk were found to slope gently enough to enable troops to wade far out to sea and board many of the little ships, although the men were almost out of their depth. The inner docks of Dunkirk had been destroyed by German bombing and could not be used by the larger ships. However, there were two wooden moles in the outer basin and one of these was still serviceable, although not designed for docking. With consummate skill, a Royal Navy destroyer contrived to moor alongside, as an example to other larger vessels, and began taking off hundreds of soldiers. About 8,000 men were rescued in the remaining few hours of the first day, 27 May.

On the first full day of operation Dynamo, 28 May, almost 18,000 men were brought to England and landed at Dover. The larger surface vessels of the Kriegsmarine were unable to interfere with this evacuation, after their severe losses in the Norwegian campaign, but U-boats and E-boats were active. The main danger came from the Luftwaffe, especially from the Ju87 Stukas which dive-bombed and sank or damaged many vessels. On the second day the rescuers managed to bring back over 47,000 men, thus exceeding the total forecast for the entire operation. By this time the number needing rescue had been swollen by the remains of the French First Army, which had also reached the Dunkirk perimeter. On the third day, 30 May, almost 54,000 were brought back, despite continuing losses.

And so the desperate operation continued, while the gallant and stubborn rearguards of the BEF and the French somehow kept the mighty Wehrmacht at bay. Over 68,000 men were brought back on the last day of the month, and still there was work to be done. The Luftwaffe resumed its attacks with increased fury, sinking many ships, but almost 64,500 men had been brought off the beaches by the end of 1 June. The number in the perimeter had shrunk, and about 26,000 of these were rescued on 2 June. But the crews of some vessels, which had made trip after trip, were dropping with exhaustion and some could do no more. The remainder of the British rearguard were awaiting rescue and the majority of the others were French. It was decided that evacuations should be restricted to the periods of darkness, to improve security, and two nights were allotted. Almost 27,000 were lifted on 3 June and about 26,000 on the last day.

The operation was closed down on 4 June, by which time over 338,000 men had been brought out, or over 366,000 if those rescued in the earlier days are included. Against this enormous achievement, six destroyers of the Royal Navy had been sunk and eleven badly damaged. The RAF had also lost heavily. Its fighters had rarely been seen over the evacuation area, partly because the pilots were well aware that they would have come under 'friendly fire' from warships. Instead, they tried to intercept enemy aircraft before they reached their targets, claiming 132 successes for the loss of 145 of their own. There was also the need to preserve sufficient fighters for the inevitable battle in the skies over Britain, yet to come, which would be a major conflict the country would have to endure.

The dictator of Italy, Benito Mussolini, saw an opportunity to share in the spoils of the victorious Germans and declared war on France and Britain on 10 June. This was an extremely unwise decision which would ultimately cost him his life and cause a great deal of misery for the people of his country, many of whom were less than enthusiastic about participating in the war. However, this development stretched the resources of the Royal Navy even further, as it now had to cope with the Mediterranean theatre as well as the possibility of Japanese aggression in the Far East.

Operation Dynamo was not the end of the evacuations from France. About 140 divisions of the Wehrmacht were still fighting against 49 of the French and the trapped 51st Highland Division. Attempts on 10 June to bring off the latter from the beaches of St-Valery-en-Caux, near Dieppe, were hampered by fog and only partially successful. About 6,000 of the men were forced to surrender on the following day. Elsewhere, over 11,000 men were rescued from Le Havre between 10 and 13 June. But even greater efforts were made at other ports between 16 and 25 June. Thousands of servicemen – British, French, Poles, Belgians and Czechs – had streamed further west. Almost 192,000 of these were taken off from Cherbourg, St-Malo, Brest, St-Nazaire and La Pallice, although about 3,000 lives were lost when the liner *Lancastria* was sunk by the Luftwaffe at St-Nazaire on 17 June. Other forces were taken off from Marseille. Apart from these evacuations, the Royal Navy brought almost 23,000 people off the Channel Islands before these were occupied by the Germans.

The Wehrmacht had occupied Paris on 14 June. Three days later its forces had crossed the Loire and France was forced to seek armistice terms, after its government had refused

A depth charge exploding after being fired from a motor gunboat of the Royal Navy's Coastal Forces. Note the gunner strapped to his gun in the foreground.
Author's collection

an offer of a political union with Britain. The terms were not ratified until 25 June, but meanwhile most of the fighting ceased. The north and west of France was occupied by the Germans, but the remainder achieved some independence under the French hero of the First World War, Maréchal Henri Pétain, with his seat of government in Vichy.

Admiral Karl Dönitz had watched all these dramatic events with intense interest, for he was about to receive a prize which must have been beyond his wildest imaginings in pre-war days. The splendid ports of western France – Brest, Lorient, St-Nazaire, La Pallice and Bordeaux – were to become available for the ocean-going types of his U-boat Arm. This would give his U-boats direct access to the North Atlantic via the Bay of Biscay and obviate the need to circumvent the north of Britain to reach the great convoys which were the lifeblood of his country's remaining enemy. About 450 miles would be cut from their journeys and they could remain on station for an extra week. A golden opportunity had been presented to him.

Dönitz visited Lorient on 23 June, before the armistice was signed, and was deeply impressed with the dockyard facilities available, for these were far more extensive than the cramped conditions in German ports. He decided that his command post should be near this port and chose a château at Larmor-Plage on the quayside at Kernéval, where the river Blavet entered the estuary. From there, a fast motorboat could take him and his staff to the main docks within minutes. Having made preparations, he then sped to Berlin, to plead once more with Hitler and Grossadmiral Raeder the need to enlarge his U-boat Arm. By then, the Führer had declared that Germany would rule Europe for the next 1,000 years, but he was not unsympathetic to these demands.

The first U-boat to enter a French port, the Type VIIA *U-30,* arrived at Lorient on 7 July, after a war cruise south-west of Ireland. This was the U-boat that had sunk the liner *Athenia* on the first day of the war. However, the total number of such U-boats had diminished slightly since the start of the war and in July 1940 stood at only twenty-eight, with twenty-three more undergoing training and trials back in German waters. All the same, those available were achieving increased successes, with over 284,000 tons of Allied shipping sunk in June. In addition, the Luftwaffe had sunk over 105,000 tons. These combined to give the highest monthly total of sinkings of the war to date, and the morale of the U-boat crews was at a peak. For the time being only about ten boats could be on station simultaneously in the North Atlantic, but there was a huge programme of expansion to back them.

The main requirement of the U-boat Arm was improved intelligence. Although the convoys were large, they were hard to find in the vast expanses of the North Atlantic, especially when visibility distance from a low conning tower was so limited. B-Dienst could decrypt many of the messages sent by the Admiralty but few of them were of any use to the U-boat Arm, for British sailing orders were not sent by wireless but handed to convoy commanders in sealed envelopes. Wireless silence was normally preserved while ships were at sea.

One solution lay with the Luftwaffe, for a long-range reconnaissance and anti-shipping aircraft had emerged in the form of the Focke-Wulf FW200C-1 Kondor. This was an adaption of a commercial airliner which originally flew in 1935. Although not entirely suitable as a military aircraft – for instance it was rather fragile and had no self-sealing tanks – it had the great advantage of a radius of action of over 1,000 miles and could thus detect convoys far out to sea when leaving or approaching British ports. It could also carry up to five 550 lb bombs. Only a handful of these machines were operational but from the end of June they were based at Bordeaux-Mérignac as No. I Staffel of I Gruppe of Kampfgeschwader 40.

These Kondors ranged far out into the Atlantic and their initial impact on convoys was devastating. The Royal Navy was so short of escort vessels in mid-1940 that there was often only one with each convoy while the merchant vessels were not armed. The Kondors could deliver low-level attacks on them and sank ship after ship. Winston Churchill called these aircraft 'the scourge of the Atlantic' and for many months there was little answer to them. Escort carriers did not exist. Although somewhat desperate measures were begun in the form of converting vessels into Catapult Aircraft Merchant Ships (CAM Ships), these could not come into service immediately. They were intended to carry a single Hurricane which could be catapulted off the deck. After shooting down the Kondor the pilot would ditch and then be picked up. Before these came into operation, however, the Kondors were able to continue their work and provided U-boats with intelligence.

Meanwhile the British were active in their preparations for the continuation of the war and some measures were taken to gain advantage in the Battle of the Atlantic, as this part of the conflict was then named. On 10 May 1940 a party of Royal Marines was carried to Iceland by two British cruisers and landed at Reykjavik, with the intention of forestalling any attempt by the Germans to establish bases on the strategically placed island. They returned home with a number of German nationals as prisoners. They also took possession of the Faeroes, the self-governing group of islands within the kingdom of Denmark, situated between the Shetlands and Iceland. From the middle of June a combination of British and Canadian troops occupied key positions in Iceland, to prevent any attack from the Kriegsmarine and to establish naval and air bases which would help cover part of the convoy routes to North America. Of course, the Icelanders did not welcome these enforced measures, even though they were far more benign than the alternative of Nazi rule.

The question of the French Navy had to be addressed after France had signed an armistice with Germany. The 'neutralisation' of this formidable force had to be achieved before it fell into the hands of the Kriegsmarine. Those warships which had entered British ports were seized, at least on a temporary basis. Four cruisers at Alexandria were immobilised by agreement with the British. A more formidable force consisting of four battleships, a seaplane carrier and several destroyers lay in port at Mers-el-Kebir in Algeria. The commander refused terms offered by the British. On 2 July 1940 these warships were bombarded by the Royal Navy, sinking one battleship, damaging others, and causing heavy loss of life. One battleship and five destroyers escaped and managed to reach Toulon. On 8 July the battleship *Richelieu* was attacked by torpedo-bombers of the Fleet Air Arm at Dakar in Senegal and put out of action for about a year. This was a melancholy period for Anglo-French relations. No more action was taken against other warships but the Admiralty continued to worry about them for over two years, until the Allies invaded North Africa and neutralised several in the French bases.

Coastal Command remained the principal air force in Britain destined to combat the U-boat peril. It was still ill-equipped, although more Sunderlands were being produced, Hudsons from the USA were replacing the elderly Ansons and long-range Catalinas were on order and would soon be delivered. The naval Mark VII depth charge of 459 lb was being modified for air attack and would soon come into service. An improved ASV system was being developed, the Mark II, having been devised by the Telecommunications Research Establishment; with a more powerful transmitter and a more sensitive receiver than the Mark I, it was expected to enter service later in 1940.

Another major step, although it might have appeared insignificant at the time, was the creation on 8 July of the Photographic Reconnaissance Unit under Coastal Command. This was formed from the Photographic Development Unit in England and 212 Squadron which had served in France, both under Wing Commander Sidney Cotton. The latter was relieved of his command and the new unit was taken over by a regular officer, Wing Commander Geoffrey W. Tuttle. This was associated with another move which had taken place slightly earlier, on 31 May, when the civilian Aircraft Operating Company at Wembley, which had carried out photographic interpretation under Sidney Cotton, was taken over by the RAF. The functions of photographic processing and interpretation, hitherto partly carried out by the Royal Aircraft Establishment at Farnborough, were incorporated in this new unit, which was named the Photographic Interpretation Unit. It was commanded by Squadron Leader Peter Riddell, the most experienced interpreter in the RAF, who had been recruited from Bomber Command. These two units were to play vital parts within British intelligence in the anti-submarine campaign and indeed in the whole conduct of the war.

Britain still had to face a major peril. On 19 July Hitler made a speech in the Reichstag directed at the obstinate people of his enemy. It was a 'last appeal to reason', aimed at a peaceful settlement between the two countries. When this was rejected with contempt by the British, he ordered operation Seelöwe (Sealion) to be put into effect.

A great invasion force of 250,000 men was being assembled and trained along the shores of northern France, under the command of Feldmarschall Walther von Brauchitsch. These were the men who had crushed the BEF and the French armies, and they were full of confidence. They were to be carried in a fleet of merchant ships, trawlers, tugs, barges and motor boats assembled by Grossadmiral Erich Raeder, to land at points between Folkestone and New Romney and between Hastings and Rye. The landings would be accompanied by a parachute division which would drop near Folkestone, while the Luftwaffe would destroy any warships of the Royal Navy which tried to interfere with the sea crossings. Once ashore, the invasion force would sweep towards London, its route ahead blasted clear by Ju87 Stuka dive-bombers, and eventually the whole of Britain would be subjugated.

It was true that an enormous amount of military equipment had been left in France by the BEF and that eleven army divisions in Britain were almost bereft of mobility or equipment except rifles and side-arms. But first the RAF had to be defeated. The bombastic and self-indulgent Hermann Goering, recently promoted to Reichsmarschall, had promised Hitler that his victorious Luftwaffe would soon accomplish this task. However, events did not work out as he planned.

The Government Code and Cipher School had managed to improve decryption of the Luftwaffe's signals and its Order of Battle was known with some accuracy. The aircraft of the new Photographic Reconnaissance Unit were able to bring back visible evidence of this intelligence from airfields occupied by the enemy. In addition, the Luftwaffe had greatly underestimated the effectiveness of the British Chain Home Radio Direction-Finding system which enabled operators to identify approaching enemy aircraft, as well as the efficiency of the Filter Room of Fighter Command's headquarters at Bentley Priory in Middlesex, which plotted these reports and those from the Observer Corps.

The German campaign is considered to have begun on 10 July 1940, mainly against convoys off the south-east coast of England. These continued until 8 August and about 50,000 tons of shipping were sunk, but the attackers lost heavily when the RAF's fighters were directed against them with surprising accuracy. The Luftwaffe chose 10 August as

Adler Tag (Eagle Day), when it would commence the destruction of the RAF. It had mustered three Luftflotten for this purpose, consisting of 3,350 bombers, fighters and reconnaissance aircraft. Opposing them were fifty-nine RAF squadrons and about 1,400 fighter pilots, including volunteers from many European countries and the USA, under the command of Air Chief Sir Hugh Dowding of Fighter Command.

The major blows fell on the radar stations and the airfields, but the Germans underestimated the ability of the British to effect repairs and remain operational. The Luftwaffe continued to suffer heavy losses, its Ju87 Stuka dive-bombers proving particularly vulnerable to Spitfires and Hurricanes. Although RAF fighters were lost, the pilots often baled out or crash-landed in home territory. Three days after the assault began, Dowding still had 672 aircraft, while German intelligence estimated the number to be only 300. Although some RAF pilots were killed or injured, more were coming through the training system while others were drawn from Bomber Command. By 21 August, Goering was dissatisfied enough to upbraid his fighter pilots and to switch some bombers to night attacks on city centres, eliciting equivalent attacks by the RAF's Bomber Command on German targets in addition to the invasion ports and enemy airfields, but continued attacks on RAF fighter airfields caused more damage and it seemed that some might become unusable.

By early September the German plans for invasion were complete and the force was waiting for Hitler's orders for the launch, expected to be on the 11th of the month. Meanwhile the British anti-invasion measures had improved, with newly built tanks and field guns at the ready. Moreover Bomber Command had caused damage in Berlin itself, to the fury of Hitler, and he ordered the Luftwaffe to concentrate by day and night on the London area. He expected civilian morale to collapse and that the country would sue for peace. Mass attacks were then made on the capital, with smaller attacks on other cities, and there were many civilian deaths and injuries as well as much destruction of property. However, the citizens stood up to the 'Blitz', as it was called, and in fact their resolve stiffened and was coupled with demands for retaliation. The Luftwaffe lost even more heavily and the climax came on 15 September when the RAF claimed 185 aircraft destroyed. The true figure was 59, but this was serious enough for the Luftwaffe. The tide had turned against it, but the raids continued. The last daylight attack took place on 30 September and thereafter the Blitz continued solely at night.

RAF Heston was bombed on 19/20 September. Several Spitfires were destroyed or damaged and preparations were made to move the Photographic Reconnaissance Unit to a more distant airfield at Benson in Oxfordshire, although this did not take place until 27 December. The premises of the Photographic Interpretation Unit at Wembley were also hit, on 1/2 October, and the personnel had to move into an adjacent row of houses. A move was proposed to Danesfield House at Medmenham in Buckinghamshire, but this did not begin until 7 January 1941 when it was renamed the Central Interpretation Unit.

On 12 October Hitler ordered the postponement of operation Seelöwe until the spring of 1941. His invasion fleet was dispersed and it was never reassembled. Hitler was already making plans for the invasion of Russia and had decided that Britain was best subdued by a combination of night bombing and a starvation of supplies by the U-boat Arm. Dowding

Fairey Swordfish I serial K8440 of 811 Squadron landing on the deck of the aircraft carrier HMS *Courageous*, 22,500 tons displacement. The squadron served on this carrier in early 1939. The Swordfish possessed superb handling characteristics, especially at low speeds, which enabled the pilot to land safely on pitching decks. The Mark I entered service with the Fleet Air Arm in February 1936, powered by a Bristol Pegasus HIM3 engine of 690 hp, and could carry a torpedo or 1,500 lb of bombs. It continued to enjoy a successful career and was joined by the Mark II in 1943, which served until the end of the war. HMS *Courageous* was torpedoed south-west of Eire on 17 September 1939 by the Type VIIA *U-29* and sank rapidly with the loss of 518 men from her complement of 840.

Author's collection

assessed the end of the Battle of Britain as the end of October 1940, although some aviation historians have chosen a different date. It is known that Fighter Command lost 537 aircrew killed in this period. The precise losses of the Luftwaffe are not known with certainty but one careful detailed study puts the number of aircrew killed as 2,662. By any computation the result was a defeat for the Luftwaffe and the reputation of Herman Goering was permanently impaired in the eyes of Hitler.

In contrast, the U-boat Arm began its most successful period of the war, with the star of Dönitz in ascendancy. His U-boats sank over 196,500 tons of shipping in July for the loss of two of their number, from a total of almost 387,000 tons lost by Britain. Those U-boats based in Lorient could range as far as 25 degrees West, almost halfway along the convoy route and beyond the range of escort vessels and air cover. There were two classes of eastbound convoys, fast and slow. The fast variety sailed from Halifax in Nova Scotia and

The aircraft carrier HMS *Eagle* of 22,600 tons displacement was completed in 1923. This photograph, showing three Blackburn Baffins and two Fairey IIIFs is evidently pre-war since the former aircraft was obsolete by September 1937. The Fairey Swordfish carrying a torpedo and apparently flying above the carrier has been superimposed on the original photograph for wartime publicity purposes. HMS *Eagle* was torpedoed south of Majorca on 11 August 1942 by the Type VIIB *U-73* and sank rapidly. Destroyers rescued 900 men from her complement of 1,160.

Author's collection

had a maximum speed of up to 14.9 knots: these were designated HX. The slow convoys sailed from Sydney in Nova Scotia, had a maximum speed of 7.5 knots and were coded SC. In the other direction the westbound convoys were not designated by their speed. Those collected from the east coast of Britain were named OA while those from the west coast and Northern Ireland were named OB. However, until wolf packs could be brought together, for the most part the U-boats still picked off the more vulnerable stragglers.

The pace quickened in August, when the French ports of Brest, St-Nazaire and La Pallice also became homes for flotillas of U-boats. In this month they sank over 267,000 tons but lost three boats from the flotillas, while about 130,000 more tons of British shipping were sunk from other causes. The morale of the U-boat crews remained high, despite the privations they suffered at sea. Much courage and fortitude was required when fifty men were crammed into a pointed steel tube of about 200 feet in length for over a month on a war cruise. The men worked, ate and slept in relays, pitched and rolled when on the surface, and experienced claustrophobic and stinking conditions when they submerged for long periods. There was also the ever-present prospect of a most unpleasant death in a steel coffin.

However, the barracks in the French ports had good amenities. There were diversions in local cafés and cabarets, with food, beer, wine and cognac, as well as more earthy pleasures in some areas. The Resistance movement in occupied France had not yet caused any difficulty. Also these ports on the west coast of France were free from the attentions of the RAF's Bomber Command, which was fully occupied with attacks on invasion ports, airfields and the German heartland.

The submarines of the Regia Marina (Italian Navy) numbered 104 when Mussolini declared war on 10 June, although ten of these were sunk within that month, one in an accident and the others by the Royal Navy, the French Navy and the RAF. On 4 September the U-boat flotillas in France were joined by twelve of these ocean-going submarines, which had left La Spezia six days earlier and passed through the Straits of Gibraltar. Mussolini had promised to supply this force on his declaration of war, and they were based at Bordeaux under the name of 'Betasom'. Dönitz allotted an area between the Azores and Spain for their war cruises, but the Italians were unused to conditions in the North Atlantic and their early efforts brought no results at all. On the other hand the new-found optimism of the U-boat men seemed to be justified in September, for they lost none of their number during the month but they and their Italian allies sank over 295,000 tons from a total of about 448,500 tons of British shipping which went to the bottom of the sea.

Dönitz took command of his new headquarters at Kernével on 16 October, after it had been suitably prepared and protected by reinforced concrete so that the ground floor looked like a blockhouse. It became known as 'the sardine can' by his men. Hitler asked him for advice about the protection needed for the U-boats in their new bases and he replied that the boats and their workshops should be under reinforced concrete. Accordingly, Hitler ordered Dr Fritz Todt, the engineer who had built the German autobahn system and had been appointed as Reich Minister for Armaments and Munitions, to begin work on U-boat shelters. These gigantic structures were constructed with roofs 16 feet thick at Brest, Lorient, St-Nazaire, La Pallice and Bordeaux. Work by the Todt Organisation continued for over a year, using forced labour and eventually slave labour. Their progress was photographed at intervals by Coastal Command's reconnaissance aircraft. Requests for attacks by heavy bombers on the incomplete structures were denied by the Air Ministry, on the grounds that these aircraft were better employed on bombing industries in Germany.

October was another good month for the U-boats and submarines, which sank almost 352,500 tons from a total of almost 443,000 lost by Britain. This was a month in which the wolf pack system took a heavy toll. The slow-moving convoy SC7 from Sydney in Nova Scotia consisted initially of thirty-five ships. Four fell out in a storm and three were picked off as stragglers by U-boats. The others continued but between the 17th and the 19th another seventeen were sent to the bottom by a wolf pack of seven U-boats which intercepted them. Another convoy, the fast HX79 of forty-nine ships from Halifax, lost

Warships of the Home Fleet preparing to resist any attempt at invasion after the fall of France, with an Avro Anson on patrol above them.

Author's collection

fourteen ships on the night of the 19th to another wolf pack, while the similar convoy HX79A lost seven more.

Another victim in October was the liner *Empress of Britain* of 42,348 tons; acting as a troopship, she was returning to Britain with servicemen and their families from the Middle East. Her course took her via Capetown and the Atlantic, but to the north-east of Northern Ireland on 26 October she was attacked by a Focke-Wulf Kondor and set on fire. Although she remained afloat, the information was passed to the Type VIIA *U-32* which torpedoed and sank her two days later. This U-boat was sunk on 30 October by the destroyers HMS *Harvester* and *Highlander*, which between them rescued thirty of the crew. It was the only U-boat lost during the month, but three Italian submarines were sunk in the Mediterranean.

The destruction of so many ships continued to cause serious anxiety at the Admiralty. The remedies were easy to diagnose but difficult to implement. More naval escorts for the convoys were a top priority but the British shipbuilding industry was unable to turn out corvettes and frigates in sufficient numbers. Winston Churchill had negotiated with President Roosevelt the transfer of fifty destroyers of First World War vintage, in return for bases in Newfoundland, Bermuda, British Guiana and the West Indies. The deal was agreed on 2 September but the destroyers, known as the 'Town Class' (or more familiarly as 'Four-stackers',) were not ideal for their intended purpose.

They were fast but did not perform well in Atlantic weather and required modifications and fitting with Asdic. Forty-four of them went to the Royal Navy and six to the Royal Canadian Navy, but they came into service slowly and for the time being made little contribution to easing the problems.

More air cover was required but by October the number of squadrons in Coastal Command had increased to only twenty-eight and there were insufficient trained aircrews. Many of the additional aircraft were cast-offs from Bomber Command and not entirely suitable for maritime work. Too few were fitted with the new ASV Mark II, for in October only forty-five of these instruments had been delivered. Production had been partially switched to Air Interception

(AI) radar for the RAF nightfighters which were hunting German bombers in the skies over Britain. However, one small step was the creation on 22 November of the Coastal Command Development Unit at Carew Cheriton in Pembrokeshire. This was commanded by Wing Commander Lawrence P. Moore, a signals officer from RAF Compton Bassett in Wiltshire. He had previously served with 217 Squadron at St Eval in Cornwall, which by then was converting from Ansons to Beauforts, and most of the initial personnel were drawn from that squadron. The only aircraft allotted to the new unit were an Anson, a Beaufort and a Hornet Moth, although a Whitley and a Hudson soon followed. The first tasks were to experiment with new forms of airborne radar and an airborne searchlight for attacks on U-boats at night. The creation of such a unit conformed with the usual British practice of 'too little, too late', but eventually it would have a significant effect on the war against the U-boats.

None of these measures had any immediate effect on the U-boats or Italian submarines, which sank over 212,000 tons in November, from a total of over 318,500 tons of British shipping lost. Some of the latter were sunk by the pocket battleship *Admiral Scheer*, which had slipped unnoticed into the North Atlantic with orders to find and tackle a convoy, provided it was not escorted by a battleship. On the 5th of the month her reconnaissance aircraft spotted the eastbound convoy HX84, which was escorted only by the armed merchant cruiser *Jervis Bay* of 14,000 tons. The convoy dispersed while the escort closed with her powerful adversary and fought courageously until she was inevitably sunk with heavy loss of life. The pocket battleship then found and sank five merchant vessels from the convoy, totalling over 38,500 tons. After this, she made for the South Atlantic and eventually for the Indian Ocean, continuing her destruction before returning to Kiel on 1 April 1941.

Two U-boats were sunk in the month of November 1940 and the total front-line force available for the campaign was reduced to only twenty-five. An Italian submarine was also sunk in the North Atlantic. The Kriegsmarine was suffering its own problems, for the German shipbuilding industry was not keeping pace with demand while many recently commissioned U-boats were still undergoing trials. Nevertheless, the U-boats and Italian submarines sank over 293,000 tons in December, from a total of almost 350,000 lost by Britain. No U-boats were sunk, although three Italian submarines were lost at sea.

During this month the cruiser *Admiral Hipper* made a foray into the North Atlantic. She found no targets but turned south and came across the convoy WS5A making for the Middle East. This was strongly escorted and the German cruiser turned away after inflicting only slight damage. Suffering from engine trouble and other defects, she entered Brest on 27 December, to undergo repairs.

The year ended on a high note for the U-boat Arm, which classed this period as its 'Happy Time', or 'Golden Time'. It ended with a continuation of anxiety for the Admiralty and those who understood the true situation in Britain. In the first nine months of the war about 800,000 tons of British shipping had been sunk. Although this had been a grievous cost in human life and suffering, the tonnage had been made good, mainly by new building but partly by captures of shipping from the enemy. Since then, the situation had deteriorated and the heavy losses were resulting in serious shortfalls in essential imports such as iron ore and timber. It is small wonder that Churchill later confessed 'The only thing that ever really frightened me during the war was the U-boat peril'.

One of the American destroyers transferred to the Royal Navy in October 1940 was the USN *Abel P. Upshur*, seen here leaving port while an Able Seaman locks the boom into position. These destroyers were twenty-five years old and required considerable overhaul and re-equipment before they could enter service.

Author's collection

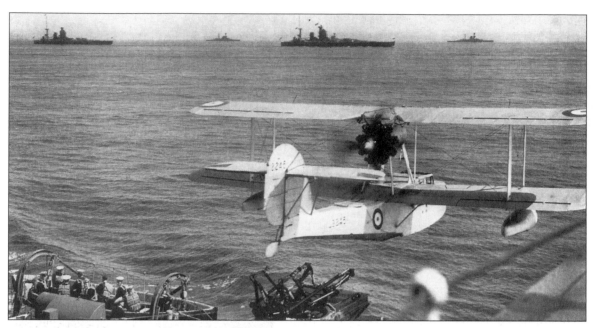

A Supermarine Walrus amphibious flying boat of the Fleet Air Arm being catapulted from the deck of the cruiser HMS *Southampton,* 9,100 tons displacement. These slow but reliable biplanes, each fitted with a Bristol Pegasus VI engine of 775 hp and a pusher propeller, were employed on reconnaissance and air-sea rescue duties. HMS *Southampton* was damaged and set on fire by German air attack when east of Malta on 11 January 1941. She was scuttled later in the day. Eighty of her men were lost.

Author's collection

The Blackburn Skua was the first British aircraft designed mainly for dive-bombing, as well as the first monoplane to enter service with the Fleet Air Arm. No. 800 Squadron on the aircraft carrier HMS *Ark Royal* received Skuas in 1938, each fitted with a Bristol Pegasus XII engine of 905 hp and armed with four .303 inch machine-guns in the wings and a single Lewis gun in the rear cockpit. The bomb-load was usually a single 500 pounder. A Skua from HMS *Ark Royal* shot down the first enemy aircraft in the war, over the North Sea, on 26 September 1939. This was Dornier Do18D-1 of 2 Staffel, Küstenfliegergruppe 106. The four crew members were picked up by the destroyer HMS *Somali*.

Author's collection

Right: The aircraft carrier HMS *Indomitable*, 23,000 tons displacement, with Fairey Albacore torpedo-bombers and a Supermarine Seafire fighter on her deck. The early Albacore, which entered service with the Fleet Air Arm in March 1940, was powered by a Bristol Taurus II engine of 1,065 hp and could carry a torpedo or up to 2,000 lb of bombs. It supplemented the older Fairey Swordfish.

Author's collection

Below: The aircraft carrier HMS *Formidable*, 23,000 tons displacement, with Grumman F-4F3 Wildcats and Supermarine Seafires on her deck. The Wildcat fighters, each fitted with a Wright R-1820-G205A engine of 1,200 hp, had been intended for delivery from the USA to France but were diverted to the Fleet Air Arm at the end of July 1940 and named Martlet Is. The Supermarine Seafire MK IB was the carrier-borne version of the Spitfire VB, powered by a Rolls-Royce Merlin engine of 1,440 hp.

Author's collection

Right: The aircraft carrier HMS *Illustrious*, 23,000 tons displacement, steaming at speed to facilitate the landing of her aircraft. A Fairey Swordfish has just landed and the ground crew are taking it to the forward lift.

Author's collection

Below: A Fairey Swordfish over the flight deck of the aircraft carrier HMS *Illustrious*, guided in by a control officer with reflector bats indicating that the pilot should land.

Author's collection

A submarine chaser of the Royal Navy cleaving through heavy seas in the North Atlantic.
Author's collection

A torpedo being greased aboard a destroyer of the Royal Navy.
Author's collection

A destroyer of the Royal Navy making smoke as a screen during a practice attack.
Author's collection

A depth-charge thrower being tested in the factory manufacturing the devices.
Author's collection

A destroyer of the Royal Navy throwing a depth charge.
Author's collection

Top: A merchant ship under construction in a British shipyard, replacing one of the many sunk by U-boats.

Author's collection

Left: A depth charge from a British destroyer exploding during an attack on a German U-boat, while other depth charges are being prepared.

Author's collection

The Type VIIA *U-31*, sunk in the Shillig Roads by a Blenheim of Bomber Command on 11 March 1940, was raised by the Germans, repaired and recommissioned at Wilhelmshaven on 30 July 1940. It left Lorient on 21 October 1940 for a war cruise under the command of Kapitänleutnant Wilfried Frellberg, but was depth-charged to the surface on 2 November 1940 when north-west of Ireland by the destroyer HMS *Antelope,* as shown here. The crew abandoned the U-boat before it sank. Forty-four men were rescued, including Frellberg, but two lost their lives.

Ref: ADM 199/2057

Coastal Command began receiving Armstrong Whitworth Whitley Vs in October 1940, when they had become obsolescent in Bomber Command. With a crew of five and armed with five machine-guns, the Whitley could carry a bomb-load of 3,000 lb for a radius of action of 825 miles. Although plagued with serviceability problems, Whitleys performed a useful role in anti-submarine patrols until more suitable aircraft arrived. This Whitley V serial Z9365 was fitted with air to surface vessel (ASV) radar by the Royal Aircraft Establishment at Farnborough. Whitleys served as stop-gaps in five Coastal Command squadrons.

Ref: AVIA 7/1493

CHAPTER THREE

British Counter-Measures

The storms and heavy seas which beset the North Atlantic in the first months of 1941 did not deter the handful of U-boats available for war cruises. In January they and their Italian allies sank over 126,500 tons of shipping from a total of over 320,000 tons lost by Britain. In addition, Dönitz received a boost to his authority, for Hitler agreed to place the Kondors of Kampfgeschwader 40 at Bordeaux-Mérignac under his direct command. Needless to say, this move met with disapproval from the commander of the Luftwaffe, Hermann Goering, who on 7 February tried to persuade him to relinquish this authority. There was acrimony when this request was refused and the two men parted bad friends.

Despite this achievement and the continued success of his U-boats, Dönitz in his Lorient headquarters was in such an unhappy mood that he was driven almost to desperation. By the end of January the number of serviceable ocean-going U-boats had fallen to twenty-two, the lowest since before the war. All boats became weatherbeaten during the four or five months after launching, when they were employed on working-up and training in the Baltic before acceptance for war cruises. After two or three war cruises in the turbulent waters of the North Atlantic, when probably more damage was sustained, it was inevitable that lengthy repair or refitting was required.

Twenty-four new U-boats were undergoing trials and training during January and an enormous expansion was planned, but insufficient were coming through the system to achieve the number Dönitz required. Unlike the British, who had achieved central control of their war production, with reasonably equitable allocation of scarce resources to the various manufacturing concerns, the Germans were poorly organised. There was no effective distribution of resources from the centre and the three services competed with one another for their share. Goering was nominally responsible for such allocations but he dispersed the function to various special commissioners. The German economy, still mainly in private hands during a time of war, was without an effective central planning authority. The Naval Ordnance Department complained of planning alterations, material and labour shortages, insufficient dockyards, transport problems and delays during air raid alarms.

Dönitz had always contended that with 300 U-boats he could bring Britain to its knees in months, and it is true that if this number had been available in the early stages of the war the result would have been catastrophic for his enemy. In February 1941 he saw the only solution to this crisis as taking over control of the U-boat expansion programme as

Director-General in Berlin, and took this proposal to Grossadmiral Raeder. It was refused on the grounds that he was indispensable in his current position.

Meanwhile, February was even more successful for the U-boats and submarines, which sank almost 197,000 tons of shipping from a total of over 403,000 tons lost by Britain. As in all months the other tonnage was sunk from a variety of causes such as aircraft, mines, surface raiders or E-boats. A few vessels were sunk without trace, for unknown reasons. Not a single U-boat was lost in the first two months of the year, although an Italian submarine was sunk in the North Atlantic on 7 January by the corvette HMS *Anemone*.

The whole situation remained grim for the Admiralty and indeed for the whole of Britain, but the general public remained unaware of the extent of these losses and their gravity. Good intelligence was always a prime requirement during the conflict. This was soon to be centred in the Admiralty's new granite building on a corner of Horse Guards Parade in London, with the forbidding appearance of a massive bunker, which was to become known as 'the Citadel'. This was where the Operational Intelligence Centre was to be situated, commanded by Rear-Admiral John Godfrey; it included the Submarine Tracking Room.

However, a decision was taken to set up another command centre, devoted solely to the war against U-boats in the Atlantic or elsewhere. The site chosen for this was Derby House in Liverpool. This building was converted into a bomb-proof centre similar to RAF Fighter Command's Operations Room at Stanmore in Middlesex. It copied the RAF system of a great wall chart for plotting purposes. At Derby House the positions of convoys, naval escorts and other warships, RAF escorting aircraft and reported U-boats were displayed. The chart was kept constantly up to date by young ladies of the Women's Royal Navy Service (WRNS). The offices of the Admiral C-in-C Western Approaches and the AOC-in-C of No. 15 Group of Coastal Command had a clear view of this huge chart. They liaised with the Citadel in London and eventually more than proved their worth.

Although no major breakthrough had occurred at the Government Code and Cipher School with the decryption of the Enigma signals sent to and from U-boats, unexpected progress was made with the more orthodox method of photo-interpretation. A person who had specialised in the Kriegsmarine in the offices of the Aircraft Operating Company at Wembley was a young civilian named David P. Brachi. He was a geography graduate from Cambridge University who had always taken an interest in warships. Slight deafness in one ear had prevented him from taking an active role in the armed services, but he was commissioned as a pilot officer in the RAFVR on 7 September 1939 and employed as a photo-interpreter in the Naval Section. From this time, and after the move to Danesfield House at Medmenham, he invariably seized on any RAF photo-reconnaissance cover of German ports which arrived, particularly those of Wilhelmshaven. Using a stereoscope, a measuring magnifier and a slide rule, he carefully examined photographs of the hulks of U-boats under construction. His assistant and partner in this work was a young WAAF, Sergeant (later Section Officer) Mary H. 'Bunny' Grierson. By comparison with the known length of the dockyards, they were able to identify the types of U-boat and arrive at an estimate for their completion as soon as keels were laid down, even though this might be as far as eleven months ahead.

In February 1941 David Brachi received a visit from Captain John Godwin of the Royal Marines, who specialised in German shipbuilding at the Admiralty. After some initial scepticism, Godwin became deeply impressed with these calculations and reported to Rear-Admiral John Godfrey, the Director of Naval Intelligence at the Admiralty. From this time British intelligence had a reasonably accurate assessment of U-boat production and was able to make operational arrangements accordingly.

No U-boats had been lost for the three months to the end of February 1941 and the morale of the German crews remained high. Action was again stepped up in March, when they and their Italian allies sank over 243,000 tons of shipping from a total of almost 530,000 tons. At the same time the British experienced another major threat to their lifeline. The battleships *Scharnhorst* and *Gneisenau* finished refitting at Kiel and in the latter part of January left for a foray in the North Atlantic. Taking a long detour to avoid detection and perhaps interception, they passed through the Denmark Strait between Greenland and the north of Iceland and then approached the sea routes on 4 February. Avoiding Convoy HX106, which happened to be escorted by the old battleship HMS *Ramillies*, they ranged down to Sierra Leone and then almost as far west as Canada, sinking 115,622 tons of shipping before entering Brest on 21 March for refitting. The cruiser *Admiral Hipper*, which had been sheltering in this port, had left during the previous month and returned to Germany.

Brest was extremely heavily defended, but Bomber Command was diverted from some of its normal tasks to try to damage these battleships. On the night of 4/5 April a 500 lb bomb fell alongside the dock occupied by the *Gneisenau* but failed to explode. The battleship was towed out of dock while demolition experts dealt with the problem, but she was photographed by a reconnaissance Spitfire in her more vulnerable position. Six Bristol Beauforts of 22 Squadron were briefed to attack from RAF St Eval in Cornwall on the night of 5/6 April but only one, flown by Flying Officer Kenneth Campbell, found its way through the adverse weather. He dropped his torpedo a few seconds before being shot down, killing all four crew members. The torpedo ran true and blew a hole about 40 feet wide in the side of the battleship, which almost sank and remained under repair for five months. Campbell was later awarded a posthumous Victoria Cross.

In spite of all the difficulties in the North Atlantic, there were indications during March 1941 of a turn-around in fortunes. The British naval escorts were more numerous, particularly with the advent of the new *Flower* class corvettes, which could cross the North Atlantic without refuelling and were being commissioned in large numbers. Some escorts were being fitted with a new seaborne radar, the Type 271, which could detect U-boats on the surface and also helped the escort commander keep the merchant vessels in their correct stations.

Five U-boats were sunk in March, and it is significant that three of them were commanded by U-boat 'aces'. The first to be lost was the Type VIIC *U-70* commanded by Korvettenkapitän Joachim Matz. On the night of 6/7 March this was drawn to the outward bound convoy OB293 south-west of the Faroes by Kapitänleutnant Günther Prien in his Type VIIB *U-47*. Matz, who was on his first war cruise, had sunk another ship ten days before but his *U-70* had suffered some storm damage which impaired its ability. On this occasion he damaged two more ships before being depth-charged to the surface by the corvettes HMS *Camellia* and *Arbutus*. These opened fire and twenty men were lost when the U-boat foundered, but Matz and twenty-five of his men were rescued to become PoWs.

The next to go was Prien's *U-47*, on 8 March. He had been driven off the convoy earlier but continued to follow it. His U-boat was detected on the surface in the early morning by the destroyer HMS *Wolverine* and then pursued by the destroyer HMS *Verity*. But Prien persisted and was sighted five hours later, once more on the surface. *Wolverine* attempted to ram but Prien crash-dived. The U-boat then received a succession of depth charges and debris came to the surface. Prien and his men, numbering forty-five in all, died in the underwater explosions. In his previous nine war cruises Prien had sunk thirty-one vessels, including the battleship *Royal Oak* in Scapa Flow, and damaged five others.

A few days later the U-boat Arm suffered two more calamities. On this occasion the convoy was the eastbound HX112, heavily escorted by five destroyers and two corvettes. It was first sighted south of Iceland by Kapitänleutnant Fritz-Julius Lemp, who by then commanded the new Type IXB *U-110*. He called up two more U-boats. One was the Type VIIB *U-99* commanded by Kapitänleutnant Otto Kretschmer, another ace who in this boat and his previous command – the Type IIB *U-23* – had sunk thirty-nine vessels and damaged five more. The other was the Type VIIB *U-100* commanded by Kapitänleutnant Joachim Schepke, yet another ace who in this boat had sunk twenty-six vessels and damaged two more.

On the first night, 15/16 March, Kretschmer and Schepke attacked the convoy but the latter's U-boat was spotted and pursued. This drew off three destroyers, enabling Kretschmer to close and torpedo five merchant vessels, four of which sank. On the following night Kretschmer sank another ship but Schepke's return to the fray met with disaster. The presence of his U-boat was detected by the destroyer HMS *Vanoc*, which was equipped with the new Type 271 seaborne radar. Hitherto, U-boats had approached convoys on the surface at night, confident that Asdic could detect them only when under water. Schepke managed to crash-dive but was blown to the surface by depth charges. Then the U-boat was rammed by HMS *Vanoc* and went to the bottom, taking with it Schepke and thirty-seven of his crew. Six survivors were picked up by the warships.

By this time Kretschmer had expended all his torpedoes and dived to escape the circling escorts. His U-boat was promptly picked up by Asdic and accurately depth-charged, wrecking the machinery. Forced to the surface, the U-boat was illuminated by a searchlight. Immediate gunfire was opened by the destroyer HMS *Walker,* but this ceased when the crew managed to flash a signal light in Morse stating that their boat was sinking. Four of the crew were killed but thirty-nine were rescued from swimming in the icy water, including Kretschmer.

The fifth U-boat to be sunk in March was the Type VIIC *U-551* commanded by Kapitänleutnant Karl Schrott. This had left Bergen on its first war cruise to operate in the North Atlantic, no doubt with the intention of eventually arriving in a French port. It sank no ships but when south of Iceland on 23 March was spotted by the trawler HMS *Vizalma*. It dived but was accurately depth-charged and lost with all forty-five hands.

The loss of these five U-boats was dismaying news for Dönitz but he accepted it philosophically, believing it to be the result of an adverse set of circumstances such as happened in war. Although he must have known via the Red Cross that some of his U-boat

```
TO I.D.8.G.                            ZTP/122.              151
FROM GERMAN NAVAL SECTION G.C. AND C.S.


5660 KC/S.                    T.O.I. 1731/9/2/41
          T.O.O. 1907/107


FROM: ADMIRAL COMMANDING U-BOATS (B.D.U.)
TO: U 37


     SO FAR AT LEAST TWO SUNK FIVE DAMAGED BY AIR ATTACK. HAVE
A GO.  ATTACK AND REPORT WHEN YOU CAN SUCCESS AND DISPOSITION OF
ESCORT.
(DEPT.NOTE:  ''HAVE A GO'' = RAN, CF. DRAN BLEIBEN, ZTP/88)


1735/17/3/41   CTC/VC
```

The Type IXA *U-37*, commissioned on 4 August 1938, left Lorient on 3 February 1941 and was on its eleventh war cruise, under the command of Kapitänleutnant Nicolai Clausen, when this signal was sent six days later. It had already sunk fifty vessels and damaged one more on its previous war cruises. On this cruise it made rendezvous with the cruiser *Admiral Hipper* and a Focke-Wulf Kondor of Kampfgeschwader 40. After sinking three more vessels, it returned to Lorient. It made only one more cruise and survived the war, to be scuttled on 8 May 1945.

Ref: DEFE 3/1

men were prisoners of war, and probably guessed that the British were providing more naval escorts, he had no knowledge of the new seaborne radar equipment which contributed to the sinkings. He assumed that the area to the south of Iceland had become more dangerous and ordered his U-boats to concentrate on an area further to the south-west. New arrivals had built up his numbers to forty-six, but with only six undergoing trials and training.

There was another development during this month, for on 6 March Winston Churchill issued his directive entitled 'The Battle of the Atlantic'. This gave top priority to the offensive against the U-boat and the Focke-Wulf Kondor. It involved such strategies as bombing U-boat building yards in ports, fitting out ships with catapult fighter aircraft, increasing the strength of Coastal Command, giving priority to ships with short-range anti-aircraft guns, taking defensive measures for key British ports, improving repair facilities for ships and directing labour resources into all such purposes.

April was another successful month for the U-boats and Italian submarines. These sank almost 250,000 tons of the total lost at sea, which reached a peak of almost 688,000 tons, for the loss of only two U-boats. German aircraft accounted for almost 323,000 tons of the balance. But Dönitz was unaware that British intelligence was taking a leap forward in the decryption of his naval Enigma code. This was being tackled in Hut 4 at Bletchley Park, but the code was proving far more intractable than those used by the Luftwaffe and the German Army.

```
                                                              181
      TO I.D.8.G.                        ZTP/147.

      FROM GERMAN NAVAL SECTION G.C. AND C.S.


      5660 KC/S.                       T.O.MI. 0541/24/2/41
                 T.O.O. 0707/116


      FROM: U 95

      TO:    ADMIRAL COMMANDING U-BOATS (B.D.U.)

           THREE SHIPS 18000 GROSS TONNAGE SUNK IN CONVOY.   HAVE EIGHT

      TORPEDOES LEFT.


         1101/18/3/41.   GT/VC                          081
```

The type VIIC *U-95* was built by Germaniawerft of Kiel and commissioned on 31 August 1940. It left Lorient on 16 February for its third war cruise, under the command of Kapitänleutnant Gerd Schreiber, and on 24 February sank three merchant vessels, resulting in this signal of the same date. The correct tonnage was 13,806. It returned safely and made three more war cruises but was sunk on the fourth. After leaving Lorient on 19 November 1941 it entered the Mediterranean and on 28 November was torpedoed by the Dutch submarine *0,21* off Algiers. Thirty-five of the crew were lost but twelve were taken prisoner, including Schreiber.

Ref: DEFE 3/1

The breakthrough happened almost by accident, resulting from a commando raid on the Lofoten Islands, north of the Arctic Circle and off the coast of Norway. During this British raid, on 4 March 1941, sailors from the destroyer HMS *Somali* boarded the German armed trawler *Krebs* (named after the constellation of Cancer), which had been under gunfire but remained afloat. This vessel was one of those employed as a weather ship, principally to provide reports for the preparation of synoptic charts for the Luftwaffe, which required regular information on the weather fronts moving over the North Atlantic. The British sailors recovered sufficient information for the cryptanalysts at Bletchley Park to read the whole of the secret radio traffic for February 1941. This was no longer of any operational use, but they had discovered the method of decryption and progressed to read the traffic for the following April. This was achieved between 22 April and 10 May, although with some delay in the process. They were then able to read most of the May traffic, the delay being between three and seven days.

One of those who had believed that the key to the decryption of the U-boat Enigma signals could lie in the German weather ships was a young Cambridge graduate at Bletchley Park, F. Harry Hinsley. He was the person who, when President of St John's College and Professor of the History of International Relations in the University of Cambridge many years later, was principally responsible for the preparation of the six official volumes entitled *British Intelligence in the Second World War*. The information from the *Krebs* revealed that the Germans were maintaining two other weather ships, one north of Iceland and the other in mid-Atlantic. This opened the opportunity of capturing more Enigma material, provided the true purpose of the Royal Naval missions could be concealed. The Admiralty became convinced of this possibility and detailed preparations were duly made.

It was decided to tackle the weather ship north of Iceland first, and a 'cutting-out operation' was accomplished on 7 May. The armed trawler *München* had not long taken up position when she was approached at speed by the destroyer HMS *Somali*, part of a force of three cruisers and four destroyers. The weather ship was boarded after a simulated attack made with guns firing dummy shells. Important material was recovered and according to Harry Hinsley's own account 'it was with her settings that CG and CS read the June traffic practically currently'.

Only two days after this episode the British were rewarded with a stroke of luck. On this occasion the westbound Convoy OB318 was attacked near Greenland by two U-boats, the Type IXB *U-110* commanded by the ubiquitous Kapitänleutnant Fritz-Julius Lemp and the Type VIIC *U-201* commanded by Kapitänleutnant Adalbert Schnee. The convoy was strongly escorted by the 3rd Escort Group commanded by Commander A.J. Baker-Creswell, consisting of three destroyers, three corvettes, three armed trawlers and an armed merchant cruiser. Lemp was a major U-boat ace on his tenth war cruise. In his earlier *U-30* and his present *U-110*, he had sunk seventeen vessels and damaged four. He was the first to attack on this occasion, torpedoing and sinking two more merchant vessels in the early morning of 9 May. Then his long period of luck ran out. His U-boat was crippled and brought to the surface by depth charges fired by the corvette HMS *Aubretia*, commanded by Lieutenant-Commander E.V. Smith. As it surfaced, the destroyer HMS *Bulldog* under Baker-Creswell was already racing towards it on a ramming course, when the commander suddenly realised that a capture might be possible and ordered the engines to be put into reverse.

Meanwhile the destroyer HMS *Broadway*, which was also racing to the scene in order to drop more depth charges, opened fire with a Lewis gun on some of the crew pouring out of the conning tower. The U-boat turned and the destroyer struck only a glancing blow, causing some damage to herself. She dropped a single depth charge. Lemp ordered his crew to abandon ship, under the impression that it would sink. Other escort warships circled the scene, hunting the evading *U-201* and picking up survivors from the two torpedoed merchant ships.

Meanwhile, HMS *Bulldog* had launched a whaler with a boarding party of nine men commanded by Sub-Lieutenant David E. Balme. This reached *U-110* when the U-boat men were already in the water and some were being picked up. The whaler was washed up on the deck of the U-boat, where it was smashed on impact. The party found the tower hatch closed but managed to open it. Their orders were to retrieve books and anything that looked important. Fortunately the U-boat did not sink and they managed to collect an Enigma machine and the code books. Another boarding party then arrived and an engineer officer stabilised the controls.

Lemp was swimming in the sea but could see that his U-boat remained afloat and ordered his watch officer, Oberleutnant zur See Dietrich Loewe, to swim back to it. Lemp probably tried to do the same but he and fourteen of his men were lost. Thirty-two others, including Loewe, were picked up by the escorts and taken prisoner. The boarding parties got a tow on to *Bulldog*, which began to move towards Iceland with her capture, the Royal

Navy men having been taken off. All went well until early the next morning when the wind increased to Force 6 and heavy waves began to rock both vessels. At mid-morning the U-boat suddenly started to go down stern first and the tow had to be released.

The sinking of *U-110* was a disappointment to the Royal Navy, but the haul of its confidential material proved a godsend to Bletchley Park. According to Harry Hinsley, it included the special signals used for 'officer only' reports and the code book used by the U-boats when making short-signal sighting reports. However, the settings for May had been destroyed. This was the only U-boat lost during May, a month in which they sank almost 325,500 tons of shipping from a total of over 511,000 tons lost by the British.

Of course, these developments were unknown to the British general public, but another dramatic event became headline news. The huge new battleship *Bismarck* left Gotenhafen on 19 May, commanded by Kapitän zur See Ernst Lindemann, and headed for Norway in company with the heavy cruiser *Prinz Eugen*. The enterprise was commanded by Admiral Gunther Lütjens. Their passage was spotted by an aircraft of the Swedish cruiser *Gotland* and the information passed to London through diplomatic channels. British intelligence was aware from Enigma decrypts that these warships intended to raid the commerce routes. On 21 May their presence at anchor off Grimstadfjord in Norway was confirmed by Spitfire I serial X4496 of No. 1 Photographic Reconnaissance Unit flown from Wick in Caithness by Flying Officer Michael F. Suckling. Another photograph taken on the following day by Maryland I serial AR720 of the Fleet Air Arm's 771 Squadron, flown from Hatston in the Orkneys by Lieutenant Noel E. Goddard, confirmed that the warships had left. The commander of the Home Fleet, Admiral Sir John Tovey, ordered most of his battleships, aircraft carriers, cruisers and other warships to patrol the Denmark Strait between Iceland and Greenland.

In the ensuing encounter on 24 May a broadside from *Bismarck* struck the battle cruiser HMS *Hood*, which immediately blew up with the loss of 1,416 lives. Only three sailors survived. The battleship HMS *Prince of Wales* was also hit but did not sink. Three of her shells caused damage to *Bismarck*, which was holed. The battle was observed by a Sunderland of 201 Squadron on a ferrying trip between Iceland and Sullom Voe in Shetlands. The pilot, Flight Lieutenant Richard J. Vaughan, shadowed the German warships for as long as his fuel permitted and reported their positions.

Admiral Lütjens decided to break off the operation and head for France. He detached *Prinz Eugen* to Brest, where she eventually arrived safely to join *Scharnhorst* and *Gneisenau*. *Bismarck* headed for St-Nazaire, where there was a dock large enough to accommodate her. With his warships in pursuit, Admiral Tovey dispatched nine Fairey Swordfish of 825 Squadron for a torpedo attack and five Fairey Fulmars of 802 Squadron for reconnaissance, all from the carrier HMS *Victorious*. They found the battleship and scored one torpedo hit but this caused little damage.

By 25 May *Bismarck* seemed to have disappeared. It was assumed that she was heading for Brest and many of the hunters were covering the wrong area. It was not until mid-morning on 26 May that she was located by Catalina I serial AH545 of 209 Squadron, recently arrived from the USA and flown from Loch Erne in Northern Ireland by Pilot Officer Denis A. Briggs. Fourteen Swordfish were dispatched from the carrier HMS *Ark Royal* during the afternoon but the weather was extremely hazy and the crews mistook the shadowing cruiser HMS *Sheffield* for their target and attacked, fortunately without causing any damage. Their torpedoes were armed with Duplex magnetic warheads, some of which exploded prematurely in the heavy area.

Then another air attack was made during the evening by fifteen Swordfish of 810, 818 and 820 Squadron from HMS *Ark Royal*, some of which had participated in the earlier attack. Led by Lieutenant-Commander Trevenen P. Coode, they headed directly for HMS *Sheffield*, which gave them the course for *Bismarck*. On this occasion their torpedoes were armed with contact pistols in the warheads. They scored three hits and one of the torpedoes wrecked the steering gear of the battleship, jamming the rudders to port.

Unable to steer correctly *Bismarck* could not head for St-Nazaire or escape her pursuers. Five British destroyers closed with her during the night, while the Type VIIC *U-556* and the Type VIIB *U-74* U-boats sped to give the German battleship some assistance. Early the next morning the battleships HMS *King George V* and *Rodney* arrived and opened a tremendous fire, knocking out all *Bismarck*'s main guns and reducing her decks to a shambles. Then the cruiser HMS *Devonshire* struck her with two torpedoes. She began to go down and the German crew abandoned ship. Rescue was rendered difficult by the presence of the U-boats. Only 110 men from her crew of 2,200 were picked up by British warships or German U-boats.*

This was the last attempt by any major German warship to raid the British supply routes, although the Royal Navy had to guard against the possibility that some would enter the Atlantic. However, a series of calamities befell these warships. On 13 June 1941 the pocket battleship *Lützow* was making an excursion south-west of Norway when she was torpedoed by a Beaufort of 42 Squadron flown from Leuchars in Fifeshire by Flight Sergeant Ray H. Loviett. Although she did not sink, repairs occupied a very lengthy period. The cruiser *Prinz Eugen*, still sheltering at Brest, was hit by a bomb dropped on the night of 1/2 July 1941 during a raid by fifty-two Wellingtons of Bomber Command. It exploded inside her hull, killing sixty-one crew members and putting her out of action for over three months. Then the battleship *Scharnhorst* left Brest on 23 July 1941 for proving trials and arrived at La Pallice. On the following day Bomber Command dispatched fifteen Halifaxes on a very dangerous daylight raid against this port. Five were shot down but all the remainder attacked. Five bombs hit *Scharnhorst*, three of which were armour-piercing and passed through the deck. She was patched up and returned to Brest for more permanent repairs, and was out of action for four months.

Henceforth the Battle of the Atlantic was conducted mainly against German U-boats. The ability of Bletchley Park to decrypt messages did not have an immediate effect on shipping losses, for the U-boats and the Italian submarines sank over 310,000 tons in June 1941 from a total of 432,000 tons lost during the month. Nevertheless, the Admiralty's Submarine

---

* Seven Bristol Beauforts of the RAF's 217 Squadron, with the author as one of the crew members, were on standby at St Eval in Cornwall ready to attack *Bismarck*. The senior survivor of the German battleship was the fourth gunnery officer, Baron Burkard von Müllenheim-Rechberg, who became a diplomat after the war. He conferred with this author when revising his book *Battleship Bismarck*, first published in 1980.

Tracking Room in London was able to begin building up a picture of the dispositions of U-boats in all waters and to take measures ensuring that convoys were routed away from them. Three U-boats were destroyed during the month. On 22 June 1941 the war with Germany expanded enormously when Hitler launched operation Barbarossa and the Wehrmacht began its advances over the Polish and Russian plains towards Moscow. This did not have any immediate effect on the Battle of the Atlantic but the Royal Navy knew that its resources might be further strained by the need to supply war materials to a new ally, over extremely difficult and icy waters in which U-boats would be active. One other noticeable effect, confirmed by decrypts of enemy signals, was the withdrawal of many squadrons of the Luftwaffe from the west to this new theatre of war.

On 28 June 1941 the Royal Navy scored another success in the intelligence war by capturing the weather ship *Lauenberg*. The date was carefully chosen since it was known she would be taking over from another weather ship and carrying the next monthly sheet of Enigma settings. The converted trawler was boarded by sailors from the destroyer *Tartar,* who did not recover an Enigma machine but brought away many secret documents. To quote Harry Hinsley again: 'With her settings GC and CS read the traffic currently throughout July.' Moreover, the situation at Bletchley Park had improved with the mounting experience in decryption methods and the recruitment of more specialist staff. They had also successfully built their 'Bombe' versions of the 'Bombas' devised by the Polish mathematicians before the war. By this time these had increased to six, with one permanently available for the naval traffic. No further attempts at captures of any weather ships were made, in case the enemy suspected the motives. The decryption of naval codes continued without any further aids. In this period the Admiralty began to use the prefix 'Ultra' for references relating to the decryption of Enigma signals concerning operations of the Kriegsmarine.

In July the U-boats and Italian submarines found far fewer targets, sinking only 94,200 tons of shipping from a total of 120,975 tons lost by Britain. They lost none of their own number, possibly since there were so few contacts with convoys and their escorts. This month thus marked the end of the first 'Happy Time' of the U-boats. Although the number of U-boats available for war cruises had increased to sixty-five and thereafter continued to mount steadily, the number of ships sunk per U-boat at sea went into reverse. There were several reasons for this decline, the ability of Bletchley Park to decrypt signals being only one of them. The increased strength of the naval escorts was undoubtedly a potent factor. In particular, the Royal Canadian Navy began to undertake escort duties in the Western Atlantic from the end of May 1941 and its willing recruits soon began to gain experience. Their advent provided a welcome relief for the Royal Navy, which was able to concentrate its efforts in the central and eastern sectors of the Atlantic. The new Type 271 radar equipment, which could identify U-boats on the surface, was being fitted to an increasing number of vessels. U-boats had lost their immunity in this respect while remaining vulnerable to the older Asdic when under the surface.

Another reason for the decline in the success of the U-boats may have been related to the fact that many of the experienced pre-war commanders had been lost. A revealing postwar analysis showed that, of about 1,171 ocean-going U-boats commissioned during the Second World War, only 321 made any attacks on ships. Of these, 25 U-boats attacked

```
TO I.D.8.G.                          ZTP 85                104
FROM GERMAN NAVAL SECTION G.C AND C.S.

    110/7760 KC/S.              T.O.I.1325/25/2/41

           T.O.O.1353.
FROM:  GRUPPE WEST
TO  :  FLEET SERIAL NO.7 (FLOTTE 7)


       ACCORDING TO PRECISE EXAMINATION OF PHOTOGRAPHS
BRX  SCAPA 24/2:  NELSON,RODNEY, KING GEORGE, ONE BERWICK, ONE

AURORA, EIGHT LIGHT CRUISERS (CLASS NOT RECOGNIZED), PROBABLY ONE

SUBMARINE, ONE DESTROYER.


1250/16/3/41/CTC/LLB
```

Notification of the presence of major British warships at Scapa Flow, photographed by a reconnaissance aircraft of the Luftwaffe on 24 February 1941.

Ref: DEFE 3/1

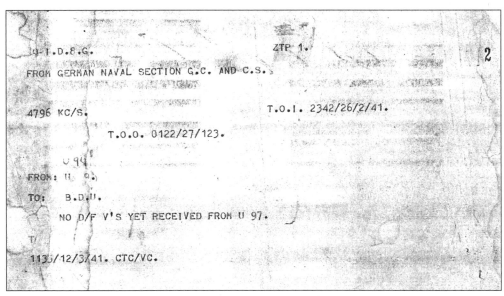

Judging from the note written in ink at Bletchley Park, this signal was sent by the Type VIIC *U-94* on 26 February 1941. This U-boat was built by Germaniaweft of Kiel and commissioned on 10 June 1940. It left Lorient on 9 January 1940 for a second war cruise, under the command of Kapitänleutnant Herbert Kuppisch. The signal was sent to the BDU (Befelshaber der Unterseeboote), or Commander-in-Chief of U-boats. It was one of the first U-boat signals to be decrypted by Bletchley Park. (See also p. 59.)

Ref: DEFE/1

and damaged or sank 20 or more ships, while 36 U-boats attacked and damaged or sank between 11 and 19 ships. Of the remainder, 70 U-boats attacked between 6 and 10 ships, while 190 U-boats attacked between 1 and 5 ships. Thus it seems that about 850 U-boats never made any attacks at all. Of course, some of these were tankers, experimental boats or commissioned in the last few months of the war, but the statistics seem surprising.

The explanation seems to lie partly in the quality of the commanders. Those who trained and qualified before the war may have found easier pickings in the first eighteen months, before the British developed effective counter-measures, but they certainly displayed skill, audacity and determination which produced favourable results. Naturally, some of the later commanders, many of whom had been junior officers before the war, emulated their predecessors, but some appear to have been more cautious when they knew the defences had strengthened against them.

By July 1941 several CAM-ships had been launched and RAF pilots were serving on them. However, the first success of a catapulted Hurricane occurred on 2 August 1941, not from a CAM-ship but from a 'Fighter Catapult Ship' of the Royal Navy. One of five such vessels, HMS *Maplin* was heading to meet an inward-bound convoy from Sierra Leone. The pilot, Lieutenant Robert W.H. Everitt of the Fleet Air Arm, shot down a Focke-Wulf Kondor after a long battle and was picked up when he ditched his Hurricane.

An unusual episode took place on 27 August 1941 when the Type VIIC *U-570* was on its first war cruise, under the command of Kapitänleutnant Hans-Joachim Rahmlow. When south of Iceland it was depth-charged by two Hudsons of 269 Squadron from Kaldadarnes. The U-boat was forced to the surface and the crew surrendered. British destroyers and an anti-submarine trawler arrived, the Germans were taken off and the U-boat was towed to Iceland. Some documents were recovered and the U-boat was closely examined, restored to serviceable condition, and later commissioned as HMS *Graph*.

Another event which took place at the end of August was a British raid on the Norwegian archipelago of Spitsbergen, where the Germans were constructing weather stations. Two cruisers and several destroyers escorted the liner *Empress of Canada,* carrying Canadian and other troops to this arctic region. They returned successfully on 3 September. The purpose was to thwart any attempts by the Kriegsmarine to set up bases for U-boats and also to play on Hitler's known fears that another attack would be made on the Norwegian mainland.

The U-boats and their Italian allies sank about 80,300 tons of shipping during August, from a total of about 130,500 tons lost by Britain. Four U-boats were lost during the month, including the capture of *U-570*. September was in some respects a more favourable month for them, for there were changes to the references in their naval grid, causing some delay while Bletchley Park worked out the new code letters. Wolf packs beset the eastbound convoy SC42, consisting of sixty-two merchant ships which left Nova Scotia on 30 August. They sank sixteen of these vessels for the loss of two of their number, the only U-boats lost in the month. U-boats accounted for 202,800 tons of the 286,000 tons of shipping lost by Britain during September.

However, there was an incident on 4 September which threatened to draw the US Navy into the Battle of the Atlantic. They Type VIIC *U-652* was south-west of Iceland when it was depth-charged by the RAF. It then fired two torpedoes at the destroyer USS *Greer,* under the impression that she was an attacker. This was within a Security Zone designated by America.

Although the destroyer avoided the torpedoes and then dropped depth charges, the incident infuriated the American public and was denounced by President Roosevelt. One outcome was the provision of four US destroyers as part of the escort to convoy HX150 which left Halifax in Nova Scotia on 16 September, although this was not intercepted by U-boats.

By October Dönitz could muster eighty ocean-going U-boats for the campaign, with as many as 118 others undergoing trials and training. The British lost a total of over 218,000 tons in the month, of which about 156,000 tons were sunk by U-boats or submarines. Only two U-boats were sunk. However, there were further incidents with American warships. In the middle of the month a strong gale forced the dispersal of the eastbound convoy SC48, which also had the misfortune to run into a wolf pack. Three merchant vessels were sunk and appeals were made for reinforcements of escorts, since some of the Canadian warships had also dispersed in the gale. Five US destroyers arrived and on 17 October the Type VIIC *U-568* torpedoed the USS *Kearney.* The destroyer did not sink but there were a number of casualties which included eleven killed. She managed to reach Iceland.

There was an even more serious encounter on 31 October, when five US destroyers were assisting in the escort of the eastbound convoy HX156. On this occasion the USS *Reuben James* was torpedoed and sunk by the Type VIIC *U-562,* resulting in the loss of 115 of her crew. Only 45 men were saved. This caused a revision of the Neutrality Act by the US Congress, enabling President Roosevelt to enter the Battle of the Atlantic although his country was not yet at war with Germany.

In November 1941 only thirteen ships totalling about 60,000 tons were sunk by U-boats and submarines, from the relatively low total of about 104,500 tons lost by Britain. Five U-boats were lost in the month. One reason for this diminution was an order given on 22 November by Hitler in his capacity as Commander of the German Armed Forces. Four days earlier the British had launched their offensive in the Western Desert under the codename of operation Crusader. Hitler required the U-boats to concentrate on the approaches to the Straits of Gibraltar or to enter the Mediterranean, in order to assist the Deutsches Afrika Korps under General Erwin Rommel, which was short of fuel following the destruction of seven supply vessels by the Royal Navy.

These new areas of operations proved most unprofitable for the U-boats and they began to suffer heavy losses in December. However, the main event this month occurred on the 7th when carrier-borne Japanese aircraft delivered an unexpected and devastating attack on the US naval base of Pearl Harbor in Hawaii. America and Japan were immediately at war. Both Hitler and Mussolini declared war on the USA on 11 December and the conflict became truly worldwide.

The entry of the USA into the war ensured that the eventual outcome would be victory for the Western Allies, but it threw an additional strain on the overall shipbuilding programme. The Lend-Lease Act had been passed on 11 March 1941 and appeals had been made to the USA for help with shipping and supplies. During the year the Americans had increased their building of fast merchant ships and handed many of these over to the British. It was hoped that new building in America and Britain would increase Britain's shipping capacity during 1942, despite losses from sinkings, but then the Americans had to replenish their own losses. The programme of supplying Britain with vital war materials was put into jeopardy.

```
TO I.D.8.G.                              ZTP.6.                      7
FROM GERMAN NAVAL SECTIONG.C AND C.S.

110/16350/7760/12040                T.O.I.1739/27/2/41.

                T.O.O. 1752.

FROM:  WEST GROUP (WESTGRUPPE)
  TO : FLEET 43 (FLOTTE 43)


    NAVAL ATTACHE WASHINGTON REPORTS CONVOY RENDEZVOUS 25TH
FEBRUARY 200 SEA MILES EAST OF SABLE ISLAND.  13 CARGO BOATS,
4 TANKERS, 100,000  TONS.  CARGO: AEROPLANE PARTS, MACHINE PARTS,
MOTOR LORRIES, MUNITIONS, CHEMICALS.  PROBABLY THE NUMBER OF THE
CONVOY IS  HX 114.

(NOTE:  THE MEANING OF FLOTTE 43 IS NOT CLEAR TO US, BUT IT IS
THOUGHT THAT IT MEANS  FLEET SERIAL NO.43).

1710/12/3/41/CTC/LLB.
```

Intelligence information emanating from the German Naval Attaché in Washington, sent to U-boats at sea on 27 February 1941.

Ref: DEFE 3/1

A Consolidated Catalina I of Coastal Command in flight. These flying boats had a remarkable endurance which could be increased to about 24 hours with extra fuel tanks.

Author's collection

Top: The Consolidated PBY-5 Catalina flying boat entered service with Coastal Command in March 1941. It was employed on maritime reconnaissance and as a long-range escort for convoys, with a radius of action of up to 2,000 miles. It had a crew of eight or nine, could carry up to 2,000 lb of bombs and was armed with a single machine-gun in the bows, two in each of the side blisters and another in a ventral position. This Catalina II serial AM266 was engaged on trials with the Torpedo Development Unit at Gosport, but Catalinas were never employed in the role of torpedo-bombers.

Ref: AVIA 16/59

Right: A depth charge exploding in early 1941, dropped by a former escort destroyer of the US Navy of 1,385 tons displacement. Forty-three of these vessels were transferred to the Royal Navy in 1940 and served under the name of 'Town' class.

Author's collection

The Type VIIC *U-70* was built by Germaniawerft of Kiel and commissioned on 23 November 1940. It left Heligoland on 20 February 1941 under the command of the highly experienced Kapitänleutnant Joachim Matz, bound for the North Atlantic. Six days later it sank a Swedish merchant vessel. Then, on 7 March, it damaged two more vessels, one British one Dutch, which were part of a convoy south-west of the Faroes. However, it was rammed by the Dutch tanker, damaging its conning tower. It then tried to escape at high speed on the surface but was pursued by the corvettes HMS *Arbutus* and *Camellia*. It submerged once more but was eventually blown to the surface by depth charges, as shown here, and came under fire. The crew scuttled their U-boat, twenty of them being lost when it sank. Twenty-six were rescued to become prisoners, including Matz.

Ref: ADM 199/2058

The Type VIIB *U-76* was built by Bremer Vulkan of Vegesack and commissioned on 3 December 1940. It left Bergen on 28 March 1941 under the command of Oberleutnant zur See Friedrich von Hippel, bound for the North Atlantic. On 3 April, when south of Iceland, it sank a Finnish merchant vessel and then a British merchant vessel on the following day. It was then pursued by the destroyer HMS *Wolverine* and the sloop HMS *Scarborough*, which depth-charged it to the surface on 5 April, as shown here. The crew abandoned the U-boat, one losing his life but forty-two being taken prisoner. The corvette HMS *Arbutus* managed to get a party aboard the U-boat shortly before it sank.

Ref: ADM 199/2058

```
                            H                                    313

  ADM

  TO I.D. 8 G.                                    ZTP/252.

  FROM G.N.S.,  G.C. AND C.S.

     15.22, 7640 KC/S                        T.O.I. 1852/16/4/41.

              T.O.O. 2040.

        FROM :  ADMIRAL COMMANDING U-BOATS.

  SHORT SIGNAL FROM U 94: 'SHALL BE OFF LORIENT AT 0830/18/4'

  HAS BEEN RECEIVED.
              2
  2035/23/4/41   AND++++

     RD   TKS
```

A further signal sent by the Type VIIC *U-94*, on this occasion on 16 April 1941 when returning from its third war cruise under the command of Kapitänleutnant Herbert Kuppisch. By this time it had sunk eight merchant vessels on its three cruises. It was eventually sunk on 28 August 1942 when east of Jamaica under the command of Kapitänleutnant Otto Ites. It was depth-charged to the surface by a Mariner of VP-92 Squadron USNAF, and then rammed three times by the corvette HMCS *Oakville*. Nineteen of the crew were killed but twenty-six became prisoners, including the commander. It had sunk a total of twenty-seven merchant vessels and damaged another during ten war cruises. (See also p. 60.)

Ref: DEFE 3/1

```
        RD TKS                                          516

  TO  I D 8 G                          ZTP/453

  FROM GERMAN NAVAL SECTION  G C AND C S

              TOO   2241/3/5/41

        FROM:   ADMIRAL COMMANDING U BOATS

        TO:    U 110

  OCCUPY AS ATTACKING AREA LINE RUNNING NORTH AND SOUTH BETWEEN

  56 DEGREES NORTH AND SQUARE AL 26.

  TOO  2331/13/5/41   WGE/EE
```

The Type IXB *U-110* was built by A.G. Weser of Bremen and commissioned on 21 November 1940. It completed a war cruise under the command of the U-boat ace Kapitänleutnant Fritz Julius Lemp (who had previously commanded two other U-boats), during which it sank three merchant vessels and damaged two more. After it left Lorient on 15 April 1941 for a second cruise, this signal was received on 3 May. Six days later *U-110* was depth-charged to the surface and then rammed by the destroyer HMS *Broadway*. The crew abandoned the U-boat after attempting to scuttle it. Thirty-two were taken prisoner but fifteen lost their lives, including Lemp. The U-boat did not sink and was boarded by a party from the destroyer HMS *Bulldog*, headed by Sub-Lieutenant David E. Balme. An Enigma machine and code books were recovered. The U-boat was taken in tow but sank two days later, on 11 May.

Ref: DEFE 3/1

```
TO  I D 8 G                    ZTP/376                    453
FROM  GERMAN NAVAL SECTION  G C AND C S

11125  KC/S                        TOI  2023/7/5/41

               TOO  2146

FROM: ADMIRAL COMMANDING U BOATS

  TO:   U 93
STEER TO SQUARE  AK  28.

TOO  1912/10/5/41  CTC/EE

RD  OK  +++LWF+++
```

The Type VIIC *U-93* was built by Germaniawerft of Kiel and commissioned on 30 July 1940. It sank nine merchant vessels during three war cruises and was on its fourth when this signal was sent on 7 May 1941, having left Lorient four days earlier under the command of Oberleutnant zur See Claus Korth. Its end came on 15 January 1942, on its seventh war cruise, when it was depth-charged to the surface in mid-Atlantic by the destroyer HMS *Hesperus*. Forty men became PoWs, including the commander, although six were lost.

Ref: DEFE 3/1

```
TO  I D 8 G                    ZTP/705                    822
FROM GERMAN NAVAL SECTION G C AND C S

TOO 2011           7640 KC/S        TOI 1846/19/5/41

FROM ADMIRAL COMMANDING U-BOATS

TO X U 94 AND U 556

THE FUEHRER HAS DECORATED BOTH CAPTAINS WITH THE RITTERKREUZ

TO THE IRON CROSS.  I WISH TO CONVEY TO YOU, ON THE OCCASION

OF THIS RECOGNITION OF THE SERVICES AND SUCCESSES OF THE BOATS

AND THEIR CREWS, MY SINCERE CONGRATULATIONS.  GOOD LUCK AND

SUCCESS IN FUTURE TOO.  DEFEAT ENGLAND.

TOO 0754/25/5/41+++AGT+++BB
```

After returning to Lorient on 18 April 1941 in his Type VIIC *U-94*, Kapitänleutnant Herbert Kuppisch learnt he had been awarded the Knight's Cross. He was killed on 30 August 1943 when commanding the Type IXD2 *U-847*. The other recipient of the Knight's Cross was Kapitänleutnant Herbert Wohlfarth, the commander of the Type VIIC *U-556*, which arrived in Lorient from its first war cruise on 30 May 1941. He had previously commanded other U-boats. He was taken prisoner on 27 June 1941 when *U-556* was sunk in mid-Atlantic by the corvettes HMS *Celandine, Gladiolus* and *Nasturtium*. (See also p. 62.)

Ref: DEFE 3/1

```
                                                        925
   TO : D 8 G                        ZTP/802

   FROM GERMAN NAVAL SECTION  G C AND C S

   21.05/7640 KC/S.                    T O :  0056/25/5/41
                   T O O  0242

   FROM: ADMIRAL COMMANDING U-BOATS.

   TO: U 73.     OCCUPY SQUARE B E 5520.  MAXIMUM ECONOMIC SPEED.

   (DEPT. NOTE:  ''MAXIMUM ECONOMIC SPEED'' = ''HOECHSTE DAUERFAHRT'').

   0614/28/5/41+++WGE

   RD
```

The Type VIIB *U-73* was built by Bremer Vulkan of Vegesack and commissioned on 30 September 1940. This signal dated 25 May 1941 was sent on its third war cruise, after it had left St-Nazaire five days earlier under the command of Kapitänleutnant Helmut Rosenbaum. It was eventually sunk on its sixteenth war cruise, under the command of Kapitänleutnant Horst Deckert, when on 16 December 1943 it was depth-charged to the surface off Oran by the US destroyers *Trippe*, *Niblack*, *Ludlow*, *Wolsey* and *Edison*. Seventeen of the crew lost their lives but thirty-four were rescued to become prisoners, including Deckert. By this time the U-boat had sunk nine merchant vessels and damaged three more.

Ref: DEFE 3/1

The Consolidated B-24C Liberator first entered service with Coastal Command in June 1941 as a 'Very Long Range' aircraft, under Lend-Lease arrangements. It was intended to close the gap in the middle of the North Atlantic which hitherto had not been covered by shore-based aircraft. The first version was known as the Liberator II. With a crew of eight and armed with ten 0.50 inch machine-guns, it provided a radius of action of about 1,200 miles when carrying depth charges. Other variants followed and eventually ten squadrons of Coastal Command were equipped with Liberators, all fitted with Air to Surface Vessel radar. The machine in this photograph was being tested in April 1942 by the Air Fighting Development Unit at Duxford in Cambridgeshire.

Ref: AIR 15/933

```
                                                                    985
ADM

TO I.D.8.G.                              ZTP/857

FROM GERMAN NAVAL SECTION G.C. AND C.S.


7640/21.05 KC/S                    T.O.I. 1658/26/5/41

              T.O.O. 1844

FROM A.C. U-BOATS

     AT 1830 BISMARK IN SQUARE BE 53, COURSE 115 DEGREES, 24

KNOTS.  CRUISER OF SHEFFIELD CLASS SHADOWING.

1500/28/5/41+++CTC/VC++
```

A signal sent to U-boats on 26 May 1941, giving the position, course and speed of the battleship *Bismarck*. The cruiser shadowing her was indeed HMS *Sheffield*.

Ref: DEFE 3/1

```
                                                                    41
RD

TO I.D.8.G.                              ZTP/976

FROM GERMAN NAVAL SECTION G.C. AND C.S.

11125 KC/S                    T.O.I. 1930/27/5/41

              T.O.O. 2059

FROM:   U 74

TO:     ADMIRAL COMMANDING U-BOATS

     AT 1930 IN SQUARE BE 6142.  THREE SURVIVORS FROM BISMARCK.

FROM THEIR ACCOUNT SHE APPEARS TO HAVE SUNK IN SQUARE BE 5330

AT ABOUT 1000.

1522/29/5/41+++WGE/VC+++
```

The Type VIIB *U-74*, under the command of Kapitänleutnant Eitel-Friedrich Kentrat, was one of the U-boats in the Bay of Biscay ordered to go to the assistance of the battleship *Bismarck*. The crew spotted gunfire in the early hours of 26 May 1941 and made contact with another U-boat, the Type VIIC *U-556*. More explosions were heard in the next few hours and Kentrat knew that the battleship had been sunk when three men in a rubber dinghy were picked up in the early evening. Their names were reported as Herzog, Höntzsch and Manthey. They were disembarked at Lorient on 30 May and taken to Group West in Paris, where they gave the first eyewitness account of the sinking of *Bismarck*.

Ref: DEFE 3/2

```
                                    √                              54
   TO I.D.8.G.              ZTP/989

   FROM GERMAN NAVAL SECTION G.C. AND C.S.

   7640 KCXS                 T.O.I. 1231/27/5/41

           T.O.O. 1416

   FROM:  ADMIRAL COMMANDING U-BOATS

   TO:    U-BOATS IN BAY OF BISCAY

       BISMARCK MUST NOW BE ASSUMED TO HAVE SUNK.   U-BOATS TO SEARCH F█

   FOR SURVIVORS IN SQUARE BE 6150 AND TO NORTH WEST OF THIS POSITION.

   1648/29/5/41+++EGT/VC+++

   RD
```

A message sent to U-boats in the Bay of Biscay on 27 May 1941, hoping that more survivors from the battleship *Bismarck* could be found. In all, only 110 men from the crew were picked up by British warships, a U-boat and a German weather ship. Attempts at rescue by the British were hampered by the knowledge that U-boats were in the area.

Ref: DEFE 3/2

```
                                                                 202
   TO I D 8 G               ZTP/1135

   FROM GERMAN NAVAL SECTION G C AND   C S

   110/7760 KC/S                  TOI 2031/27/5/41

              TOO 2156
   FROM WESTGRUPPE

   TO    SACHSENWALD W 10

   ENEMY REPORT:

   PROCEED AT ONCE TO SQUARE B E 6142, WHERE SURVIVORS OF BISMARCK

   HAVE BEEN PICKED UP BY U 74.  U BOAT IS SENDING D/F V'S ON 852

   METRES.

   TOO 0415/30/5/41+++AGT+++
```

The weather ship *Sachsenwald,* a converted trawler under the command of Leutnant zur See Wilhelm Schutte, was en route to home after fifty days at sea when she received this signal on 27 May. She hunted fruitlessly from the morning of the following day for survivors of *Bismarck,* finding only wreckage and corpses in life jackets. Then three red flares were seen at around 2230 hours and she picked up two men in a rubber raft. These were Matrosenfreiter Otto Maus and Maschinengefreiter Walter Lorenzen. They were disembarked in the Gironde on 1 June and taken to Group West in Paris for interrogation.

Ref: DEFE 3/2

329

```
TO I D 8 G                            ZIP/ZTP/2314

FROM G N S

5660 KC/S.                        T O I  0214/9/6/41

              T O O   0330

FROM:  U 46

TO: ADMIRAL COMMANDING U-BOATS

     FOUR TORPEDO FAILURES, OF WHICH THREE DEFINITELY (DUE TO)

PISTOL.  ЬNE MORE FREIGHTER OF 5000 TONS.   SQUARE B D 6245.

(DEPT. NOTE:  FIRST SENTENCE IN ORIGINAL READS:-

         4 TORP. VERSAGER, DAVON MIT SICHERHEIT 3 PI)

0521/9/6/41+++WGE

RD
```

The Type VIIB *U-46* was built by Germaniawerft of Kiel and commissioned on 2 November 1938. It was on its eleventh war cruise, under the command of Kapitänleutnant Englebert Endrass, when this signal was sent on 9 June 1941, before returning to St-Nazaire three days later. Torpedo failures were a constant source of annoyance to U-boat commanders. Nevertheless, by this time it had sunk twenty-three merchant vessels and damaged four more. It was later decommissioned and used as a gun platform, and was scuttled at the end of the war.

Ref: DEFE 3/3

On 13 June 1941 several Beaufort Is of 42 Squadron were dispatched from Leuchars in Fife to hunt the German heavy cruiser *Lützow*, which was known from Enigma decrypts to be off the coast of south-west Norway. One of these, serial L9939 flown by Flight Sergeant Ray H. Loveitt, came across the cruiser escorted by destroyers and achieved a surprise attack. His torpedo scored a hit and put the warship out of action for several months. Loveitt was awarded a DFM. He is shown here, fourth from left, with his crew kitted out for flying and watching a torpedo being loaded on another Beaufort.

Author's collection

```
TO I D 8 G                    ZIP/ZTPG/16                        16
FROM GNS
5660/8365 KC/S          TOO 2210          TOI 2351/15/6/41
          FROM: U 557
            TO: ADMIRAL COMMANDING U-BOATS
HAVE AVOIDED TORPEDO TRACK IN SQUARE C C 3656. FOLLOWED WITH HELP
OF LISTENING APPARATUS BUT ENGLISH S/M THAMES TYPE ESCAPED ON
SURFACE COURSE 310 DEGREES.

0445/16/6/41          EGT/EGT
RD TKS
```

The Type VIIC *U-557* was built by Blohm & Voss of Hamburg and commissioned on 13 February 1941. It was on its first war cruise when this signal was sent on 15 June 1941, having left Kiel on 13 May 1941 under the command of Kapitänleutnant Ottokar Paulshen. It sank one merchant vessel on this cruise, before arriving at Lorient on 10 July 1941. The end came on its third war cruise, after it had entered the Mediterranean. On 16 December 1941 it was accidentally rammed by the Italian torpedo boat *Orione* when south-west of Crete and lost with all forty-three hands.

Ref: DEFE 3/20

```
TO I D 8 G                    ZIP/ZTPG/1054                      56
FROM N S
6180 KC/S                          T O I  0354/25/6/41
          T O O   0539
FROM:  ADMIRAL COMMANDING U-BOATS
TO:  U 561
SEND SHADOWING REPORTS AT ONCE.
0726/25/6/41+++WGE
NOTE: THE GERMAN TEXT READS DISTINCTLY: U 561
RD
```

The Type VIIC *U-561* was built by Blohm & Voss of Hamburg and commissioned on 13 March 1941. It was on its first war cruise when this signal was sent to it on 25 June 1941, having left Kiel on 25 May 1941 under the command of Kapitänleutnant Robert Bartels to operate in the North Atlantic. It arrived safely at Lorient on 1 August 1941, without achieving any sinkings. Its end came on 12 July 1943 when operating from Toulon on its fifteenth war cruise, under the command of Oberleutnant zur See Fritz Henning. It was torpedoed at the northern end of the Straits of Messina by HMS *MTB-81* and sunk with the loss of forty-two crew members. Five men were rescued to become prisoners. By this time *U-561* had sunk seven vessels and damaged another.

Ref: DEFE 3/21

```
TO ID8G                    ZIP/ZTPG/1369                    383
FROM NS

7640 KC/S                     TOI 1641/27/6/41

          TOO 1150

FROM: ADMIRAL COMMANDING U-BOATS

     U 69 REPORTS NO CONTACT WITH CONVOY.

(DEPT.NOTE:  SEE ZTPG/1368)

1320/27/6/41+CTC/VC+

RD OK TKS++
```

The Type VIIC *U-69* was built by Germaniawerft of Kiel and commissioned on 2 November 1940. It was on its third war cruise when this signal was sent on 27 June 1941, having left Lorient on 5 May 1941 under the command of Kapitänleutnant Jost Metzler. Despite this report, it sank two large merchant vessels on the same day, bringing its total score by then up to nine sunk and one damaged during its cruises. It returned safely from this cruise but was sunk in the North Atlantic on its eleventh, on 17 February 1943, when under the command of Kapitänleutnant Ulric Gräf. The destroyer HMS *Fame* depth-charged it to the surface and then rammed it. All forty-six crew members lost their lives. By this time it had sunk sixteen vessels and damaged another.

Ref: DEFE 3/21

```
TO ID8G                    ZIP/ZTPG/1616                    646
FROM NS                                                     118

11125 KC/S               TOI 1328/29/6/41

          TOO 1425

E' 709

FROM: U 123

     ENEMY CONVOY IN SIGHT IN SQUARE DG 9421, STEERING 315

DEGREES, SPEED 7 KNOTS, OPEN FORMATION.

1620/29/6/41++WGE/VC+

RD
```

The Type IXC *U-123* was built by A.G. Weser of Bremen and commissioned on 30 May 1940. It was on its fifth war cruise when this signal was sent, having left Lorient on 8 June 1941 under the command of Kapitänleutnant Reinhard Hardegen. It returned to Lorient on 23 August 1941, twenty-three merchant vessels having been sunk during its five cruises. It then continued a long and eventful career under various commanders. The Germans blew up this U-boat at Lorient on 19 August 1944, after it had become unseaworthy. By this time it had completed thirteen war cruises, sunk a total of forty-seven vessels and damaged five more.

Ref: DEFE 3/21

```
TO I D 8 G                          ZIP/ZTPG/1749              784

FROM N S

     11125 KC/S                    T O I 1524/30/6/41

          T O O 1643

FROM: ADMIRAL COMMANDING U-BOATS

     TWO OUTPOST VESSELS WILL BE AT POINT 32 AT 1000/1/7 AS

ESCORT FOR U 371.    A SPERRBRECHER WILL TAKE STATION AHEAD OF

YOU AT POINT B 1.    FOLLOW AT A DISTANCE OF 200 METRES.

(DEPT NOTE:  POINT 32 IS 48 DEGREES 03.00 MINUTES NORTH

05 DEGREES 10.00 MINUTES WEST.

          POINT B 1  IS 48 DEGREES 16.00 MINUTES NORTH

04 DEGREES 49.7 MINUTES WEST).

1913/30/6/41/WGE/LLB++++
```

The Type VIIC *U-371* was built by Howaldtswerke of Kiel and commissioned on 15 March 1941. When this signal was sent on 30 June 1941, it was returning from its first war cruise after having left Kiel on 5 June 1941 under the command of Kapitänleutnant Heinrich Driver, during which it had sunk two merchant vessels. The 'Sperrbrecher' was a mine-exploding vessel with a reinforced concrete bottom, which preceded it into Brest on the following day. This U-boat continued a very eventful career, mainly in the Mediterranean, but was forced to scuttle itself on 3 May 1944 when north-north-west of Bougie in Algeria, on its eighteenth war cruise and under the command of Oberleutnant zur See Horst-Arno Fenski. It submerged after being chased by British and French destroyers as well as an American minesweeper. Finally the French destroyer *Senegalais* depth-charged it to the surface, despite being torpedoed. Three of the crew lost their lives but forty-eight were taken prisoner. By this time it had sunk twelve merchant vessels, damaged two more, and damaged two destroyers.

Ref: DEFE 3/21

```
        PAPER OK NOW                                          120

  TKS

    TO  I D 8 G                          ZIP/ZTPG/2113
  FROM  N S

  7640 KC/S        TOO 2322        TOI 2145/3/7/41

  FROM:  ADMIRAL COMMANDING U BOATS

  U 559 WILL BE OFF LORIENT IN 36 HOURS.

  (DEPT. NOTE: CF. ZTPG/2108).

  0235/4/7/41++++EE
```

The Type VIIC *U-559* was built by Blohm & Voss of Hamburg and commissioned on 27 February 1941. It left Kiel on 4 June 1941 for its first war cruise, under the command of Kapitänleutnant Hans Heidtmann, and arrived at St-Nazaire on 5 July 1941 without scoring any successes. The end came on 30 October 1942 on its tenth war cruise under the same commander, about 60 miles north-east of Port Said. By this time it had sunk an Australian sloop and four merchant ships and damaged another. It was depth-charged to the surface by the destroyers HMS *Pakenham, Petard, Dulverton* and *Hurworth*. The crew scuttled the U-boat but it was boarded before sinking. An Enigma machine, code books and charts were recovered, enabling Bletchley Park to break into the new four-wheel system. Two of the Royal Navy boarders, Lieutenant Anthony Fasson and Able Seaman Colin Grazier, went down with the U-boat along with seven of the crew. Forty-one, including the commander, were rescued.

Ref: DEFE 3/22

```
      ADM                                                    502
    TO  ID8G
    FROM NS                          ZIP/ZTPG/2470
    9420 KC/S                        TOI 1755/7/7/41
              TOO 1920
    FROM: ADMIRAL COMMANDING U-BOATS
    TO: U 103
          ITALIAN S/M REPORTS CONVOY, 10 SHIPS, AT 1600 IN SQUARE
    CG 8856, COURSE 205 DEGREES, 10 KNOTS.   THERE ARE SEVERAL
    ITALIAN S/MS IN SQUARE CG.
    2107/7/7/41+++AND/DE
    RD
```

The Type IXB *U-103* was built by A.G. Weser of Bremen and commissioned on 5 July 1940. It was on its fourth war cruise when this signal was sent to it on 7 July 1941, having left Lorient on 1 April 1941 under the command of Kapitänleutnant Victor Schültze to operate off West Africa. It had already sunk a total of twenty-eight merchant ships during its cruises, including this cruise, and damaged two more. It returned safely to Lorient on 12 July 1941 and continued a successful career, sinking sixteen more vessels and damaging another before being destroyed on 15 April 1945 during a bombing raid on Kiel by the US Eighth Air Force.

Ref: DEFE 3/22

```
ADM        =3?                                                    3   776

  TO I D 8 G                                    ZIP/ZTPG/2727
  FROM NS

  5660 KC/S              TOO 0053/10             TOI 2319/9/7/41

       FROM: ADMIRAL COMMANDING U-BOATS

  ACCORDING TO SHORT SIGNAL U 553 HAS BEGUN RETURN PASSAGE.

  0313/10/7/41++++EGT
```

The Type VIIC *U-553* was built by Blohm & Voss of Hamburg and commissioned on 23 December 1940. It left St-Nazaire on 7 June 1941 for its second war cruise, commanded by Kapitänleutnant Karl Thurman, and sank two ships in the North Atlantic before sending this signal on 9 July 1941 and reaching port ten day later. It did not return from its tenth war cruise under the same commander, after reporting 'periscope failure' on 20 January 1943 when in the North Atlantic. It was lost with all forty-seven crew members. By this time it had sunk fifteen merchant ships.

Ref: DEFE 3/22

```
ADM                                                                  138

  TO I D8 Q                                     ZIP/ZTPG/3130
  FROM N S

       11125 KC/S                       T O I 0931/14/7/41
                    T O O 1102

  FROM: ADMIRAL COMMANDING U BOATS
  TO :   U 202

       RETURN BY STAGES IN ACCORDANCE WITH STATE OF FUEL.
  SQUARES BD 20, BD 30 AND BE 10 APPEAR TO OFFER GOOD PROSPECTS.

  1220/14/7/41/CEL/LLB++++
  RD
```

The Type VIIC *U-202* was built by Germaniawerft of Kiel and commissioned on 22 March 1941. It left Kiel on 17 June 1941 for its first war cruise, commanded by Kapitänleutnant Hans-Heinz Linder, and received this signal on 14 July 1941 before arriving in Brest a week later without scoring any successes. The end came on 1 June 1943 in the North Atlantic on its ninth war cruise, under the command of Kapitänleutnant Günther Poser, when it was depth-charged to the surface by the sloop HMS *Starling* and then repeatedly hit by gunfire. Eighteen crew members were killed but thirty were taken prisoner, including Poser. It had sunk nine merchant vessels and damaged four more during its career.

Ref: DEFE 3/23

```
ADM                                                      549

TO ID8G

FROM NS                              ZIP/ZTPG/3522

7640 KC/S                            TOI 1635/18/7/41

          TOO 1810

FROM: ADMIRAL COMMANDING U-BOATS

TO: U 141

     CONVOY PROCEEDING FROM NORTH TO EAST WILL PASS LANDS END AT

ABOUT 0500/19/7.

1925/18/7/41+++AND/DE

RD
```

The Type IID *U-141* was built by Deutschewerke of Kiel and commissioned on 21 August 1940. It left Lorient on 14 July 1941 for its third war cruise, commanded by Oberleutnant zur See Philip Schüler, to operate off the Scilly Isles. By this time it had sunk two merchant vessels and damaged another. No successes were scored on this cruise, despite this signal of 18 July 1941. It made one more war cruise, sinking two small vessels. It was relegated to training duties in September 1941 and scuttled off Wilhelmshaven at the end of the war.

Ref: DEFE 3/23

```
     DD                                                  561
ADM
TO I D 8 G                              ZIP/ZTPG/4544

FROM N S

10819 KC/S                             T O I 2336/26/7/41

          T O O   0128/27

E' 874.
FROM : U 331.

     ENEMY CONVOY IN SIGHT, SQUARE B E 8565, (COURSE) 135.

0158/27/7/41    AND+++

RD
```

The Type VIIC *U-331* was built by Nordseewerke of Emden and commissioned on 31 March 1941. It left Kiel on 2 July 1941 for its first war cruise, commanded by Oberleutnant zur See Hans-Dietrich Baron von Tiesenhausen, and sent this signal on 26 July 1941. Despite the sighting of a convoy in the North Atlantic, it sank no vessels and arrived at Lorient on 20 August 1941. It then entered the Mediterranean and was bombed and crippled on 17 November 1942 by three Hudsons of the RAF's 500 Squadron, when on its ninth war cruise under the same commander and about 35 miles north-west of Algiers. An Albacore of the Fleet Air Arm's 820 Squadron from the carrier HMS *Formidable* then torpedoed and sank it. Thirty-two crew members were killed but the commander and seventeen men were taken prisoner. By this time it had sunk five vessels, including the battleship HMS *Barham*.

Ref: DEFE 3/24

```
ADM                                                        595
TO  I  D  8  G
FROM  N  S                              ZIP/ZTPG/5572
11068 KC/S                          T O I  1535/5/8/41
              T O O  1704
FROM: U 204
TO: ADMIRAL COMMANDING U-BOATS
      SQUARE AL 7191.    DURING NIGHT HIT ON ABOUT 14000 TON (SHIP).
DRIVEN OFF BY ESCORT.    8 PLUS 2 TORPEDOES.    XX 72 CUBIC METRES.
NO CONTACT.    ENGINE OVERHAUL.
1543/12/8/41+++WGR/DE
RD
```

The Type VIIC *U-204* was built by Germaniawerft of Kiel and commissioned on 8 March 1941. It left Brest on 22 July 1941 for its second war cruise, commanded by Kapitänleutnant Walter Kell, and sank a merchant vessel of 4,922 tons on the day this signal was sent, 5 August 1941. It returned safely from this cruise but was sunk on the next, after depth-charging by the sloops HMS *Rochester* and *Mallow* when west of Gibraltar on 19 October 1941. There were no survivors from the crew of forty-six. By this time it had sunk seven vessels.

Ref: DEFE 3/25

```
ADM                                                        335
TO  I  D  8  G              ZIP/ZTPG/5326
FROM   N  S
5560/7770 KC/S     TOO 0504      TOI 0334/7/8/41
FROM:  ADMIRAL COMMANDING U-BOATS
U 97 WILL BE OFF PORT OF ARRIVAL AT 1600/8/8.
2051/10/8/41++++WGE/EE
RD
```

This signal of 7 August 1941 informed the U-boat authorities at St-Nazaire that the Type VIIC *U-97*, under the command of Kapitänleutnant Udo Heilmann, would return from its fourth war cruise on the following day. The U-boat had been built by Germaniawerft of Kiel and commissioned on 28 September 1940, and had already sunk nine merchant vessels and damaged another. It then entered the Mediterranean but was sunk on 16 June 1943 during its fifteenth war cruise when under the command of Kapitänleutnant Hans-Georg Trox. A Hudson IIIA of 459 (RAAF) Squadron, flown from Lydda in Palestine by Flight Sergeant David T. Barnard, bombed and depth-charged it 50 miles west of Haifa, suffering damage itself. Twenty-seven crew members were killed, including Trox, but twenty-one were taken prisoner. By this time it had sunk sixteen vessels and damaged another.

Ref: DEFE 3/25

```
ADM                                                                    935
TO I D 8 G                          ZIP/ZTPG/5878
FROM N S
8365 KC/S                              T O I 2047/17/8/41
                    T O O 2232
E' 472

FROM: U 201

SQUARE A L 9611.   ENEMY STEERING WESTERLY COURSE.

0110/19/8/41+++WGE/AGT+++

RD
```

The Type VIIC *U-201* was built by Germaniawerft of Kiel and commissioned on 25 January 1941. It was on its third war cruise when this signal was sent on 17 August 1941, having left Brest three days earlier under the command of Kapitänleutnant Adalbert Schnee, heading for an area west of Spain. It had sunk two merchant vessels and damaged another on its previous cruises. It was sunk on its tenth war cruise, on 17 February 1943, while under the command of Oberleutnant zur See Günther Rosenberg. In mid-Atlantic it was depth-charged to the surface by the destroyer HMS *Viscount* and then rammed. There were no survivors from the crew of forty-nine. By this time it had sunk twenty-three vessels and damaged two more.

Ref: DEFE 3/25

```
                                                                       920
TO I D 8 G                          ZIP/ZTP/1883
FROM N S
        7640 KC/S                      T O I 1456/2/7/41
                    T O O 1645
E' 867
FROM: U 108
    ENEMY CONVOY IN SIGHT SQUARE  BE 7176, WESTERLY COURSE, SLOW

SPEED.
```

The Type IXB *U-108* was built by A.G. Weser of Bremen and commissioned on 22 October 1940. It was on its third war cruise when this signal was sent on 2 July 1941, having left Lorient on 25 May under the command of Korvettenkapitän Klaus Scholtz. It sank seven merchant vessels on this cruise, bringing its total score up to ten, and returned safely to Lorient. In all, it completed twelve war cruises in a successful career under various commanders, sinking a total of twenty-three vessels before being decommissioned on 1 June 1944.

Ref: DEFE 3/21

```
ADM                                                                      661
TO I D 8 G                                    ZIP/ZTPG/6633
  FROM N S
4595 KC/S                                     T O I  0053/26/8/41
                T O O    0125
FROM : U 101
TO   : ADMIRAL COMMANDING UXBOATS

  HAVE SEEN NOTHING SO FAR.  STRONG AIR PATROLS EAST OF 15 DEGREES.

  75 CUBIC METRES. (WIND) SOUTHEAST 2, CLOUDY.  VISIBILITY MODERATE

  TO GOOD.  SQUARE A M 1719.

0006/29/841    EE/AND+++

  RD
```

The Type VIIB *U-101* was built by Germaniawerft of Kiel and commissioned on 11 March 1940. It was on its ninth war cruise when this signal was sent on 26 August 1941, having left Lorient nineteen days earlier under the command of Kapitänleutnant Ernst Mengersen. It returned to Lorient on 4 September 1941 and made one more war cruise before being relegated to training duties on 1 January 1942. By this time it had sunk twenty-two merchant vessels, damaged two more, and sunk a British destroyer. It surrendered after the war and was scrapped.

Ref: DEFE 3/26

```
TO I D 8 G                        ZIP/ZTPG/6243              254
FROM NS

7640 KX:S            TOO  1153            TOI 1011/23/8/41
     FROM: U 75
        TO: ADMIRAL COMMANDING U BOATS
GIBRALTAR CONVOY NO SUCCESS.  18 CUBIC METRES. SQUARE C G 2717.

NAZAIRE.

0554/25/8/41+++++WGE/EGT
```

The Type VIIB *U-75* was built by Bremer Vulkan of Vegesack and commissioned on 19 December 1940. It was on its third war cruise when this signal was sent on 23 August 1941, having left St-Nazaire on 29 July 1941 under the command of Kapitänleutnant Helmuth Ringlemann. It then returned to St-Nazaire and was sent to the Mediterranean. It was sunk on its fifth cruise, on 28 December 1941, off Mersa Matruh by the destroyer HMS *Kipling*. Fifteen crew members were killed, including Ringlemann, but thirty were taken prisoner. It had sunk a total of six vessels.

Ref: DEFE 3/26

The Type VIIC *U-570,* built by Blohm & Voss of Hamburg and commissioned on 15 May 1941, entered history as the first U-boat to be captured by the British. It left Trondheim on 23 August 1941 for its first war cruise, under the command of Kapitänleutnant Hans Joachim Rahmlow. Four days later, when south of Iceland, it was spotted by a Hudson of 269 Squadron flown from Kaldadarnes by Sergeant Mitchell, who attacked but his depth charges failed to release. The crew called in another Hudson on patrol, flown by Squadron Leader J.H. Thompson, who dropped depth charges and began machine-gunning the deck of the U-boat when it surfaced. Then the RAF men were surprised to see a white flag flying from the conning tower and the crew gathering on deck. Unknown to them, chlorine gas had escaped within the hull of the U-boat. The Hudson signalled for help and remained on station until Catalina serial AH553 of 209 Squadron, flown by Flying Officer E.A. Jewiss, arrived about three hours later from Reykjavik.

Ref: AIR 27/1568

The first Catalina was relieved about two hours later by another of 209 Squadron's Catalinas, serial AH545 flown from Reykjavik by Flight Lieutenant B. Lewin. The anti-submarine trawler HMS *Northern Chief* also arrived in the evening, while *U-570* remained afloat. The seas were so rough on the first day that the U-boat crew could not be rescued. During the next morning the trawler HMS *Kingston Agathe* and the destroyers HMS *Burwell* and *Niagara* also arrived, when this photograph was taken.

Ref: AIR 15/473

Lieutenant H.B. Campbell of HMS *Kingston Agathe* eventually crossed in an inflatable dinghy (normally used as a life raft) to accept the surrender, as shown here. All the German crew members were taken off and the U-boat was towed to Iceland. It yielded some intelligence but the Enigma machine and code books had been thrown overboard. After restoration, the U-boat was recommissioned as HMS *Graph*.

Ref: AIR 27/1568

```
ADM                                                              71
    TO ! D 8 G                          ZIP/ZTPG/7678
FROM N S
        7640 KC/S                 T O ! 1842/8/9/41
                 T O O 2017
FROM: U 206
    WILL BE AT (POINT) N 1 AT 0600/10/9.  REQUEST LUGGAGE AND
POST BE SENT FROM LORIENT TO NAZAIRE.
    1322/12/9/41/CEL/LLB++++
```

The Type VIIC *U-206* was built by Germaniawerft of Kiel and commissioned on 17 May 1941. It was on its first war cruise when this signal was sent on 8 September 1941, having left Trondheim on 5 August 1941 under the command of Kapitänleutnant Herbert Opitz. It arrived at St-Nazaire two days after the signal and made another war cruise from this port, sinking a British corvette and a merchant vessel. It left St-Nazaire again on 29 November 1941, bound for the Mediterranean, but disappeared with the loss of all forty-six crew members including Opitz. It is believed that it struck a mine.

Ref: DEFE 3/27

Author's note: as a matter of minor interest, my squadron was dropping magnetic mines near the entrance to St-Nazaire at this time. I recollect, on a very clear night, being able to put one exactly between the marker buoys leading to and from the port.

```
ADM                                                             588
    TO ! D 8 G                          ZIP/ZTPG/8 7564
FROMN S
        9420 KC/S                 T O ! 1152/11/9/41
                 T O O 1229
FROM: ADMIRAL COMMANDING U BOATS
TO :    U 575
    OPERATE AGAINST CONVOY OF U 432 AT CRUISING SPEED.
    2220/11/9/41/EE/LLB+++
```

The Type VIIC *U-575* was built by Blohm & Voss of Hamburg and commissioned on 19 June 1941. It was on its first war cruise when this signal was sent on 11 September 1941, having left Trondheim on 8 August 1941 under the command of Kapitänleutnant Günther Heydemann. It arrived at St-Nazaire on 9 October 1941 and carried out nine more war cruises. The end came north of the Azores on the tenth cruise, after leaving St-Nazaire on 29 February 1944 under the command of Oberleutnant zur See Wolfgang Boehmer. On 13 March 1944 it was attacked by a Leigh Light Wellington of 172 Squadron, backed by a Fortress of 206 Squadron and another of 220 Squadron, followed by aircraft from the carrier *USS Bogue*. Depth charge attacks followed from the frigate HMCS *Prince Rupert* and the destroyers USN *Haverfield* and *Hobson*. The U-boat was eventually forced to the surface. Sixteen of the crew were killed and thirty-eight were taken prisoner, including Boehmer. It had sunk eight merchant vessels and damaged three more during its career.

Ref: DEFE 3/27

```
ADM                                                                    785
TO  I D 8 G                          ZIP/ZTPG/8755
FROM  N S

  5660 KC/S          TOO 2315        TOI 2325/16/9/41

  FROM:  GYSAE

  IN SQUARE  C P  2476, AFTER 3 HOURS' DEPTH-CHARGING, SIGHTED

CONVOY ON EASTERLY COURSE.   TWO SHIPS (SUNK) SO FAR.

  (DEPT. NOTE:  T O I  ABOVE IS OF RE-TRANSMISSION FROM RXU').

2336/18/9/41+++WGE/EE
```

Kapitänleutnant Robert Gysae, commanding the Type VIIC *U-98*, sent this signal on 18 September 1941. The U-boat had been built by Germaniawerft of Kiel and commissioned on 12 October 1940. It was on its fourth war cruise, having left St-Nazaire on 31 August 1941, and brought its total score up to nine merchant vessels sunk. It continued war cruises but was sunk on its ninth. On 15 November 1942, when commanded by Oberleutnant zur See Kurt Eichmann and west-south-west of Cape Vincent, it was depth-charged by the destroyer HMS *Wrestler* and lost with all forty-six crew members. It had sunk a total of ten merchant vessels in its career.

Ref: DEFE 3/28

```
ADM                                                                    490
TO  I D 8 G                          ZIP/ZTPG/9460
FROM N S

5660 KC/S                            T O I   0751/22/9/41
                  T O O   0926

FROM: U 84

TO: ADMIRAL COMMANDING U-BOATS

AM PROCEEDING IN BEHIND ESCORT.

0709/25/9/41+++EGT/WGE
RD
```

The Type VIIC *U-84* was built by Flenderwerft of Lübeck and commissioned on 29 April 1941. It was on its first war cruise when this signal was sent on 22 September 1941, having left Bergen on 9 August 1941 under the command of Kapitänleutnant Horst Uphoff. It arrived at Lorient on the same day and thereafter carried out six more war cruises. It was sunk on the seventh, after leaving Brest on 10 June 1943. When about 800 miles south-west of the Azores on 24 August 1943, it was attacked with homing torpedoes by Avengers from the carrier USS *Core* and was lost with all forty-six crew members including Uphoff. By this time it had sunk six merchant vessels and damaged another.

Ref: DEFE 3/29

```
ADM                                                          762
TO I D 8 G                        ZIP/ZTPG/12727

FROM .N S
        4796 KC/S                 T O I 2324/17/10/41
                T O O 2355/17/10/41

FROM:      ROSENSTIEL
TO:        ADMIRAL COMMANDING U-BOATS
        AM IN SQUARE 5137.    KEPT UNDER WATER BY AIRCRAFT UNTIL
DUSK.    HEAVY OIL TRACE AT TIMES.    CANNOT CARRY OUT SUPPLEMENTARY
ORDER OWING TO DISTANCE.    SO FAR ONE HIT — 'SVEND FOYN'.
2018/20/10/41++EE/VSN++
```

Above: Kapitänleutnant Jürgen von Rosenstiel was in command of the Type IXC *U-502* when he sent this signal on 17 October 1941. The U-boat had been built by Deutschewerft of Hamburg and commissioned on 31 May 1941. It had left Kiel on 29 September 1941 and was heading for Lorient, which it reached on 9 November 1941 after damaging the British merchant vessel *Svend Foyn*. The U-boat made another war cruise but was sunk on its third, after leaving Lorient on 22 April 1942 and then returning from the Caribbean. The end came on 6 July 1942 in the Bay of Biscay when it was attacked by a Wellington VIII of 172 Squadron equipped with a Leigh Light and flown from Chivenor in North Devon by an American, Pilot Officer Wiley B. Howell. All fifty-two crew members were killed, including von Rosenstiel. By this time it had sunk a total of fourteen merchant vessels and damaged two more.

Ref: DEFE 3/32

Opposite Top: The Type VIIC *U-576* was built by Blohm & Voss of Hamburg and commissioned on 26 June 1941. It left Kirkenes on 6 October 1941 for its first war cruise, in the Arctic under command of Kapitänleutnant Hans-Dieter Hienicke, but evidently experienced trouble in operating the Enigma machine, according to this signal of 22 October 1941. The cruise seems to have been uneventful and it returned to Kirkenes on 5 November 1941. It then left for St-Nazaire and carried out three more cruises. It was sunk on its next cruise, when it was attacked on 15 July 1942 by aircraft of VS-9 Squadron and the US Auxiliary *Uncoi,* which subjected it to gunfire and then rammed it. All forty-five crew members lost their lives, including Heinicke. By this time it had sunk five merchant vessels and damaged another.

Ref: DEFE 3/33

Opposite Bottom: The Type VIIB *U-83* was built by Flenderwerft of Lübeck and commissioned on 8 February 1941. It was on its second war cruise when this signal was sent on 24 October 1941, having left Brest on 28 September 1941 under the command of Kapitänleutnant Hans-Werner Kraus to operate in the North Atlantic. It seems probable that the attacker was a Sunderland of the RAF. The U-boat returned safely to Brest and was then sent to the Mediterranean. The end came on 4 March 1943, during its thirteenth war cruise. It had left La Spezia under the command of Kapitänleutnant Ulrich Wörisshoffer and was attacked on the surface about 50 miles south-east of Capa de Palos in Spain by a Hudson of 500 Squadron flown from Blida in Algeria by Sergeant G. Jackimov. Some men were seen in the water but none of the crew survived. By this time it had sunk six merchant vessels and damaged another.

Ref: DEFE 3/33

```
ADM

TO  I  D  8  G
FROM N S                                          ZIP/SZTPG/13463

    7825 KCS                             T.O.I. 0920/22/10/41
                        T.O.O. 0848
FROM: U 576

TP: ADMIRAL COMMANDING NORWAY OPERATIONAL STAFF.

  POSITION SQUARE 9769.

  ENIGMA MACHINE WORKING AGAIN. APPARENTLY MISTAKE IN DOCUMENTS.

  REQUEST SETTINGS FOR 20/21 OCTOBER BE USED UNTIL I ARRIVE.
2333/24/10/41+++LWF+++
```

```
ADM

TO  I  D  8  G                    ZIP/ZTPG/13559
FROM N S

    2032 KC/S                    T O I 2032/24/10/41
                T O O 1915
FROM: U 83

  ATTACKED WITH BOMBS BY FLYING BOAT WHILE SURFACING IN

SQUARE 8177.   NO HITS.

1757/25/10/41/EE/LLB+++
CORRN LAST WORDS    NO HITS.
```

Top: The aircraft carrier HMS *Ark Royal*, of 22,000 tons displacement and capable of carrying sixty aircraft, listing east of Gibraltar on 13 November 1941 after being hit by a single torpedo fired by the Type VIIC U-boat *U-81*. The destroyer HMS *Legion* of 1,920 tons is alongside.

Author's collection

Left: The crew of the aircraft carrier HMS *Ark Royal* were rescued on 13 November 1941 by the destroyer HMS *Legion*. Only one man was lost. The aircraft carrier was taken in tow but became increasingly flooded and foundered on the following day.

Author's collection

This photograph taken over the port of Brest on 18 November 1941 shows the old French cruiser *Gueydon* with two smaller vessels of about 250 feet being attached to give her the length to act as a decoy for *Prinz Eugen*.

Another photograph taken over Brest on 7 December 1941 showed the work nearly completed, with the three vessels probably fastened together with steel girders. The superstructure of *Gueydon* was altered to resemble that of *Prinz Eugen*. It was a good imitation from a vertical view, but distant oblique photographs revealed the irregularity of the hull.

Ref: AIR 34/239

The destroyer HMS *Kandahar*, 1,685 tons displacement, ploughing through choppy seas at full speed in the North Atlantic. She struck a mine and sank north of Tripoli on 19 December 1941 when attempting to assist the cruiser HMS *Nelson* which had struck several mines. Her crew of 174 were rescued.

Author's collection

The heavy cruiser *Admiral Hipper* photographed from low level on 26 January 1941 in dry dock at Brest. The open hatch amidships is the aircraft hangar.

Ref: AIR 34/239

CHAPTER FOUR

A Critical Year

Hitler's order to Dönitz to concentrate on the approaches to Gibraltar was partly responsible for the loss of ten U-boats during the month of December 1941. Three of these were sunk during a long battle with Convoy HG76 which left Gibraltar for Britain on 14 December with an escort of sixteen warships which included the escort carrier HMS *Audacity*. This was one of five merchant ships converted in the USA with a flight deck suitable for operations with single-engined aircraft. The convoy was involved in numerous encounters with a U-boat wolf pack and Focke-Wulf Kondors, spread over six days. Not only were the three U-boats sunk but two Kondors were shot down by Grumman Martlets of the Fleet Air Arm from the escort carrier. One merchant vessel was sunk, as was the destroyer HMS *Stanley* on 19 December and then the carrier HMS *Audacity* two days later. However, Dönitz considered the German losses too heavy a price to pay.

Three of the other U-boats lost in the month were within the Mediterranean. Operating in this almost landlocked sea was not popular with the crews, who termed the Straits of Gibraltar 'The Mousetrap', since the prevailing currents assisted entry but impeded exit, while the waters were more confined, clearer and shallower than the Atlantic. One of these U-boats was lost in a collision with an Italian torpedo boat off Crete, after having left Lorient on 19 November. The other two were already based at Salamis in Greece but were sunk by the Royal Navy while operating off Tobruk and Mersa Matruh.

However, the Type VIIC *U-331* commanded by Kapitänleutnant Hans-Dietrich Baron von Tiesenhausen had already torpedoed and sunk the battleship HMS *Barham* on 25 November 1941 between Crete and Libya, causing heavy loss of life. The month of December 1941 was even more disastrous for the capital ships of the Royal Navy. On 10 December the battleships HMS *Prince of Wales* and *Repulse* were sunk with huge loss of life by Japanese torpedo-bombers when sailing between Malaya and French Indo-China. On 19 December the two remaining battleships in the Mediterranean Fleet, HMS *Queen Elizabeth* and *Valiant*, were sent to the bottom of Alexandria harbour by six very audacious Italian frogmen in diving suits who rode astride 'human torpedoes' and fixed explosive charges to the hulls below the waterlines.

By comparison with these disasters, an achievement by the British forces on 27 December 1941 was a very minor affair. This was the first combined operation when the Royal Navy landed Commandos on the Norwegian islands of Vaasgö and Maalöy near Bergen, at the same time as the RAF raided the nearby airfield of Herdla. The German garrisons were overcome, installations destroyed, merchant ships totalling 16,650 tons were sunk and then Norwegian volunteers were brought back to join the armed services. This was yet another attempt to convince Hitler that British forces would eventually attempt to open up another front in Norway.

Overall, the U-boats and submarines sank 124,000 tons of Allied shipping in December 1941, from a total of about 583,700 tons lost. An unusually high proportion of the latter, over 431,500 tons, was lost in the Pacific following the unexpected aggression by Japan at Pearl Harbor on 7 December and the creation of a huge new theatre of war.

After the entry of the USA into the war, far easier pickings were potentially available for the U-boat Arm off the eastern seaboard of America. However, Dönitz was unable to take immediate advantage of this opportunity, for most of his U-boats were employed elsewhere. He had ninety-one available for war cruises by 1 January 1942, but twenty-three of these were already in the Mediterranean, six were employed off the Straits of Gibraltar, four were engaged off the Norwegian coast and thirty-six others were undergoing servicing at various ports. This left twenty-two available for the North Atlantic, but half of these were either en route to their operational areas or returning to ports. Only eleven could be spared for the eastern seaboard of America, and five of them set out for these waters at the end of December 1941.

The commanders of these five U-boats found the situation in the new waters beyond their wildest dreams. There was no blackout along the coast and buildings were ablaze with light, enabling them to pinpoint their positions accurately. They could submerge during daylight hours and hunt on the surface without hindrance at night. Merchant vessels were unarmed and sailing independently, without any protection from naval escorts. The commanders could sink them at will, sometimes even by gunfire instead of expending their limited stocks of torpedoes. The US Navy, commanded by Admiral Ernest J. King, had not adopted the principle of forming merchant vessels into convoys and protecting them with warships. Instead, all the anti-submarine warships which could be spared from the war in the Pacific were sent out on patrols hunting U-boats, seemingly using the policy advocated by Churchill early in the war. These forays were completely fruitless, for the U-boats operated only at night and remained undetected.

These five U-boats made a major contribution to the 327,500 tons of Allied shipping sunk by U-boats and submarines during January 1942, from a total of almost 420,000 tons lost by the Allies. It was the beginning of what became known as the 'Second Happy Time' by the German crews. Three U-boats were sunk elsewhere in the North Atlantic during this month, two by the Royal Navy and one by the RAF. Two Italian submarines were also sunk by the Royal Navy in the Mediterranean.

On 1 February a serious setback occurred in the British intelligence war against U-boats. On this day the U-boat command added a fourth wheel to the Enigma machines used for signals to and from U-boats operating in the Atlantic and the Mediterranean. This was achieved not by replacing any of the Enigma machines but by fitting four slimmer wheels in the space previously occupied by three. Bletchley Park could not understand what had happened but was no longer able to decode these all-important signals or to identify the location of the U-boats on their war cruises. However, this innovation was not employed by the U-boats in Norwegian waters or the Baltic and it did not apply to the surface

An example of the four-wheel Enigma machine, which was employed by the U-boat Command from 1 February 1942 and caused an interruption in the ability of 'Station X' at Bletchley Park to decrypt the signals.

Author's collection

warships of the Kriegsmarine. Bletchley Park was able to obtain some information from these sources, but the Atlantic convoys could seldom be routed away from wolf packs and some suffered enormous losses.

An additional hazard occurred in the month of February, for the German B-Dienst was able to break Cypher No. 3 used by the Royal Navy. This carried the majority of the Allied signals relating to Atlantic convoys and thus enabled the U-boat Command to direct its wolf packs to prime targets. These two developments in intelligence were calamitous for the Allies. In February 1942 the U-boats and Italian submarines sank 476,500 tons of shipping from a total of over 679,500 lost by the Allies, without losing any of their own number in any theatre of war.

There was another event at sea during this month which was humiliating for the British forces and was later described as a fiasco. Decrypts on 5 February had established that the German officer commanding battleships, Vizeadmiral Otto Ciliax, had hoisted his flag over *Scharnhorst* in Brest and that the major warships in this port were carrying out exercises. It was already believed that Hitler would order his battleship to return to Germany, together with *Gneisenau* and the cruiser *Prinz Eugen,* in order to guard against a British invasion of Norway. This view was reinforced by other decrypts which showed that fighters of the Luftwaffe as well as warships of the Kriegsmarine were being strongly reinforced along the Channel coast and the Hook of Holland, indicating that a passage would be attempted through the Straits of Dover. British preparations were implemented under operation Fuller, consisting of air and submarine patrols, the redistribution of torpedo-bombers of RAF Coastal Command and the Fleet Air Arm along or near the south coast of England*, and the movement of destroyers to the Thames Estuary. However, the date of the German operation was not known.

The three German warships left Brest at 2245 hours on 11 February and steamed west and then north to the English Channel. By coincidence, the submarine on patrol off Ushant, HMS *Sealion,* had moved about 30 miles away to recharge its batteries. Two Hudsons of Coastal Command on patrol had returned to base since in both cases their ASV radars had failed. After dawn on the next day the German heavy warships were joined by minesweepers which preceded them, steaming undetected at about 28 knots up the Channel. Destroyers and E-boats formed screens for the convoy. About 250 fighter aircraft, Messerschmitt Bf110s and Bf109s with Focke-Wulf Fw190s, provided relays of air cover by hopping from airfield to airfield in northern France in order to refuel. The Germans succeeded in creating interference with RAF radar stations and it was not until 1030 hours that one near Beachy Head detected enemy aircraft circling over the Channel. Two Spitfires took off twenty minutes later to reconnoitre and spotted the German warships about 15 miles west of Le Touquet. The alarm was raised at last, but it was far too late for effective combined action to be taken.

The German formation reached the Straits of Dover before any action was taken against it. Several 9.2 inch guns were fired from the shore but the range was too great for these to be effective. Five motor torpedo-boats of the Royal Navy attempted to reach the battleships but could not penetrate the German destroyer screen and their torpedoes were fired from too far away.

Six Fairey Swordfish of the Fleet Air Arm's 825 Squadron took off at 1225 hours from Manston in Kent but became separated from their ten Spitfire escorts in bad weather. They attempted to drop their torpedoes but all were shot down. Their leader, Lieutenant-Commander Eugene Esmonde, was awarded a posthumous Victoria Cross. Five Beauforts of 217 Squadron took off at slightly different times from Thorney Island in Sussex but their fighter escorts failed to make contact with them. They approached the enemy convoy off the Hook of Holland at about 1540 hours but one was shot down and all their torpedoes missed. However, unknown to them the battleship *Scharnhorst* had struck a magnetic mine at 1531 hours, shortly before this attack, and had fallen back with the destroyer *Z29* in attendance. These warships came under attack from aircraft sent out by Bomber Command, but the bombs fell about 100 yards away. The magnetic mine was one of those previously dropped by Bomber Command against this contingency, under operation Fuller.

---

* The majority of the Beauforts of the author's squadron, no. 217, had already been moved from St Eval in Cornwall to Thorney Island in Sussex. The aircrews were aware that the German warships were potential targets but knew nothing about the decryption of enemy signals. They assumed that the source of intelligence was the French Resistance in Brest.

A British destroyer undergoing trials in 1942, steaming at full speed with her decks awash.
Author's collection

Shortly afterwards, at 1605 hours, *Scharnhorst* got under way again in the gathering darkness. Meanwhile, seven Beauforts of 42 Squadron which had flown down from Leuchars in Fifeshire attacked the main formation but their torpedoes scored no hits. Bombs dropped by five Hudsons of Coastal Command all missed. The German formation was attacked at 1645 hours by five destroyers of the 16th and 21st Flotillas of the Royal Navy from Harwich in Essex, but these were subjected to heavy gunfire and all their torpedoes missed. Two more Beauforts of 217 Squadron from Thorney Island attacked later, without result. Twelve other Beauforts of 86 and 217 Squadrons, which had flown from St Eval in Cornwall to Coltishall in Norfolk, tried to find the enemy in darkness, without success, and two failed to return. Bomber Command dispatched 242 aircraft in these ill-coordinated attacks but only 39 were able to bomb, without scoring any hits, and 15 did not return. Fighter Command dispatched 398 aircraft and some strafed the escort vessels, but 17 failed to return. Only three Fw190s, one Bf109 and three Dornier Do17s were lost on this operation.

On the following day the British Press was scathing about the success of the German warships in reaching their home country but the editors did not know the extent of the damage they had suffered. At 1955 hours *Gneisenau* had struck another of the magnetic mines, dropped previously by the RAF off Terschelling, but she had continued her journey and reached the mouth of the Elbe with *Prinz Eugen*. At 2134 hours *Scharnhorst* had struck yet another of these magnetic mines off Terschelling but had managed to reach Wilhelmshaven the following morning. This was by no means the extent of their misfortunes. It was known by British intelligence from Enigma decrypts that the purpose of this German operation was the gathering of warships in Trondheim, where the great new battleship *Tirpitz,* sister-ship of *Bismarck,* was located behind torpedo nets. On 23 February the undamaged cruiser *Prinz Eugen* was nearing this port when she was torpedoed by the submarine HMS *Trident.* She managed to reach shelter but was out of action for the rest of the war. On the night of 26/27 February the battleship *Gneisenau* was under repair in Kiel when she was hit by a bomb dropped by Bomber Command. This killed 116 of her crew and put her completely out of action. Her guns were removed and she was towed to Gdynia but also took no further part in the war. Of these three warships only the battleship *Scharnhorst* remained under repair as a potential threat in the longer term.

Although more numerous, U-boats proved elusive in March, partly owing to the limited ability of Bletchley Park to decrypt the relevant German signals. In March 1942 they and the Italian submarines sank about 538,000 tons of shipping from a total of 834,000 tons lost by the Allies, while losing three U-boats and three submarines in the process. One operation in this month ensured that the Battle of the Atlantic continued entirely against U-boats and submarines. The battleship *Tirpitz* constituted a major threat since she might break out of Trondheim and potentially obliterate Allied convoys. The only dry dock in western France capable of receiving this giant was at St-Nazaire, built originally to accommodate the liner *Normandie.* On the night of 27/28 March the former American destroyer HMS *Campbeltown,* flying the colours of the Kriegsmarine and loaded with 3 tons of high explosive, was rammed against the dock gates while motor launches landed Commandos and naval forces as a diversion. The operation resulted in many deaths among these British forces but the explosives blew up some hours later and wrecked the dock gates as well as killing numerous Germans who had gathered on board the destroyer.

This operation also had an effect on Dönitz's U-boat headquarters at Kernéval, near Lorient. Hitler had already anticipated that the British would mount a raid against this centre, and he was probably correct. The destruction of the dock gates at St-Nazaire confirmed his suspicions and he ordered the headquarters to be moved to Paris, which was generally recognised as an 'open city'. This move took place in mid-April and henceforth the headquarters were situated in a large apartment block in the Avenue Maréchal Maumory.

The war at sea against German and Italy continued almost entirely against the underwater menaces. In April these sank about 431,500 tons of shipping from a total of 674,500 tons lost by the Allies, while suffering the loss of three U-boats but no Italian submarines during the month. The enemy operations became more effective in this month with the introduction of the Type XIV 'Milch Cow' U-boats, which were able to resupply the fighting types with fuel, ammunition, food and water in distant regions. These were helping the growing fleet of U-boats to become an even more dangerous and effective fighting force.

In May U-boats and submarines sank over 607,000 tons of shipping from a total of 705,000 tons lost by the Allies, while four U-boats but no Italian submarines were sunk. June was an even worse month for the Allies, with over 700,000 tons of shipping sunk by U-boats and submarines from a total of about 834,000 tons sunk in all areas. The Kriegsmarine lost three U-boats while the Marina Italiana lost two in the Mediterranean, with RAF aircraft beginning to play an increased role in their destruction. The inability of Bletchley Park to discover the whereabouts of U-boats from decrypts continued to be a serious disadvantage to the Allied maritime operations.

Up to this time most of the lost U-boats and submarines had been destroyed by Allied surface warships, while there had been insufficient aircraft to play a major role in the process. However, this situation was steadily changing with the introduction of long-range aircraft in RAF Coastal Command and the provision of similar aircraft in the US Navy Air Force.

Another factor which caused considerable perturbation to the enemy was the sudden appearance of an instrument fostered by the Coastal Command Development Unit and known as the Leigh Light after its inventor, Squadron Leader Humphrey de Verde Leigh. This was a cylinder fitted under the fuselage of a Vickers Wellington, containing a brilliant light which could be switched on when a U-boat or a submarine seemed to appear on the aircraft's ASV radar screen. It was first used operationally on the night of 3/4 June when four Wellingtons of 172 Squadron took off from Chivenor in North Devon to hunt in the Bay of Biscay. One found two targets and on the first occasion dropped depth charges over the Italian submarine *Luigi Torelli,* which was seriously damaged but managed to beach on the coast of northern Spain. It was towed off three days later and limped back to Bordeaux. The other target attacked was the Italian submarine *Morosini*, which continued its war cruise to the Caribbean but was lost for unknown reasons after sending its last signal on 8 August.

The Leigh Light caused considerable difficulties for the U-boat Arm, for the boats usually sailed on the surface in the Bay of Biscay during the night, in order to conserve or recharge their batteries. After one was sunk at night on 6 July by a Leigh Light Wellington and several others were attacked, Dönitz ordered them to remain submerged when crossing the Bay. During this month they and their Italian allies sank 476,000 tons of shipping, from a total of 618,000 tons lost by the Western Allies. Eleven U-boats and two Italian submarines were destroyed in the month, with aircraft continuing to play an increasing part in these successes.

Another measure in favour of the Allies at the beginning of July was the sudden introduction of the convoy system by the US Navy off the eastern seaboard of their country. This resulted in an immediate setback to the crews of the U-boats, who no longer enjoyed easy pickings in these waters. Some of the long-range U-boats and Italian submarines moved to more southerly latitudes of the Atlantic, where so far there had been less activity in the sinking of the merchant ships or in anti-submarine measures.

Both sides continued to grow in strength during July. The U-boat Arm could deploy 140 boats, with as many as 191 more undergoing training and trials. On the Allied side, surface escorts had become more numerous and a system of refuelling in mid-ocean enabled some of them to cross the entire Atlantic instead of turning back when part-way across. These duties were mainly shared by the Royal Navy and the Royal Canadian Navy, since most American warships were serving in the Pacific. Rescue ships were introduced

The 'Hedgehog' device for firing a salvo of depth charges, mounted on the forecastle of a British destroyer. It was introduced in 1942, increasing the effectiveness of depth charges against U-boats.

Ref: ADM 199/2059

into convoys, augmenting the facility of picking up survivors from sunken vessels. Depth charges containing the new and more powerful explosive 'Torpex' had been introduced. The knowledge that U-boats could submerge to far greater depths than believed hitherto began to result in an increase in settings to as low as 800 feet. Simulation training in Britain helped naval officers to understand the best and latest techniques in combating U-boats.

Perhaps even more important, air cover was increasing steadily, with some of the long-range aircraft such as the Liberator closing the 'Atlantic Gap'. This was an area in the middle of the Atlantic which previously had been beyond the range of aircraft based in Northern Ireland, Newfoundland or Iceland. It was about 600 miles wide and stretched from Greenland to the Azores. This was the region where wolf packs had congregated and previously enjoyed immunity from an enemy the crews loathed, an aircraft which could arrive suddenly and unexpectedly, machine-gunning men on deck and dropping sticks of depth charges.

The Germans were familiar with the radar the RAF used for locating U-boats, the ASV Mark II, and were experimenting with a set they had captured. They recognised that a new radar device for U-boats had become necessary to counter this instrument. A receiver known as the R600A, or 'Metox', was developed, which could pick up transmissions on the same frequency as the ASV Mark II. French companies were ordered to begin producing the Metox in bulk for fitting to U-boats. Apart from restricting Allied air operations in the further reaches of the Atlantic, it also curtailed the effectiveness of Leigh Light aircraft hunting over the Bay of Biscay. The Allies lost about 544,500 tons of shipping to U-boats and Italian submarines in August, from an overall total of about 661,000 tons sunk from all causes. Nine U-boats and three Italian submarines were sunk, including *Morosini* mentioned above.

The Royal Navy made a determined attempt in September to bring supplies to the Russians, who were counter-attacking the German forces on the Eastern Front. Their previous convoy, PQ17, which had left Iceland on 27 June with thirty-six merchant ships under the escort of eight destroyers, two anti-aircraft ships, four corvettes and two submarines, had resulted in a massacre. Since Bletchley Park had not broken the Enigma keys the disposition of U-boats and enemy surface vessels was uncertain. Attacks on the convoy by U-boats and torpedo-bombers began on 1 July, without resulting in any sinkings, but two merchant ships were sunk three days later. Then the Admiralty gave the convoy orders to scatter, under the mistaken impression that *Tirpitz* was approaching. Twenty-three of the ships were picked off and only eleven reached Kola in Russia. The huge losses in the sunken ships included 210 aircraft, 430 tanks, 3,350 vehicles and about 100,000 tons of stores.

Precautions were taken in September to avoid a repetition of this disaster with the next convoy, PQ18. RAF Coastal Command had been given authority to set up a strike force at Vaenga airfield in North Russia. This was intended to consist of thirty-two Handley Page Hampdens of 144 Squadron and 455 (RAAF) Squadron, converted to the role of torpedo-bombers, but nine of these aircraft were lost on the flight to the new base. Also based at the same airfield was a flight of three Spitfire PR 1Ds for photo-reconnaissance over the Norwegian fjords. In addition, Catalinas of 210 Squadron were ordered to carry out a dual function from their base at Sullom Voe in the Shetlands and from Grasnaya in North Russia. They were to maintain patrols looking for enemy surface vessels and to provide air escorts over the convoy armed with depth charges.

Convoy PQ18 left Iceland on 11 September, consisting of thirty-nine merchant ships escorted by two destroyers, two anti-aircraft vessels, four corvettes, three minesweepers, four trawlers and two submarines. It was also arranged that more escorts would join this convoy in the most dangerous stretches of its passage. These were a light cruiser and sixteen destroyers, as well as the escort carrier HMS *Avenger*, carrying Sea Hurricanes and Swordfish of the Fleet Air Arm. In addition, other forces were at sea. These were a covering force of three cruisers and another of two battleships, a cruiser and five destroyers.

Attacks on the convoy began on 13 September, from torpedo-carrying Junkers Ju88s and Heinkel Helll1s, and continued throughout the next day. The attackers met the Sea Hurricanes and twenty-two of their number were shot down. Three Hurricanes were forced to ditch but the pilots were picked up. More attacks continued in the next few days, on a lesser scale, until 20 September. Seven more torpedo-bombers were shot down, as well as six dive-bombers and two reconnaissance aircraft. The German aircraft scored some successes against vessels, as did the U-boats, but twenty-seven merchantmen reached Russia.

U-boats and submarines sank about 485,000 tons of shipping in all waters during September, from a total of about 567,000 tons lost by the Allies. Ten U-boats were sunk in this month, one from a collision, as well as a single Italian submarine. A very distressing incident occurred on the 12th of the month when the liner *Laconia* of 19,559 tons was torpedoed and sunk near the equator by the Type IXC *U-156*. She was carrying about 1,800 Italian prisoners to Britain, as well as 160 Polish former prisoners and 268 British personnel, and of course her own crew. The commander of the U-boat realised the calamity and broadcast an international appeal for help in English. French warships managed to rescue about a thousand survivors, but there was serious loss of life.

During October U-boats and Italian submarines sank about 619,500 tons of shipping from a total of about 638,000 tons lost by the Allies. Sixteen U-boats were sunk, ten of them by air attack, but no Italian submarines were lost. By this time the military situation in Britain was nearing crisis point. Imports of food and raw materials had become insufficient to feed the population or sustain the war effort. Fuel oil for the Royal Navy alone was down to only two months' supply and the entire military and political establishment of the country was becoming extremely nervous. The only solution would be to destroy or avoid the armada of U-boats and submarines which was causing this immense problem. One means of achieving this would be to crack the 'Shark' code used by the U-boat Arm with its four-wheel Enigma machines, and thus enable the Admiralty to resume its 'Ultra' signals warning of the presence of wolf packs. Pressure was mounting on the cryptanalysts at Bletchley Park to somehow achieve what appeared to be impossible.

However, an event took place on 30 October which proved a providential gift for the Allied armed forces in their efforts to defeat the enemy in the Battle of the Atlantic. It began at 0248 hours north-east of Port Said in the eastern Mediterranean when the presence of a submarine was picked up by the ASV of Sunderland III serial W4023 of 230 Squadron flown from Aboukir in Egypt by Flight Lieutenant E.F. Thornicroft. The crew searched the area but nothing was seen and it appeared possible that the submarine had crash-dived. A message was sent to base and the Royal Navy was alerted.

The destroyer HMS *Hero* sped to the scene, followed by four other destroyers from the Twelfth Destroyer Flotilla, HMS *Petard*, *Pakenham*, *Dulverton* and *Hurworth*. These hunted for as long as fifteen hours and used cross bearings of Asdic to locate the position of a submarine. Many depth charges were dropped over a period of several hours, without apparent result. However, the Asdic on HMS *Petard* indicated that the submarine was lying as deep as 500 feet. The commander ordered soap to be stuffed into the holes of the depth charges, so that pressure built up more slowly and caused the explosions to occur at a lower level. These seemed to produce a result, for the target moved.

More attacks continued, and it is now known that eventually a charge scored a direct hit on the bow and stove in some plates. With its air almost exhausted, the submarine was forced to the surface at 2240 hours, where it immediately came under fire from the destroyers. The crew surrendered and were taken off, under searchlights, although seven of them were lost. The survivors had counted as many as 288 explosions during their long travail. It was a Type VIIC U-boat, *U-559*, commanded by Kapitänleutnant Hans Heidtmann, on its tenth war cruise. Three of these cruises had been in the Atlantic, before it arrived at Salamis in Greece on 20 October 1941. Six other cruises had been from this port, before it docked at Messina in Sicily on 21 October 1942. It was returning to this port from its tenth patrol when it met this fate.

The U-boat did not sink immediately and one officer with two seamen from HMS *Petard* managed to swim over, climb aboard and conduct a search of the interior. The lights were still on and they recovered code books as well as what was later discovered to be a four-wheel Enigma machine, all of which were handed to other men alongside in a whaler. Two men were still searching for more material inside the U-boat when it suddenly sank, taking both of them with it. They were Lieutenant Anthony B. Fasson and Able Seaman Colin Grazier, both of whom were recommended for posthumous Victoria Crosses. These were not awarded since their action had not been in the presence of the enemy, but each was granted a posthumous George Cross. Boy Seaman Thomas Brown, who had entered the interior with them and brought up the material, was in the conning tower when it sank. He managed to jump clear and was rescued by the whaler. He was only 16 but had lied about his age to join the Royal Navy. He was awarded a George Medal.

The documents recovered proved to be the *Wetterkurzschlussel* (Short Weather Book) and the *Kurzsignalheft* (Short Signal Book), which were normally used by U-boats for reports of positions, situations and sightings. Together with the four-wheel Enigma machine, they were received as 'manna from heaven' by cryptanaylsts in Hut Eight at Bletchley Park. However, the only Bombes available were three-wheel and it seemed that it might take as long as several weeks for these to decrypt U-boat signals sent on a single day. Meanwhile it was seen that the Short Weather Book recovered from *U-559* gave only three-letter settings and that the fourth wheel in the Enigma machine was set in a neutral position when messages were encoded and sent. Eventually it was realised that messages in the codes of the Short Signal Book, which constituted the majority, were also being sent by the same method, with the fourth wheel remaining in neutral and thus cancelling its advantage. The cryptanalysts needed to work through only twenty-six additional possibilities for the fourth wheel, instead of the colossal number which would otherwise have been necessary.

This work on the Bombes continued to be carried out by skilled young ladies of the WRNS who spent long hours on monotonous shift work, but they knew that the results were essential for the prosecution of the war. From time to time they were given talks which demonstrated the supreme importance of their work. All were sworn to absolute secrecy and none betrayed their trust. Churchill called them 'The geese who laid the golden eggs and never cackled'.

It was 13 December before the decryption process resulted in translated U-boat signals being passed to the Submarine Tracking Room in the 'Citadel'. An officer who had worked in this department from January 1941 was a former barrister, Rodger Winn. Childhood poliomyelitis had prevented him from joining any front-line service but he had offered himself for intelligence duties in the Royal Navy Volunteer Reserve and been given the rank of Temporary Commander in the Special Branch. He had proved brilliant at re-routing convoys to avoid wolf packs or individual U-boats, based mainly on information fed to the Tracking Room by Bletchley Park. It was clear that his prescience had prevented numerous sinkings in the period up to February 1942, when the decryption of signals from U-boats had ceased. Since then, he had become distraught at the enormous tonnage of merchant vessels sunk in the Atlantic. It was his rest day when the momentous news arrived from Bletchley Park and was conveyed to him, but unexpectedly he did not drop everything and rush round to the Admiralty. Instead, it was learnt that he had collapsed. His doctor reported that he was suffering from total mental and physical exhaustion, and advised that he should leave his post. This was extremely bad news for the Admiralty, for he was regarded as irreplaceable, but fortunately he returned to duty after only four weeks.

In the meantime U-boats and Italian submarines had sunk the appalling total of over 729,000 tons of shipping in November 1942, from a total of over 807,500 tons lost by the Allies. Their own casualties had not been light, for thirteen U-boats and three Italian submarines had also been sunk, with aircraft continuing to play an increasing part in these actions.

There were other events on the world stage in this month which were also significant in the Battle of the Atlantic. The US Eighth Air Force had arrived in England and was building up its strength to become a major component in the air war against Axis forces on the European mainland. Many of its initial attacks were being made against the U-boat ports in western France. Their bombs could not penetrate the immensely strong roofs of the U-boat shelters but they could destroy general facilities in the dock areas. It was recognised that these attacks would cause casualties among French civilians, but this was accepted as an inevitable consequence of the war. At the same time the RAF's increasingly powerful Bomber Command was paying more attention to U-boat construction yards in Germany, such as those in Kiel, Lübeck and Rostock.

The Anglo-American landings in north-west Africa had begun on 8 November under operation Torch, following the successful campaign of the British Eighth Army which drove the Afrika Korps out of Egypt and Libya. Hitler responded to the landings by occupying the whole of Vichy France on 14 November, gaining the country's ports in the Mediterranean. The fighting in Africa resulted in the diversion of more U-boats to the Straits of Gibraltar and the western Mediterranean. Seven of these U-boats were lost in this area, from the thirteen sunk in the month.

As usual, the winter weather restricted U-boat operations in the North Atlantic during December, but the ability of Bletchley Park to resume decrypting signals contributed to a huge reduction in Allied shipping losses. Sinkings fell to about 262,000 tons, within an overall total of about 349,000 tons, while five U-boats and three Italian submarines were sunk.

The year of 1942 had brought the heaviest sinkings of merchant ships of the war in the Battle of the Atlantic. About 5.6 million gross tons, mostly British-controlled, had been sunk worldwide during this critical year. President Roosevelt had recognised that the British need for help was beyond dispute and had done his best to respond to Churchill's requests, but shipbuilding in his country had not yet been able to meet the huge demand. However, the future looked more promising, and there was a general belief that American ships would materialise in enormous numbers in 1943. British commitments in the war were entered into on this basis. Allied intelligence could face the forthcoming year with far more confidence in a successful outcome to the war at sea.

This oblique photograph of the battleship *Tirpitz* at Aas fjord in Norway, taken at low level on 15 February 1942, shows floating camouflage units surrounding her bow and stern, with netting draped between her port side and the shore. This was an attempt to break up the outline of the battleship.

Ref: AIR 34/239

The Italian submarine *Asteria,* the first of six of this class built after Italy's entry into the war, left Naples on 11 February 1942 for its eighth patrol in the Mediterranean. On the night of 16/17 February, when in an area between Algiers and Bougie, the destroyers HMS *Wheatland* and *Easton* picked up an Asdic signal at a range of about 1,300 yards, which turned out to be *Asteria* steaming west at about 8 knots. The Italians spotted the two warships in poor visibility and the captain ordered diving stations. HMS *Wheatland* dropped five depth charges set to 50 feet, which caused some damage, and the hunt continued for about an hour until contact was lost for two further hours. HMS *Easton* then made a very effective attack which put all *Asteria*'s motors out of control, eventually forcing the submarine to the surface and resulting in a surrender. All but four of the crew of fifty-two were rescued before the submarine sank at 0940 hours.

Ref: ADM 199/2060

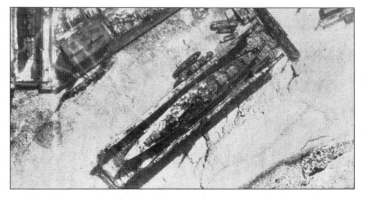

The battleship *Gneisenau*, photographed at Kiel on 2 March 1942, after her passage from Brest through the English Channel and the North Sea. Photo-interpreters could see that work was in progress and that deck plating had been removed from her bows.

Ref: AIR 34/239

A remarkable low-level oblique of the battleship *Tirpitz* in Aas fjord near Trondheim, taken from 200 feet on 28 March 1942 by a Spitfire of No. 1 Photographic Unit based at Wick in Caithness.

Ref: AIR 34/239

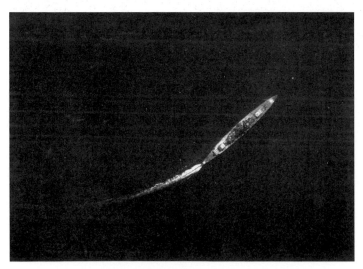

The pocket battleship *Admiral Scheer* photographed on 30 April 1942 on a south-westerly course in Trondheim fjord. She had carried out a war cruise in the Atlantic in the latter part of 1940. Her end came on the night of 9/10 April 1945 during a raid on Kiel by RAF Bomber Command, when she was hit and collapsed in an inner dockyard basin.

Ref: AIR 34/744

The port of Keroman in Lorient photographed on 1 May 1942. Photo-interpreters were able to identify:
1. a group of U-boat pens under construction, in an area where considerable evacuation work had been
identified in previous photographs; and 2. a cradle which supported a U-boat and travelled laterally to
the entrance of the pen where it would be received.

Ref: AIR 34/744

```
ADM                                                                    295
    TO:    I D 8 G                        ZIP/ZTPG/53289
    FROM:    N S

    4860 KC/S                             T O I   1103/31/5/42

                        T O O   1255

    FROM:  U. 520


    HAVE SURFACED AND AM COMMENCING RETURN PASSAGE TO U/BOAT BASE AT KIEL.


    1630/31/5/42    CEL/AH++++
```

Above: The Type IXC *U-520* was built by Deutschewerft of Hamburg and commissioned on 19 May 1942, shortly before this signal was intercepted. It left Kiel on 3 October 1942 under the command of Kapitänleutnant Volkmar Schwarzkopff, bound for the Canadian coast. On 30 October 1942 it was bombed by Douglas B-18 Digby serial 742 of 10 (BR) Squadron RCAF, when east of Newfoundland. It was sunk with all fifty-three hands.

Ref: DEFE 3/104

Opposite Top: The cruiser *Prinz Eugen* photographed on 17 May 1942 on a north-north-easterly course off the south-west coast of Norway. Photo-interpreters noted the squared-off stern, about 30 feet having been cut away after torpedo damage from the submarine HMS *Trident* on 23 February 1942. An Arado aircraft is visible amidships on the catapult.

Ref: AIR 34/744

Opposite Bottom: The Type VIIC *U-71* was built by Germaniawerft of Kiel and commissioned on 14 December 1940. After carrying out six war cruises, it left St-Nazaire on 4 June 1942 for another cruise, under the command of Kapitänleutnant Walther Flachsenberg. On the following day it was attacked about 140 miles west of Bordeaux by Sunderland II serial W3986 of 10 (RAAF) Squadron flown from Mount Batten in Devon by Flight Lieutenant S.R.C. Wood, who dropped eight depth charges. The U-boat crash-dived but then resurfaced and an exchange of gunfire took place, as shown here. The U-boat then dived once again. The Sunderland was damaged and during its return flight was engaged in combat with a Focke-Wulf Fw200 Kondor, when further damage was sustained. The U-boat was also damaged but managed to return to St-Nazaire for repairs. It carried out five more war cruises before being relegated to training duties in June 1943. By this time it had sunk five merchant vessels. It was scuttled at Wilhelmshaven on 2 May 1945.

Ref: AIR 15/470

This further photograph of the docks at Keroman in Lorient was taken on 9 June 1942. Photo-interpreters were able to identify: 1. the first cover showing a U-boat on the travelling cradles utilised to transfer the vessels from pen to pen; 2. the entrance lock; 3. a further set of pens under construction; 4. a radial slip with turntable (below centre of photograph); and 5. an armed merchant vessel.

Ref: Air 34/744

The pocket battleship *Lützow,* originally named *Deutschland,* photographed at anchorage in Bogen fjord on 11 June 1942. She was sunk on 18 April 1945 by RAF Bomber Command when in Kaiserfahrt Canal, Swinemunde. Although refloated, she was scuttled on 4 May 1945.

Ref: Air 34/239

The 'Mousetrap' projector for firing depth charges was introduced in 1942 for installation in small anti-submarine vessels, such as patrol craft which could not withstand any great amount of deck thrust. The device consisted of two groups of rails, each containing four projectiles. The latter were similar to the larger 'Hedgehog', but with rocket motors in the tail.

Ref: ADM 199/2059

```
ADM
                                                                            446
TO I D 8 G                                    ZIP/ZTPG/62449

FROM N S

4860 KC/S                                     TOI 0735/16/7/42

              T O O 0920

FROM:  U 602

TO:   5TH U/B FLOTILLA

    AM ABOUT TO DIVE 2 MILES NORTH OF ARKONA

2236/17/7/42+CEL/AM
```

The Type VIIC *U-602* was built by Blohm & Voss of Hamburg and commissioned on 29 December 1941. This signal was sent on 16 July 1942, before it began its war cruises. These took place from 26 September 1942 when it left Bergen to operate in the North Atlantic under the command of Kapitänleutnant Phillipp Schüler. It sank no ships but was destroyed on its fourth war cruise, when bombed off Oran by a Hudson of 500 Squadron operating from Gibraltar. There were no survivors from the crew of forty-eight.

Ref: DEFE 3/181

A very clear photograph of the battleship *Tirpitz* taken on 17 July 1942 when she was moored in Bogen fjord near Narvik. Details of deck and armament are clearly visible. The arrows point to two anti-aircraft guns, believed to be 37mm and either twin or single. No aircraft can be seen but the catapult amidships shows plainly.

Ref: AIR 34/744

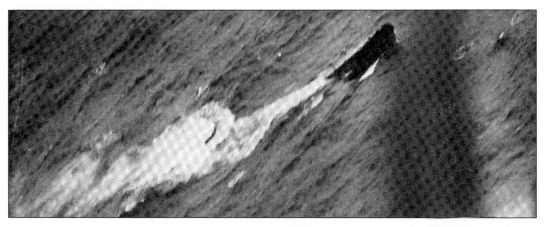

The Type VIIC *U-751* was built by Kriegsmarinewerft of Wilhelmshaven and commissioned on 31 January 1941. It made six war cruises in the North Atlantic, under the command of Kapitänleutnant Gerhard Bigalk, sinking five merchant vessels and damaging another, as well as sinking the escort carrier HMS *Audacity*. It then left St-Nazaire on 14 July 1942 for a seventh cruise, bound for the North Atlantic. About 200 miles west-north-west of Cape Ortegal in Spain three days later, it was attacked by a Whitley VII of 502 Squadron, flown from St Eval in Cornwall by Pilot Officer A.R. Hunt. Anti-submarine bombs were dropped and several machine-gun attacks were made, as shown in this photograph. About an hour later Lancaster I serial R5724 of 61 Squadron arrived, flown from St Eval by Flight Lieutenant P.R. Casement. This was one of several Lancasters of Bomber Command on detachment to Coastal Command for a short experimental period. Two attacks were made with depth charges and anti-submarine bombs, as well as with machine-guns. As the Lancaster left, some German crew members were seen to shake their fists. The U-boat sank with the loss of all forty-eight crew members.

Ref: ADM 199/2059

```
ADM                                                              680

    TO I D 8  G                        ZIP/ZTPG/79662

    FROM N S

    4860 KC/S                                    TOI: 0828/11/10/42

                  T O O 0958

FROM: U 38

    Ø    21ST  U/B FLOTILLA

         W/T MESSAGE 0826  DECYPHERED HERE.1000  POSITION: 545242

         NORTH 1841  EAST.

    1644/13/10/42+AGT/PG
```

The Type IXA *U-38* was built by A.G. Weser of Bremen and commissioned on 24 October 1938. It made eleven war cruises under various commanders, sinking thirty-three merchant vessels and damaging another. It was relegated to training duties on 1 January 1942, after returning to Bergen. This signal on 11 October 1942 gave its position north of the Gulf of Danzig. It was scuttled in the outer Weser Estuary on 5 May 1945.

Ref: DEFE 3/198

This reconnaissance photograph of Gdynia taken on 20 August 1942 shows: 1. the northern floating dock from Kiel, ready to accommodate the battleship *Gneisenau*; 2. the battleship *Gneisenau*, which had been extensively stripped after the serious damage sustained during an attack on Kiel by RAF Bomber Command on the night of 26/27 February 1942; and 3. the incomplete aircraft carrier *Graf Zeppelin*, covered with netting camouflage. Work on this vessel was never completed.

Ref: AIR 40/347

The Type VIIC *U-597* was built by Blohm & Voss of Hamburg and commissioned on 20 November 1941. It left Brest on 16 September 1942 for its second war cruise, under the command of Kapitänleutnant Eberhard Bopst, having scored no successes on its first cruise. On 12 October 1942, when south-south-west of Iceland, it was picked up on the radar of Liberator I serial AM929 of 120 Squadron, flown by Flight Lieutenant Terence M. Bulloch on escort for convoy ONS 130. Bulloch dived and dropped depth charges, which sank the U-boat with all forty-nine hands. This was the first success for Terry Bulloch, who became the RAF's top-scoring pilot in attacks against U-boats.

Ref: AIR 15/470

The bomb-proof roof of a new U-boat bunker at St-Nazaire is clearly visible in this photograph taken on 9 November 1942 by Spitfire PR IVB serial AD427 of A Flight, 543 Squadron, flown from St Eval in Cornwall by Flying Officer D.K. McQuaig.

Ref: ADM 205/30

The Type VIIC *U-660* was built by Howaldtswerke of Hamburg and commissioned on 8 January 1942. After a war cruise in the North Atlantic, during which it sank a merchant vessel, it left Brest on 3 October 1942 under the command of Kapitänleutnant Götz Baur and entered the Mediterranean. It sank another merchant vessel and damaged yet another before arriving at La Spezia in Italy. It left this port on 24 October 1942 for another war cruise but on 12 November, while attacking Convoy TE3 north of Oran in Algeria, it was depth-charged to the surface by the corvettes HMS *Lotus* and *Starwort*. Brought to the surface, it was abandoned before sinking. Two of the crew were killed but forty-two were rescued to become prisoners, including Baur.

Ref: ADM 199/2060

The US Eighth Air Force dispatched fifty-two B-17 Flying Fortresses and thirteen B-24 Liberators in daylight on 18 November 1942 to bomb U-boat bases in western France. The thirteen Liberators attacked Lorient, with the results shown in this photograph taken later the same day. The Central Interpretation Unit at Medmenham in Buckinghamshire reported that there was no damage to the U-boat shelters, although there were a number of craters and points of damage in the vicinity. These included seventeen craters near the radial slips at the head of the Bassin Long. These damaged sheds, the railway and the roadway.

Ref: AIR 40/369

Some Handley Page Halifax IIs began to enter service with Coastal Command at the end of 1942, becoming known as GR IIs. The machines were fitted with Air to Surface Vessel radar and employed on anti-submarine and meteorological duties, but later versions occasionally carried out bombing attacks against enemy ports. The Halifax GR II had a radius of action of about 1,200 miles with a bomb-load reduced from the maximum of 13,000 lb. This example was undergoing trials at the Air Fighting Development Unit in 1941.

Ref: AIR 16/933

```
ADM
   TO: I D 8 G                        ZIP/ZTPGU/2767              802
FROM: N S
4540 KC/S                            TOI 0534/20/11/42
                 TOO 0512
FROM: WALKERLING
'EELS' CANNOT BE DRAWN OUT OF TUBES 1, 2 AND 5. 'EEL' IN TUBE 3
HARD TO MOVE. TORPEDO RIPPED, BATTERY AND MOTOR CHAMBER FULL OF
WATER, MOTOR BURNT OUT. TUBE 4 IN ORDER, DEPTH GEAR IN THE
'EEL' HARD TO MOVE. ALL 'EELS' . REQUEST ORDERS.
0527/7/1/43 +++EEL/FA
```

This signal was sent on 20 November 1942 by Kapitänleutnant Heinz Walkerling, the commander of the Type VIIC *U-91*. This U-boat had been built by Flenderwerft of Lübeck and commissioned on 28 January 1942. It was on its second war cruise, having left Brest on 1 November 1942 for the North Atlantic. During its first war cruise it had succeeded in sinking the destroyer HMCS *Ottawa*, but was evidently having technical trouble with its torpedoes (known as 'eels') on this second cruise. It returned to Brest on 26 December 1942, without scoring any successes.

Ref: DEFE 3/705

```
   ADM
   TO I D 8  G                        ZIP/ZTPGU/767              112?
FROM N S
10510 KC/S                    ,    TOI: 1547/3/12/42
             T O O 1531
FROM: BERTELSMANN
   NAVAL   GRID SQUARE  BE 8454.  SEVERAL  PIECES OF  WRECKAGE
AND   A DRIFTING, EMPTY   LIFEBOAT.
0951/24/12/42+EGT/PG
```

Oberleutnant zur See Hans-Joachim Bertelsmann was the commander of the Type VIIC *U-603* when he sent this signal on 3 December 1942. The U-boat had been built by Blohm & Voss of Kiel and commissioned on 2 January 1942. It was on its first war cruise, having left Bergen on 23 November 1942 for the North Atlantic. There were no sinkings on the cruise and it arrived in Brest six days after this signal. It carried out two more cruises but was sunk on the next, after leaving Brest on 5 February 1944 under the same commander. About 580 miles north of the Azores on 1 March 1944 it was depth-charged by the destroyer USS *Bronstein* and lost with all fifty-one crew members. It had sunk four merchant ships during its career. (See also p. 143.)

Ref: DEFE 3/705

```
    ADM                              ZIP/ZTPGU/715              1070

    FROM:    N S

    TO:      I D 8 G

    4444 KC/S                                 T O I  1740/4/12/42

                    T O O    1700

    FROM:  KOENNENKAMP

    SQUARE 3197, 2 BATTLESHIPS, 2 AIRCRAFT CARRIERS, 1 CRUISER,

    8 DESTROYERS, 070 DEGREES, 16 - 18 KNOTS, DEPTH CHARGES FROM

    DESTROYER(S).

    2311/23/12/42    EE/AH++++
```

The Type VIIC *U-375* was in the Mediterranean on its sixth war cruise when its commander, Kapitänleutnant Jürgen Könenkamp, sent this signal on 4 December 1942, after leaving Pola in Yugoslavia on 14 November 1942. The U-boat had been built by Howaldtswerke of Kiel and commissioned on 19 July 1941. It returned from this cruise but was sunk on its tenth, on 30 July 1943, under the same commander. About 30 miles south-east of Pantellaria it was depth-charged by the patrol craft USS *PC624* and lost with all forty-five crew members. It had sunk seven vessels and damaged two more during its career.

Ref: DEFE 3/705

```
    ADM                                                        192
    TO:- I D 8 G                     ZIP/ZTPGU/175

    FROM:- N S

    5650 KC/S                              T O I: 2251/6/12/42

                    T O O: 2307

    FROM:- GILARDONE

        HAVE BEEN DRIVEN OFF . CONTACT LOST. LAST POSITION OF CONVOY AT 0
        1800 SQUARE AJ 6887.

    0950/14/12/42          EGT/BMS+
```

Kapitänleutnant Hans Gilardone was the commander of the Type VIIC *U-254* when he sent this signal on 6 December 1942. The U-boat had been built by Bremer Vulkan of Vegesack and commissioned on 8 November 1941. It was on its third war cruise, having left Brest on 21 November 1942 for the North Atlantic. The position was about 300 miles south-east of Cape Farewell on the southern tip of Greenland. However, it was sunk on the same day, following a collision with the Type VIIC *U-221* commanded by Oberleutnant zur See Hans Trojer. Four of the crew were rescued by *U-221* but forty-one were lost, including Gilardone. It had sunk three merchant vessels during its war cruises.

Ref: DEFE 3/705

The U-boat bunker at La Pallice in France was built by the Todt Organisation and completed in the summer of 1942. The bomb-proof roof can be seen clearly in this photograph taken on 9 December by Spitfire PR IVB serial AD427 of A Flight, 543 Squadron, flown from St Eval in Cornwall by Pilot Officer G.B.D. Greenwood.

Ref: ADM 205/30

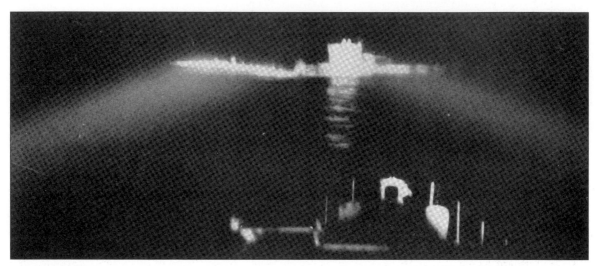

The Italian submarine *Uarsciek* was on its twenty-fifth patrol on 15 December 1942 when sighted at 0305 hours in a glassy calm sea by lookouts in the destroyer HMS *Petard*. The latter was in company with the Greek destroyer HHMS *Queen Olga,* en route from Benghazi to Malta and about 50 miles from her destination. The submarine dived but HMS *Petard* obtained Asdic contact and dropped depth charges. The submarine went out of control and shot to the surface, when HHMS *Queen Olga* also attacked, causing more damage. HMS *Petard* switched on a searchlight, as shown here, and opened fire with her pom-poms and Oerlikons, killing the captain and some crew members. The Italians surrendered and the submarine was taken in tow but sank some hours later. The number of those killed, wounded or taken prisoner is not recorded.

Ref: ADM 199/2060

```
    ADM                                                          985
      TO I D 8 G                                ZIP/ZTPGU/1938
      FROM N S
      10510 KC/S                            T O I 1117/16/12/42
                        T O O 1111
      FROM: RUPPELT
            AT 0115 SINGLE SHOT AGAINST TANKER 5000 GRT WITH
      'PI 39', DEPTH 4, UNHEATED . WENT UP IN THE AIR WITH 3
      EXPLOSIONS . 88 CBM .

      1035/4/1/43++++++++EE/EW
```

Oberleutnant zur See Günther Ruppelt was the commander of the Type VIIC *U-356* when he sent this signal on 16 December 1942. The U-boat had been built by Flensburger Schiffbau and commissioned on 20 December 1941. It was on its second war cruise, having left St-Nazaire on 5 December 1942 to operate near the Azores. The vessel it sank was the Norwegian *Bello* of 6,125 tons. It sank three more vessels and damaged another on this cruise, but on 27 December 1942 when about 400 miles north of the Azores was depth-charged by the destroyer HMCS *St Laurent,* the frigate HMCS *St John* and three Canadian corvettes. It was sunk with the loss of all forty-six crew members.

Ref: DEFE 3/706

```
ADM                                                              937
   TO:   I D 8 G                        ZIP/ZTPGU/586

   FROM:   N S

   3210 KC/S                              T O I  0657/18/12/42

                    T O O    0738

RUDLOFF REPORTS AT 0726:

3 STEAMSHIPS IN NAVAL GRID SQUARE BD 3334, COURSE 250 DEGREES,

SPEED 7 KNOTS.


1715/22/12/42   EE/AH++++
```

Kapitänleutnant Klaus Rudloff sent this report on 18 December 1942 when he commanded the Type VIIC *U-609*. The U-boat had been built by Blohm & Voss of Hamburg and commissioned on 12 February 1942. It was on its third war cruise, having left St-Nazaire on 30 November 1942 for the North Atlantic, and returned safely from the operation. The next war cruise was its last, for after leaving St-Nazaire on 16 January 1943 it was depth-charged on 7 February 1943 when about 600 miles east-south-est of Greenland by the French corvette *Lobelia* and lost with all forty-six crew members, including Rudloff. It had sunk two merchant ships during its first war cruise.

Ref: DEFE 3/705

```
   ADM                                                            30
   TO:   I D 8 G                        ZIP/ZTPGU/1027

   FROM:   N S

   7640 KC/S                              T O I  2344/25/12/42

                    T O O   2300

   FROM:   U 92

AT 2200 IN NAVAL GRID SQUARE BE 9738 DESTROYER WITH LOCATION

HORIZONTAL 147 CM. AND STEAMSHIP HIGH SPEED, COURSE SOUTH ,

16 CUBIC METRES, FLAT CALM.

   2313/26/12/42   EE/AH++++
```

The Type VIIC *U-92* was built by Flenderwerft of Lübeck and commissioned on 3 March 1942. It was on its second war cruise when this signal was sent on 25 December 1942, having left Brest on 24 October 1942 under the command of Kapitänleutnant Adolf Oetrich for the North Atlantic. It returned safely, after sinking one merchant ship. It made nine war cruises and arrived at Trondheim on 29 September 1944, after the Kriegsmarine evacuated the port of Brest. On 4 October 1944 it was badly damaged during a raid by RAF Bomber Command on the U-boat pens at Bergen and took no further part in the war. Its total score had been one vessel sunk and two damaged.

Ref: DEFE 3/706

```
ADM                                                             658

TO   I D 8 G                        ZIP/ZTPGU/1623

FROM   N S


        T O O   1141/30/12/ 42  B'  GCL


    CONVOY IN SQUARE AB 6394, 6 TO 10 SHIPS, ENEMY'S

COURSE 100 DEGREES.   WEAKLY PROTECTED CONVOY.

                                    SJ.  ( U 354).



1313/1/1/43++EGT+EMP
```

The Type VIIC *U-354* was built by Flensburger Schiffsbau and commissioned on 22 April 1942. It was on its second war cruise in the Arctic when this signal was sent on 30 December 1942, having left Narvik on 19 December 1942 under the command of Kapitänleutnant Karl-Heinz Herbschleb. It survived a total of ten cruises in the Arctic but was lost on the eleventh, after leaving Narvik on 21 August 1944 under the command of Oberleutnant zur See Hans-Jurgen Sthamer. Near Bear Island on 24 August 1944 it was depth-charged by the destroyer HMS *Keppel,* the frigate HMS *Loch Dunvegan* and the sloops HMS *Mermaid* and *Peacock.* There were no survivors from the crew of fifty-one. It had sunk two merchant vessels and a British destroyer escort during its career, as well as damaging another merchant vessel and a Canadian escort carrier.

Ref: DEFE 3/706

CHAPTER FIVE

The Height of the Battle

T he leaders of two of the Allied powers, the USA and Britain, met at Casablanca in Morocco for a conference which began on 13 January 1943, under the code name 'Arcadia'. These were President Franklin Roosevelt and Prime Minister Winston Churchill, with Generalissimo Chiang Kai-Shek of China in attendance. The Russian dictator Josef Stalin had been invited but declined. The conference lasted for ten days, with the purpose of formulating a military strategy for the remainder of the war. It was decided that the defeat of Germany must be the main priority and that the 'unconditional surrender' of all enemy countries would be demanded. This was a stipulation which Hitler would never accept, and it ensured that the war would continue until the Wehrmacht was completely crushed.

Both Roosevelt and Churchill were fully aware of the major threat posed by U-boats and both were determined to devote all possible resources to their destruction. Their concern partly rested on the knowledge that supplies of fuel oil in Britain had fallen to a dangerously low level. Fears were intensified when news arrived at the beginning of the conference of the fate of Convoy TM1. This consisted of nine tankers from Trinidad, escorted by one destroyer and three corvettes, destined for Gibraltar with supplies for the American forces in North-West Africa. It had had the misfortune to be intercepted on 8 January by a U-boat which sank one tanker and then called a whole group to the attack. The combined U-boats sank six more from this valuable convoy. This was one of the factors which prompted the leaders at Casablanca to make an immediate decision.

The Commander-in-Chief of the RAF's Bomber Command, Air Chief Marshal Sir Arthur Harris, received instructions from the Air Ministry on 14 January to 'devastate the whole area in which are located the submarines, their maintenance facilities and the services of power, light, communications, etc, and other resources upon which their operations depend'. These attacks were to take place at night and the order of priority was given as Lorient, St-Nazaire, Brest and La Pallice. Thus the system of 'area bombing', which Bomber Command had adopted over cities and towns in the German heartland after the destruction caused by the Luftwaffe in British residential districts, was unexpectedly extended to these four French ports.

Harris responded immediately, making four raids on Lorient with fairly small numbers of bombers before the end of the month, dropping high explosives and showers of incendiaries. The new US Eighth Air Force under the command of General Ira C. Eaker, which was already engaged on attacking U-boat ports in daylight, also received orders to attack the same targets. Eaker sent a small force of heavy bombers, B-17 Fortresses and B-24 Liberators, to Lorient on one occasion during the month. At this early stage in its formation, the Eighth was not equipped with long-range fighters and cover was provided by Spitfires of the RAF's Fighter Command. In total, 564 bombers from both forces attacked Lorient during January, losing fourteen aircraft in the process. Alarmed by their civilian casualties, the Lorientais began to evacuate thousands of children and other vulnerable people to the interior of France, assisted by the Red Cross.

U-boats and Italian submarines sank about 203,000 tons of Allied shipping during January, from a total of about 261,500 tons lost from all causes. Huge winter storms with winds of up to 150 mph were frequent in the North Atlantic, making conditions extremely difficult for warships, merchant ships and their attackers alike. Yet the ability of Bletchley Park to decrypt U-boat signals and the return of Rodger Winn to his duties in the middle of the month, with the consequent re-routing of convoys, must have limited the tonnage sunk. Six U-boats and three Italian submarines were lost during the month.

On 30 January Hitler promoted Dönitz to the highest rank in the service, Grossadmiral, and appointed him to command the entire Kriegsmarine in replacement for Grossadmiral Erich Raeder, who had resigned after being castigated by Hitler. The failure of the pocket battleship *Lützow,* the heavy cruiser *Hipper* and six destroyers to wipe out convoy JW51B headed for Murmansk at the end of 1942, under the escort of two light cruisers and five destroyers of the Royal Navy, had infuriated Hitler. During the engagement in the Barents Sea on 31 December the German destroyer *Friedrich Eckoldt* had been sunk by gunfire from the cruiser HMS *Sheffield,* while *Hipper* had been damaged by *Sheffield* and the cruiser HMS *Jamaica.* The German formation had failed to sink a single vessel.

This appointment did not separate Dönitz from command of the U-boat Arm but he relied more on the decisions made by his competent head of operations in Paris, Konteradmiral Eberhard Godt. Henceforth, Dönitz's headquarters were in the Charlottenburg district of Berlin, where he was brought into frequent contact with Hitler and was thus privy to the highest reaches of power in the Third Reich. He was a highly competent and professional officer but also a fervent adherent to the Nazi doctrine. After the war he protested that he was never aware of its vicious depredations, and there may have been some truth in this assertion since he was concentrating so intently on prosecuting the war at sea.

On 6 February the German forces suffered their most serious defeat of the war with the surrender of the entire Sixth Army under Feldmarschall Friedrich von Paulus to Russian forces in the Battle of Stalingrad. This represented a major turning point in the Second World War and was the first of a long succession of defeats for the Wehrmacht.

Meanwhile the winter storms in the North Atlantic continued into February. Valuable intelligence was not confined to the British, for B-Dienst was able to decrypt a signal from the Admiralty concerning the eastbound convoy SC118, bringing supplies for both Britain and Russia. This consisted of sixty-three merchant ships, escorted by five destroyers and two US coastguard cutters. About a hundred U-boats were operating in the Atlantic in early 1943 and twenty of these were directed to the path of this convoy. The area chosen as the most favourable was the 'Atlantic Gap', although by this time this was being partly covered by small numbers of Fortresses and Liberators of the RAF operating from Iceland.

The extremely hard-fought battle began on 4 February and continued for five days. At the end of the engagements thirteen merchant ships had been sunk while three U-boats had been destroyed and four more badly damaged. On the Allied side it was evident that the escort vessels lacked coordinated training while the aircraft were almost ineffective at night, since they were not fitted with Leigh Lights.

Although the U-boats gained some success in this battle, they lost heavily in February, with no fewer than fifteen destroyed in all waters, while their Italian allies lost three more submarines. They sank eighty-three merchant ships totalling about 369,000 tons in the month, from a total of about 403,000 tons lost by the Allies. It was clear that both sides were gathering strength and that the war at sea would be intensified in the coming months.

The agony suffered by Lorient continued, in what was described by a French air historian as the 'martyrdom' of the port. The fledgling US Eighth Air Force made no attacks on this port in February, although it sent small numbers of bombers to St-Nazaire and Brest. However, RAF Bomber Command dispatched 128 aircraft to Lorient on the night of 4/5 February, 323 on 7/8 February, 466 on 13/14 February and 377 on 16/17 February, losing sixteen bombers during these operations. At the end of these huge attacks, which as usual included incendiaries, about 3,500 of the 5,000 homes in the centre of Lorient had been destroyed plus almost 1,000 more in nearby suburbs. Many other homes had been damaged. Almost all municipal buildings had been destroyed as well as three churches. Civilian casualties since the beginning of January amounted to 184 dead and at least 162 injured.

All this was completely valueless from a military standpoint, since the heaviest bombs carried by the RAF were 4,000 lb and these could do no more than chip the surfaces of the concrete roofs of the U-boat shelters built by the Todt Organisation. RAF Bomber Command had left these untouched during their construction period, when they were vulnerable to air attack. By February 1943 the U-boat men with their vessels and equipment were safe within these shelters, although some men were dispersed in the early evenings to outlying districts.

Having destroyed Lorient, RAF Bomber Command turned its attention to St-Nazaire, dispatching 437 aircraft on the night of 28 February/1 March and dropping the usual combination of high explosives and incendiaries. These caused widespread destruction, including about 60 per cent of the houses. Fortunately the citizens had anticipated more air attacks and most had evacuated the port. Only 39 were killed and 36 injured, according to the records. Despite this destruction, Bomber Command dispatched 357 more aircraft to this target on 23/24 March and 323 more on 28/29 March, losing two aircraft. On these occasions the bomb-loads fell primarily on the dock areas. Soon afterwards, it was realised from photo-reconnaissance and intelligence reports that these attacks were doing little harm to the Germans. Mass raids on ports in western France were discontinued, although smaller attacks on the docks and minelaying in the sea approaches took place.

However, many of the operations being carried out in March by RAF Coastal Command were having a more favourable effect on the Battle of the Atlantic. The Command had expanded to fifty-two squadrons and six flights, of which about thirty squadrons were mostly engaged on operations against U-boats. Six were equipped with Sunderlands, five

```
    ADM                                                              263
    TO:-  I D 8 G                       ZIP/ZTPGU/3243

    FROM:- N S

  3210 KC/S                                T O I: 1752/11/1/43

           T O O: 1444

  FROM:- STEIN

  REFERENCE SERIAL NO.374 OF 11/1:

       NOTHING OBSERVED AFTER SALVO OF 4 AT DESTROYER OF 'GLEAVES'

       TYPE. IT IS NEVERTHELESS POSSIBLE AND INDEED PROBABLE THAT
              and
       IT WAS HIT AS SANK , AS SUBSEQUENTLY WHILE FIRING ON THE TANKER

       NO OPPOSITION WAS OFFERED ME AND ABOUT 5 MINUTES AFTER THE

       SALVO A DULL EXPLOSION WAS FELT IN ONE BOAT , WHICH DID NOT

       COME FROM THE TANKER. ALTHOUGH WE SEARCHED , NOTHING COULD BE

       SEEN OF THE DESTROYER.

  0551/14/1/43      EGT/BMS+
```

Oberleutnant zur See Heinz Stein was in command of the Type VIIC *U-620* when he sent this signal on 11 January 1943. The U-boat had been built by Blohm & Voss of Hamburg and commissioned on 30 April 1942. It was on its second war cruise, having left La Pallice on 19 December 1942 to operate near the Azores. On the day of this signal it scored its only success, sinking the tanker *British Dominion* of 6,983 tons. On 13 February 1943, about 180 miles north-west of Cape St Vincent on its return journey, it was depth-charged by Catalina IB serial FP223 of 202 Squadron flown from Gibraltar by a Canadian, Flight Lieutenant Harry R. Sheardown, and was lost with all forty-six crew members.

Ref: DEFE 3/708

with Catalinas, five with Wellingtons, five with Liberators, three with Whitleys and one with Fortresses. The others were Hudson squadrons, engaged on somewhat shorter-range operations. Two of the Liberator squadrons were part of the USAAF while one of the Catalina squadrons was part of the USNAF, coming under temporary control of the RAF. The Whitleys were a short-term expedient, being obsolescent in RAF Bomber Command, but were employed on anti-shipping work until more of the 'Very Long Range' aircraft arrived from the USA.

The collaboration of these Coastal Command squadrons with the Royal Navy was producing positive results, especially in the steady closure of the 'Atlantic Gap', which was still a favourite killing area for U-boats. Of the aircraft supplied from the USA, the Consolidated Liberator was found to be very effective for this purpose, being a heavy bomber adapted for maritime work. It was well-armed, had a crew of eight, and could carry a load of depth charges for a range of about 2,300 miles. Nine RAF squadrons were eventually equipped with this machine.

Not all the convoys which crossed the Atlantic were beset by U-boats. Many were routed around the wolf packs known to be hunting for them and and arrived at their destinations completely unmolested. The officers at U-boat headquarters in Paris may have been puzzled at the difficulty they experienced in intercepting convoys after December 1942, by comparison with the ease earlier in the year, but they did not suspect that the coded messages sent on their Enigma machines were being decrypted and read by the British.

However, some notable engagements took place. One of these occurred when the eastbound convoy SC121, consisting of fifty-nine merchant ships escorted by the cutter USS *Spencer,* the destroyer USS *Greer* and four corvettes, ran into a heavy storm in mid-Atlantic in the first week of March and began to straggle. It managed to pass through the first wolf pack on 5 March, consisting of twenty-four U-boats, but the Type VIICs *U-566* and *U-230* made contact on the night of 6/7 March and sank one merchant ship. Contact was then lost in the storms but regained a day later. Although reinforced with two more cutters and another destroyer, the convoy lost twelve more ships from attacks by twenty-seven U-boats during the next three days. Not a single U-boat was lost in an action which was classed as a triumph by Konteradmiral Godt.

In the middle of these catastrophes, on 10 March Bletchley Park suffered a blackout in its ability to read the Enigma 'Triton' short-signal reports, after the U-boat Command introduced a new code book. This was rated as a calamity by the Admiralty's Tracking Room, for it was believed that several months might elapse before the problem was overcome. However, Bletchley Park managed to start re-reading the signals after only nine days, although there were some delays after that date. It was fortunate that, by this time, there were sixty three-wheel Bombes available at Bletchley Park to assist in this process.

In the interim the unfortunate convoy SC121 was only one of those intercepted in March, for U-boats and submarines sank 108 vessels totalling over 627,000 tons during the month, comprising the great majority of the 693,000 tons lost by the Allies. Their own losses were not insignificant, for fifteen U-boats were sunk and an Italian submarine was lost in a collision. The fact that eight of these U-boats were sunk by air attack provided a harbinger of the fate of many others in the future. Nevertheless, the U-boat Arm ended March on a high note, with as many as 240 boats in operational service and 185 more undergoing training and trials. This was a peak for the number of operational U-boats during the entire war. From this time events began to move inexorably against the U-boat Arm, and it would never again achieve this level of sinkings.

At the beginning of April many U-boats operating in the North Atlantic were compelled to return to their bases in France in order to refuel, only one U-tanker being available for them at sea. There was a short remission for the convoys, but increased numbers of U-boats soon returned to the fray. They found that conditions were changing. Although there were increased numbers of merchant vessels, mostly built in America, there were fewer convoys and these were more elusive than in March. On the recommendation of Professor Patrick Blackett, a highly respected authority who had moved from his advisory position in RAF Coastal Command to the Admiralty, the number of ships in a convoy had been increased from about thirty-two to about fifty-four. This facilitated an increase in the

```
ADM                                                              819

  TO I D 8 G                              ZIP/ZTPGU/3785

  FROM N S

  13768 KC/S                              TOI 1327/22/1/43

              TOO 1407

  HELLRIEGEL IS TO REPORT THE CONVOY'S COURSE AT ONCE. STICK

  TO IT. REPORT CONTACT. DO NOT ATTACK.

  131724/1/43/    EGT+++MRT+++
```

Oberleutnant zur See Hans-Jürgen Hellriegel was in command of the Type VIIC *U-96* when this signal was sent to him on 22 January 1943. The U-boat had been built by Germaniawerft of Kiel and commissioned on 14 September 1940. It had already had a long operational career, being on its eleventh war cruise after leaving St-Nazaire on 26 December 1942 and having been responsible for sinking twenty-eight vessels as well as damaging three more. However, this was its last, for it was relegated to training duties after arriving at Königsberg on 8 February 1943. It was destroyed during a raid on Wilhelmshaven by the US Eighth Air Force on 30 March 1945.

Ref: DEFE 3/708

escort vessels from an average of six to nine. Thus the convoys were better protected, not only by warships but by aircraft.

The first escort carrier to sail with the Atlantic convoys was already in operation. This was USS *Bogue,* which took its place in the centre of the formation and was equipped with single-engined Grumman TBF Avengers and Grumman F4F Wildcats of the US Navy. These operated in pairs, with the Avenger carrying homing torpedoes while the Wildcat was armed with six forward-firing 0.50 inch machine-guns. This combination could be deadly for any U-boat found on the surface. The five escort carriers commissioned into the Royal Navy, most of which had been engaged in the operations off North-West Africa, were also becoming available for the North Atlantic. These included HMS *Archer* and HMS *Biter,* both of which scored successes in the following month, as did USS *Bogue.*

Other developments were taking place to counter the activities of U-boats. There were more 'Very Long Range' RAF aircraft operating in the North Atlantic and these were equipped with a new radar, the ASV Mark III. This was fitted with a revolving trace which could pick up the dot of a U-boat on the surface, and was far more effective than the single column on the screen of the ASV Mark II. Some of the naval escorts were equipped with a new weapon known as a 'Hedgehog'. This was fitted in the bows and fired a pattern of twenty-four small bombs containing high explosive, intended to destroy a diving U-boat before it reached a safe depth.

There was a drop in the sinkings of Allied merchant vessels during April, mainly as a result of the successful re-routing of the convoys by the Admiralty Tracking Room. U-boats and submarines sank about 328,000 tons in all waters, from a total of about 344,500 tons lost overall. The U-boats lost fifteen of their number, eight of them as a result of air attack, while one Italian submarine was sunk in the South Atlantic, also from air attack.

The month of May 1943 represented the climax of the anti-submarine war in the Atlantic. Ninety-one U-boats were deployed in these waters but thirty-eight of them were destroyed as well as three others in the Mediterranean. Two Italian submarines were also sunk in the Atlantic and two more in the Mediterranean. So far as can be ascertained, twenty-one of the U-boats were destroyed solely by air attack (three of them by carrier-borne aircraft), fourteen solely by warships, three from a combination of aircraft and warships, two in a collision and one from unknown causes. Two of the Italian submarines were destroyed by air attack, one by a warship and one by unknown reasons. Thus there was a variety of factors for this huge increase in sinkings, but the increase of air cover and its collaboration with the escort vessels was largely responsible for the successes. Combined with these was the ability of Bletchley Park to identify the whereabouts of U-boats.

It was obvious to Dönitz that the loss of over 40 per cent of the U-boats deployed in a single month in the Atlantic could not be sustained. On 24 May he ordered his remaining U-boats to withdraw to an area south of the Azores, but several of them were sunk while doing so. The total number lost was not his only problem, for many of the remaining U-boats arrived back at port in a damaged state and were in need of extensive repair. Together with those who did not return, their crews had managed to sink almost 265,000 tons of shipping, from an overall total of 299,500 tons, but at a terrible price. Among the men lost were many of the cream of the service, who could only be replaced by newly trained and inexperienced men arriving through the system in Germany and the Baltic. Dönitz later admitted that Germany had lost the Battle of the Atlantic.

This was not the end of Germany's woes in this period, for the Allies had mopped up the last pockets of resistance of the Axis forces in North-West Africa. All the German and Italian aircraft that were airworthy had left Tunisia and the armies had no means of evacuation by sea, for all their warships and transport vessels had been destroyed or forced to withdraw. The remaining enemy ground forces had no option but to surrender on 14 May. In all, about 250,000 of the enemy fell into Allied hands during this hard-fought campaign. Meanwhile it had occupied a huge amount of the Royal Navy's resources in maintaining seaborne supplies and protecting the convoys. Pressure on the service had now lessened, but an Allied invasion of southern Europe was being actively planned.

The month of June was far quieter in the North Atlantic. Only four merchant vessels were sunk, although sixteen others were sunk by U-boats and Italian submarines in the South Atlantic, the Mediterranean and the Indian Ocean. The tonnage amounted to about 95,500, from a total of about 124,000 tons lost from all causes. However, the attackers lost almost the same number of vessels as those they sank, seventeen U-boats and one Italian submarine. Once again it was aircraft which were responsible for the majority of the enemy's losses, accounting for ten U-boats and the submarine. This was more gloomy news for Dönitz.

June was also the month when the Allies began to acquire more merchant ships than were being sunk. This resulted partly from the activities of the American Maritime Commission and the enormous industrial capacity of its country. Over 200 so-called 'Liberty' ships of 7,176 gross tons were built in 1943, each in prefabricated sections which were then welded together. These carried huge quantities of war material across the North Atlantic.

In addition, the great ocean liners such as the *Queen Mary, Queen Elizabeth, Ile de France* and *Nieuw Amsterdam* had been converted temporarily into troopships and were bringing many thousands of American troops to Britain, travelling safely at full speed without interference from U-boats. This was the beginning of the great military build-up which would culminate in the D-Day invasion of Normandy a year later.

On 10 July Anglo-American forces from Tunisia and Libya landed on the southern and eastern shores of Sicily, preceded by airborne forces. The enterprise was codenamed operation Husky and involved as many as 2,000 vessels of all types. The troops drove inland against stiff German opposition and made headway to the Straits of Messina and the toe of Italy. The majority of the Italian people had become disillusioned by a succession of military failures and most of them detested their German allies. The dictator Benito Mussolini was ousted by the Fascist Grand Council on 23 July. His powers were transferred to the monarchy and his place was taken by Marshal Pietro Badoglio. It was evident that the resolution of the country was wavering and that most people longed for peace. One effect of the Allied invasion was the destruction of nine Italian submarines in the month, mainly by escort vessels. The Regia Marina Italiana had become almost a spent force.

Three U-boats were lost in the Mediterranean during July, and elsewhere the results were catastrophic for Dönitz. Thirty-four others were sunk, mostly in the Atlantic. Aircraft accounted for thirty of the total of thirty-seven U-boats lost. One reason for this was that the U-boat commanders had been ordered to cross the Bay of Biscay in groups and in daylight for their common protection. They had been fitted with increased anti-aircraft armament, replacing the 88 mm deck gun. However, RAF aircraft had swooped on them and destroyed many. During the month U-boats and submarines sank forty-six ships amounting to about 252,000 tons, from a total of 365,500 tons. About 80,500 tons of shipping were sunk in the Mediterranean, in connection with the action taking place in that region. At the end of the month the number of operational U-boats was reduced to 170, with about 200 more undergoing training and trials. The rate of attrition was exceeding the rate of replacement, and the U-boat Arm was in decline.

The practice of sailing on the surface across the Bay of Biscay was reversed in August. The U-boat commanders were ordered to remain submerged during daylight hours, unless they had to surface to recharge their batteries. They sank sixteen ships totalling about 86,000 tons of shipping but lost twenty-five of their own number, of which seventeen were the result of air attack. The Allies lost a total of about 120,000 tons during the month. The Italians lost one of their submarines from the tiny force left to them.

On 8 September the Italians announced their unconditional surrender, having signed the instrument five days before. The battleships of the Regia Marina Italiana managed to reach Malta, apart from one which was sunk en route by the Luftwaffe, but the Italian cruisers, destroyers, torpedo boats and corvettes fell into German hands. One of the remaining Italian submarines had the misfortune to be sunk the day before this announcement. Most of the Regia Aeronautica flew to North-West Africa in September and formed squadrons to fight alongside the Allies. Benito Mussolini, who had been imprisoned near the Gran Sasso mountain, was rescued by German parachutists and remained at liberty until he was executed by Italian partisans later in the war.

The roof of the large U-boat bunker at St-Nazaire had been cleverly camouflaged by the time this photograph was taken on 3 February 1943 by Spitfire PR IVB serial AD427 of A Flight, 543 Squadron, flown from St Eval in Cornwall by Sergeant G.H. Evans.

Ref: ADM 205/30

On 3 September Anglo-American forces landed across the the Strait of Messina, beginning an invasion of the mainland against determined opposition from the Wehrmacht. Six days later they landed further up the coast at Salerno. U-boats in the Mediterranean continued to operate from such ports as Toulon in southern France, Pula (Pola) in Yugoslavia and Salamis in Greece, and reinforcements were sent from the western ports of France. Later, on 13 October, the Italian government declared war on Germany.

U-boats managed to sink twenty vessels in September, amounting to almost 119,000 tons, with many of these sinkings taking place in the Mediterranean. They lost nine of their own number, with aircraft accounting for five of these. A new defensive ship sailed in one of the convoys attacked, ON202. This was the merchant vessel *Empire MacAlpine,* which still carried cargo but had been modified with a flight deck of about 450 feet. Although there was no hangar, she carried four Swordfish of the Fleet Air Arm. This was the first of nineteen such vessels, known as 'Merchant Aircraft Carriers' or 'MAC Ships', which operated under the Red Ensign but provided additional air support for convoys.

The Royal Navy made an astonishing attempt in this month to disable German warships which continued to threaten the Arctic convoys. These were the battleships *Tirpitz* and *Scharnhorst* and the pocket battleship *Lützow,* which had been located by air reconnaissance in inlets off Altenfjord in Norway. On 11 September six submarines of the Royal Navy left the north-west coast of Scotland on operation Source, towing midget submarines known as X Craft. Each of these was manned by a crew of four volunteers and the armament consisted of a ton of high explosive charges carried on each side of the hull.

Two of these X-Craft were lost during the passage across the North Sea: one accidentally foundered and another was damaged after the premature explosion of her charges. The other four parted from their parent submarines in the evening of 20 September and entered Altenfjord. By coincidence, *Scharnhorst* had left her anchorage for gunnery practice but the X-craft managed to return to a parent submarine. One of the other three, making for *Tirpitz* in Kaa Fjord, disappeared for some unknown reason, but the other two managed to slip past an anti-submarine boom on 22 September.

These were *X6* commanded by Lieutenant D. Cameron and *X7* commanded by Lieutenant B.C.G. Place, both of which contrived to drop their charges under the hull of the battleship. Cameron and his crew in *X6* came under small arms fire and were picked up by the *Tirpitz* after scuttling their craft, but *X7* became entangled in nets and only Place and one of his officers survived to be taken prisoner. In the subsequent explosions *Tirpitz* received massive damage to her hull and rudder, and it was six months before she could be repaired. Both Cameron and Place were awarded the Victoria Cross.

The number of operational U-boats had declined to 175 by October. A huge replacement programme was in progress, with as many as 237 more boats undergoing training and trials, but these and their crews were unable to keep pace with the rate of sinkings. October was another appalling month for the U-boat Arm, for it lost twenty-six more boats, with nineteen of them falling victim to the burgeoning number of Allied aircraft in the skies above. Some of these aircraft had the additional advantage of a base in the Azores, following an agreement with the Portuguese government, and thus were able to cover the

```
    ADM
                                                                    545
    TO I D 8 G                              ZIP/ZTPGU/4527
    FROM N S

    3920 KCXS                               TOI: 2215/5/2/43

                     TOO: 2136

    FROM: KESSLER

        AT 2030 FORCED UNDER WATER BY DESTROYER IN

        NAVAL GRID SQUARE AK 8237.  AFTER DEEP DIVE

        PORT OUTER EXHAUST CUT-OUT WILL NOT CLOSE.

        AM MOVING OFF.  REQUEST RETURN PASSAGE

        37 CUBIC METRES.

        ((WEATHER REPORT)).

    0454/7/2/43+++EGT+++DG
```

Kapitänleutnant Horst Kessler was in command of the Type VIIC *U-704* when he sent this signal on 5 February 1943. His U-boat had been built by Stülcken Sohn of Hamburg and commissioned on 18 November 1941. It was on its fourth war cruise, having left La Pallice on 7 January 1943 for the North Atlantic. In its previous cruises, it had sunk one merchant vessel, damaged another, and made an unsuccessful attack on the liner *Queen Elizabeth*. There were no successes on this cruise, nor on the next. It was then relegated to training duties in Germany and finally scuttled at Vegesack on 3 May 1945.

Ref: DEFE 3/709

'Atlantic Gap' even more effectively. In return, the U-boats sank only twenty merchant ships, amounting to 97,500 tons, from a total of about 140,000 tons lost by the Allies.

There was no improvement in the situation for U-boats in November. They sank fourteen merchant vessels amounting to about 66,500 tons but lost nineteen of their own number in the process, ten of which were to aircraft. This ratio of losses did not justify the work of the U-boat Arm, which was suffering far more than its enemy. The Allies lost a total of 144,500 tons in the month, with enemy aircraft accounting for 62,500 tons and the Mediterranean being the worst area for the losses.

December brought the usual reduction in activity on the high seas but the U-boats sank thirteen ships totalling about 87,000 tons while losing eight of their own number in the month. The Allies lost 168,500 tons in all waters, the Mediterranean continuing to be the main area of conflict and enemy air activity causing most of the sinkings. One of the most dramatic events in the month took place in the Arctic, where B-Dienst decrypts and U-boat sightings revealed that the British had resumed convoys to Russia in the winter season, taking advantage of the long periods of darkness in those northern latitudes. The knowledge that supplies of war materials were reaching Russia, enabling the Red Army to continue its advance westwards, was infuriating to Hitler.

Convoy JW55B, consisting of twenty-two ships escorted by three cruisers with several destroyers and smaller vessels, left Loch Ewe in Scotland on 20 December. This coincided with the journey of the homeward-bound convoy JW55A from Archangel. After JW55B was sighted by the Luftwaffe and U-boats, the battleship *Scharnhorst* in Altenfjord was put on three hours' notice. Morale among the crew of this battleship was high, for the men believed that they represented the cream of the Kriegsmarine and welcomed the prospect of action. Further orders were awaited by Konteradmiral Erich Bey, the commander of the Northern Task Force, and Kapitän zur See Fritz Hintze, the captain of *Scharnhorst*. The Royal Navy was already aware of this standby, from signals decrypted by Bletchley Park. The battleship HMS *Duke of York* and the cruiser HMS *Jamaica* with four destroyers, under the command of Admiral Sir Bruce Fraser, was already at sea to cover the two convoys in the hope of intercepting a German formation. Bletchley Park continued to decrypt the enemy signals, and these were passed to Admiral Fraser.

Unaware of the British battleship and the cruiser, Dönitz ordered Bey to put to sea on Christmas Day, together with six destroyers. The formation left at 1800 hours, with Bletchley Park aware of this movement. Reports by B-Dienst that the Luftwaffe had sighted the British battleship do not seem to have reached the Kriegsmarine. The two formations began to close with each other on Boxing Day. Fraser ordered convoy JW55A to put about for three hours, in order to keep clear of the forthcoming sea battle. Meanwhile the heavy German destroyers experienced problems in very rough seas. They found no convoy and Bey ordered them back to base while *Scharnhorst* continued alone.

In the subsequent engagement *Scharnhorst* was damaged by gunfire from the British cruisers and turned for home. She managed to hit the cruiser HMS *Norfolk,* causing serious damage, and straddled HMS *Duke of York* without scoring hits. The sea battle lasted for several hours, illuminated by British starshells, until the German battleship ceased firing at 1830 hours. She then become a target for torpedoes fired by destroyers and the cruiser HMS *Jamaica* and went down at 1945 hours in the icy seas. Both Bey and Hintze were lost, together with 1,801 of the crew who had fought against impossible odds. Only thirty-six men were picked up the Royal Navy. The major threat to the Arctic convoys had been destroyed, leaving the U-boat Arm as the main enemy.

Another sea battle took place on 28 December, after a German force of destroyers and torpedo boats had made a sortie into the Bay of Biscay to escort the inbound blockade runner *Alsterufer,* unaware that this had been sunk the day before by Coastal Command. The cruisers HMS *Glasgow* and HMS *Enterprise* made contact with four of these warships and sank the destroyer Z.27 and the torpedo boats *T.25* and *T.26,* although they rescued 168 men from the three boats.

The year ended after a string of disasters for the U-boat Arm and the whole of the Kriegsmarine. Moreover, although the precise figures could not be known in Germany, in July 1943 Allied gains from new merchant shipbuilding had overtaken the cumulative losses sustained since September 1939. Primarily from the great powerhouse and shipyards of the USA, about 19 million gross tons had been launched, equalling the total of merchant ships sunk from all causes. After this month new gains had begun to greatly exceed losses, which were falling away sharply. Yet Dönitz remained determined and resolute, although he must have known from operational reports that he was fighting a losing battle.

At 1758 hours on 13 February 1943 Sunderland III serial DV961 of 461 (RAAF) Squadron, flown from Hamworthy in Dorset by Squadron Leader Samuel R. Wood, was about 75 miles north-west of the north-westerly tip of Spain when a U-boat was spotted on the surface. Wood climbed into cloud at 6,000 feet, turned and dived to attack. The bomb distributor was unserviceable and the depth charges were released in a salvo instead of a stick. The U-boat, which was a large ocean-going type, was covered in spray but did not appear to have been damaged. The tail-gunner, rear gunner and mid-gunner of the Sunderland fired many rounds at it. The U-boat fired back but did not score any hits. There are no records of a U-boat sunk or damaged on that day.

Ref: CN 1/36

```
    ADM                                                             131
       TO: I D 8 G                        ZIP/ZTPGU/6122

       FROM: N S

       4540 KC/S                          TOI 0421/17/2/43

                 TOO 0513

       FROM: M 6TH U/B FLOTILLA

       TO:     U.608 FOR STOKER HAMPEL

       DAUGHTER SIGRID HAS ARRIVED. HEARTY CONGRATULATIONS.

    0840/17/2/43++++CEL/FA
```

This compassionate signal was sent to Stoker Hampel when he was serving in the Type VIIC *U-608* on 17 February 1943. The U-boat had been built by Blohm & Voss of Hamburg and commissioned on 5 February 1942. It was on its third war cruise, having left St-Nazaire on 20 January 1943 for the North Atlantic under the command of Kapitänleutnant Rolf Struckmeier. It made a total of nine war cruises and sank four merchant vessels. On 9 August 1944, after leaving Lorient bound for La Pallice under the command of Oberleutnant zur See Wolfgang Reisener, it was depth-charged and damaged by Liberator VI serial EV877 of 53 Squadron flown from Thorney Island in Sussex by the commanding officer, Wing Commander R.T.F. Gates. The attack was continued by the sloop HMS *Wren*. All fifty-one crew members were rescued by British warships and became prisoners.

Ref: DEFE 3/711

The Type VIIC *U-205* was built by Germaniawerft of Kiel and commissioned on 3 May 1941. It completed two war cruises in the North Atlantic and then, on 3 November 1941, left Lorient for the Mediterranean. After eight more war cruises, during which it sank the anti-aircraft cruiser HMS *Hermione* of 5,450 tons displacement, it left Salamis in Greece on 2 February 1943 under the command of Kapitänleutnant Friedrich Bürgel but on 17 February was picked up on the Asdic of the destroyer HMS *Paladin,* one of four warships escorting Convoy TXI about 80 miles north-east of Benghazi in Libya. The *Paladin* and a Bristol Bisley of 15 (SAAF) Squadron, flown by Captain C.R. Brinton from Amriya in Egypt, depth-charged *U-205.* This was brought to the surface and came under fire from the *Paladin,* the destroyer HMS *Jervis* and the Bisley. The U-boat surrendered, eight of the crew being killed and forty-two rescued.

Ref: CN 1/35

The *Flower* class corvette HMS *Gloxinia* then arrived on the scene and took *U-205* in tow, although the U-boat appeared to be in danger of sinking, and headed for Ras el Hilal on the Libyan coast. Two seamen from HMS *Paladin* went out in a cutter and boarded the U-boat. After a while they were given permission to venture inside and, in spite of almost complete darkness, found books and other material which they passed to the cutter. But the U-boat was slowly settling and the two men were taken off. It went down just short of Ras el Hilal but a diver went down later and recovered more material, including an Enigma machine.

Ref: CN 1/35

```
    ADM (2)                                                        461
    TO I D 8  G                            ZIP/ZTPGU/6448
    FROM N S
    13768 KC/S                                     TOI: 1640/18/2/43
              T O O : 1725
       U 403  SIGHTED  AT 1716  ONE  DESTROYER, ONE  STEAMSHIP
    IN  NAVAL  GRID  SQUARE  BC 3473, COURSE 270  DEGREES.
    2222/20/2/43+EGT/PG
```

The Type VIIC *U-403* was built by Danzigerwerft and commissioned on 25 June 1941. It was on its eighth war cruise when sending this signal on 18 February 1943, having left Bergen on 9 January to operate in the North Atlantic under the command of Kapitänleutnant Heinz-Ehlert Clausen. It had sunk one merchant vessel on its previous cruises and then sank another on the day after this signal. It arrived at Brest on 2 March 1943 and made another war cruise, sinking a third ship. The end came on its tenth cruise, under the command of Kapitänleutnant Karl-Franz Heine. When off Dakar on 17 August 1943, it was depth-charged by a Hudson III of 200 Squadron flown from Yundum in the Gambia by Flying Officer P.R. Horbat; this was followed by another attack by a Wellington of the Free French Air Force flown from Bel Air near Dakar. There were no survivors from the crew of forty-nine.

Ref: DEFE 3/711

The Type IXC *U-508* was built by Deutschewerft of Hamburg and commissioned on 20 October 1941. After a war cruise from Kiel and then another from Lorient, during which it sank eleven merchant ships, it left Lorient for a third cruise on 22 February 1943, under the command of Kapitänleutnant Georg Staats. Four days later it was attacked in mid-Atlantic by Liberator II serial AL507 of 224 Squadron flown from Beaulieu in Hampshire by Squadron Leader Peter J. Cundy, as shown here. Four depth charges were dropped, but the crew of the Liberator could see no results and continued their patrol. Unknown to them, the U-boat was forced to return to Lorient for repair. It was eventually sunk on 12 November 1943 in the Bay of Biscay by a Liberator of VP-103 Squadron, US Navy, flown by Lieutenant Ralph B. Brownell. In turn, the Liberator was shot down and all crew members were killed. There were no survivors from the fifty-seven crew members of the U-boat.

Ref: AIR 15/470

```
ADM (2)                                                    991
   TO: I D 8 G                          ZIP/ZTPGU/7948
   FROM: N S
   4540 KC/S                          OI 0210/10/3/43
                TOO 0058
   FROM: GELHAUS
      HAVE SEARCHED FOR CONVOY ON NORTHERLY AND NORTHWEST
      COURSES, IN VAIN.   CONSISTED OF LARGE TRANSPORTS,
      ASSUME HIGH SPEED.
   1653/12/3/43+++TZ/SMH
```

Kapitänleutnant Harald Gelhaus was in command of the Type IXB *U-107* when he sent this signal on 10 March 1943. His U-boat had been built by A.G. Weser of Bremen and commissioned on 8 October 1940. It was on its eighth war cruise, having left Lorient on 30 January 1943 to operate in the Azores area. Up to this time its score had been thirty-two merchant vessels sunk and another damaged. It made five more war cruises, sinking six more merchant vessels and damaging three others. The end came on 18 August 1944 when under the command of Leutnant der Reserve Karl-Heinz Fritz and sailing from Lorient to La Pallice. It was spotted south-west of Belle Ile by the crew of Sunderland III serial EJ150 of 201 Squadron flown from Pembroke Dock under the captaincy of Flight Lieutenant Les H. Baveystock. A stick of depth charges destroyed the U-boat with the loss of all fifty-eight men on board.

Ref: DEFE 3/712

```
ADM                                                       515
   TO I D 8 G                          ZIP/ZTPGU/10507
   FROM N S
   4412 KC/S                        T O I 0724/15/3/43
             T O O 0655
   FROM: BOTHE
      AT 0900/14/3 BOMBED IN NAVAL GRID SQUARE AL 8836.
   DIESEL OIL TANK '2 I' CRACKED, PORT MAIN COUPLING AND MAGNETIC
                                       ZL
   COMPASS DEFECTIVE. AM IN SQUARE ZA 3191.
   1701/9/4/43+AND+DJL
   PLEASE READ LAST LINE - +) 3191
   ZL 3191
```

This signal was sent on 15 March 1943 from *U-447*, commanded by Kapitänleutnant Friedrich-Wilhelm Bothe, when west of Eire. This was a Type VIIC U-boat, built by Schichau of Danzig and commissioned on 11 July 1942. It had left Kiel on 20 February 1943 for its first war cruise and the attack probably came from a Sunderland of 201 Squadron from Castle Archdale in Northern Ireland. The U-boat arrived safely in Brest, despite this incident. Then it left Brest on 27 April 1943, bound for the Mediterranean. Eight days later it was engaged in a gun battle with an LCT (Landing Craft, Tank). On 7 May 1943, when about 170 miles south-west of Cape St Vincent, it was caught on the surface by two Hudson IIIs of 233 Squadron flown from Gibraltar by Sergeant J.V. Holland and Sergeant J.W. McQueen. These dropped depth charges which destroyed the U-boat, with the loss of all forty-eight crew members.

Ref: DEFE 3/715

Two U-boats were sunk by a convoy escort in the North Atlantic on 11 March 1943. One was the Type VIIC *U-444*, built by Schichau of Danzig and commissioned on 9 May 1942. This left La Pallice on 1 March 1943 for its second war cruise, commanded by Oberleutnant zur See Albert Langfeld. It damaged a merchant vessel on 11 March but was then depth-charged by the destroyer HMS *Harvester*. Blown to the surface, it was rammed by the destroyer and the two vessels remained stuck together for about ten minutes. Once freed, *U-444* began to escape on the surface, leaving the destroyer disabled with damage to a propeller. However, the U-boat was then located by the French corvette *Aconit* and rammed again. It sank with the loss of forty-one crew members, including the commander. Five men were rescued.

The other was the Type VIIC *U-432*, built by Schichau of Danzig and commissioned on 26 April 1941. This had already made seven war cruises and sunk twenty-one vessels and damaged another. It left La Pallice on 14 February 1943 for its eighth war cruise, under the command of Kapitänleutnant Herman Eckhardt, and torpedoed the disabled HMS *Harvester*, causing heavy loss of life. However, it was then depth-charged to the surface by the French corvette *Aconit* and subjected to gunfire, as shown in this photograph. Twenty-six crew members were killed, including the commander, but twenty were rescued to become prisoners.

Ref: ADM 199/2060

Prisoners from *U-432* on board the French corvette *Aconit*.

Ref: ADM 199/2060

In the afternoon of 22 March 1943 the crew of Whitley V serial Z6950 of No. 10 Operational Training Unit, flown from St Eval in Cornwall by Sergeant J.A. Marsden, spotted a U-boat on the surface about 300 miles west of St-Nazaire. Marsden turned and dropped six depth charges, which straddled the U-boat. It was the Type VIIC *U-665,* commanded by Oberleutnant zur See Hans-Jürgen Haupt, which had been built by Howaldtswerke of Hamburg and commissioned on 22 July 1942. It was on its first war cruise, having left Kiel on 20 February 1943 and already sunk one merchant vessel. It was lost with all forty-six crew members.

Ref: AIR 28/741

This signal was sent on 5 April 1943 by the Type VIIC *U-563,* having torpedoed and damaged the US merchant ship *Sunoil* of 9,005 tons when south-west of Iceland. This U-boat had been built by Blohm & Voss of Hamburg and commissioned on 27 March 1941. It was on its seventh war cruise, having left Brest on 20 March 1943 under the command of Kapitänleutnant Götz von Hartmann. Its total score during these cruises was five vessels sunk and one damaged. It returned safely to Brest from this cruise, on 18 May 1943. (see also p. 145.)

Ref: DEFE 3/715

```
ADM(2)

TO I D 8 G                               ZIP/ZTPGU/10127        124
FROM N S


12950 KC/S                            T O I 1549/5/4/43)M
              T O O 1149
FROM: U 563

1) AT 1145 HIT XX ON 7,000 GRT. TANKER ASTERN OF CONVOY. THREW
2 ''WIBOS'' INEFFECTIVELY ON ACCOUNT OF DESTROYER. DEFECTS IN
DIESEL AND HYDROPLANE. DIVED UNTIL 1600.
2) AM IN NAVAL GRID SQUARE AK 1831. AM OPERATING FOR A FINISHING
SHOT. REQUEST ORDERS' AS BY THEN SHALL BE TOO FAR ASTERN OF CONVOY
AND THE PORT BLOWER IS DEFECTIVE.
3) 80 CUBIC METRES. TWO ''T3''. ONE DEFECTIVE, SIX ''T2'' PLUS TWO
''A'' TORPEDOES.
4) SERIAL NO. 843 MISSING.
(DEPT NOTE: ''WIBO''. ''T2'' AND ''T3'' ARE NEW TO US)
1949/6/4/43+EE+DJL
```

```
      8470 KC/S                                          TO: 0053/7/4/43
                             TOO 1334/6
                                                                  273
    FROM: U 509

           26/3 OPERATING AGAINST 5 STEAMSHIPS WESTRLY COURSES IN
           NAVAL GRID SQUARE A ERXH GR 5341.  KEPT CONTINUALLY UNDER
           WATER BY LOCATING AIR. . THEREAFTER WENT NORTHWARD ALONG 50
           FATHOM LINE.   ON 2/4 IN SQUARE GJ 8144 2 STEAMSHIPS 2 ESCORTS
           COURSE 160 DEGREES, 4 FAN FIRED ACCORDING TO HYDROPHONE IN
           FOG.   1 EXPLOSION FROM HIT.   FOUND NOTHING.   5/4 IN SQUARE
           J 4312 DOUBLE MISS ON TRAWLER ESCORT 6/4 SQUARE J 1616
           HARBOUR EMPTY, 1 ESCORT.   'METOX' FOR SOME TIME EFFECTIVE ONLY
           WITH VERTICAL CABLE.   STILL 4 WEEKS PROVISIONS.   8 'A'
           TORPEDOES 2 'E' TORPEDOES 2 T3, 82 CBM.   RETURN PASSAGE.
      0913/7/4/43+++EGT/SHH
```

This signal from *U-509* was sent on 7 April 1943. It was a Type IXC U-boat, built by Deutschewerft of Hamburg and commissioned on 4 November 1941. It was on its third war cruise, having left Lorient on 23 December 1942 under the command of Kapitänleutnant Werner Witte to operate off South Africa. During these three cruises it sank four merchant vessels and damaged four more. It returned safely to Lorient but left again on 3 July 1943, with Witte promoted to Korvettenkapitän, again bound for South Africa. This proved to be its last cruise, for on 15 July 1943 it was caught south-west of the Azores by two aircraft of VC-29 Squadron from the escort carrier USS *Santee*. Strafed by a Wildcat flown by Lieutenant J.D. Anderson and then hit by a 'Fido' homing torpedo dropped by an Avenger flown by Lieutenant C.N. Barton, it went to the bottom with all fifty-four crew members.

Ref: DEFE 3/715

```
    ADM (2)                                                    968
    TO:  I D 8 G                          ZIP/ZTPGU/10953
    FROM: N S
    11068 KC/S                            TOI 1313/11/4/43
                     TOO 1449
    FROM: KAPITZKY
    AM IN NAVAL GRID SQUARE AK 5740. COMMANDER NOT YET FIT BECAUSE
    OF SPLINTERS IN RIGHT SHOULDER AND UPPER ARM AND PERHAPS FRACTURE
    OF COLLAR BONE. REQUEST RETURN PASSAGE.
    1155/16/4/43+++EGT/FA
```

The commander of the Type VIIC *U-615*, Kapitänleutnant Ralph Kapinsky, sent this signal on 11 April 1943. His U-boat had been built by Blohm & Voss of Hamburg and commissioned on 26 March 1942. It was on its third war cruise in the North Atlantic and Kapinsky had just been wounded after sinking his third victim, the American Liberty ship *Edward B. Dudley* of 7,177 tons. His wounds had not been caused by the enemy action but by splinters when the ship blew up. The U-boat returned safely to La Pallice. It left La Pallice again on 12 June 1943 and sank another merchant ship, this time in the Caribbean. The end came on 6 August 1943 when it was bombed by Mariner aircraft of VB-130, VP-204 and VP-205 Squadrons, US Navy, as well as others of 10 Squadron, USAAC. Five of the crew were killed but forty-three were rescued to become prisoners, including Kapinsky.

Ref: DEFE 3/715

```
ADM (2)                                                         57
   TO: I D 8 G                          ZIP/ZTPGU/11055
FROM: N S
8362 KC/S
                    1057/17/4/43 B' Z G J

     AM MAINTAINING CONTACT.

                          CA (U 175)

1933/18/4/43+++CEL/SMH
```

Above: The Type IXC *U-175* was built by A.G. Weser of Bremen and commissioned on 5 December 1941. It made two war cruises under the command of Kapitänleutnant Heinrich Bruns, during which it sank ten merchant vessels. It left Lorient on 10 April 1943 for its third war cruise, Bruns having been promoted to Korvettenkapitän. This was its last signal, sent on 17 April 1943 when west-south-west of Eire and indicating contact with a convoy. On the same day it was located with H/F D/F by the coastguard cutter USS *Spencer*. Depth charges brought it to the surface, and it came under gunfire before sinking. Thirteen men were killed, including Bruns, but forty-one survivors were rescued by the cutters *Spencer* and *Duane*.

Ref: DEFE 3/716

Opposite Top: Depth charges from the coastguard cutter USS *Spencer* exploding before bringing the Type IXC *U-175* to the surface.

Ref: ADM 199/2060

Opposite Bottom: The Type IXC *U-175* photographed from the coastguard cutter USS *Spencer* on 17 April 1943.

Ref: ADM 199/2060

```
ADM
    TO: I D 8 G                                    ZIP/ZTPGU/10834    855
    FROM: N S
    ℞ 12950 KC/S                                      TOI 1243/11/4/43
                          TOO 1316
    FROM: MOEHLMANN
        AT 0735 IN SQUARE 9682 OUT OF LUEDDEN'S CONVOY (ABOUT 30
        UNITS) SANK 7500 ((TON)) FREIGHTER.   SINKING OF 6000 ((TON))
        FREIGHTER PROBABLE.   THIRD HIT PROBABLY ON UNIDENTIFIED UNIT.
        FOR 4 HOURS HYDROPHONE HUNT WITH HEAVY DEPTHCAHRGING.   AM
        EFFECTING REPAIRS.   SQUARE AJ 9691.   ((WEATHER REPORT.))
        85 CUBIC METRES, 8 'E' TORPEDOES, 2 'A' TORPEDOES.
    0504/16/4/43+++EE/SMH
```

This signal of 11 April was sent from the Type VIIC *U-571*, commanded by Kapitänleutnant Helmut Möhlmann. The U-boat was on its eighth war cruise, in the North Atlantic, after leaving La Pallice on 25 March 1943. It had been built by Blohm & Voss of Hamburg and commissioned on 22 May 1941. It had sunk five merchant ships and damaged three more on its previous cruises. This report was not completely correct, for on this occasion it sank only one vessel, the Norwegian *Ingerfire* of 3,835 tons. The U-boat was sunk on its tenth war cruise, when under the command of Oberleutnant zur See Gustav Lüssow. On 28 January 1944, about 180 miles west of the mouth of the river Shannon, it was depth-charged and sunk by Sunderland III serial EK577 of 461 (RAAF) Squadron, flown from Pembroke Dock by Flight Lieutenant Richard D. Lucas, and was lost with all fifty-two crew members.

Ref: DEFE 3/715

The Type IXC/40 *U-189* was built by A.G. Weser of Bremen and commissioned on 15 August 1942. It left Kristiansund South on 3 April 1943 under the command of Korvettenkapitän Hellmut Kurrer to report on ice limits in the area of the Denmark Strait. It was spotted on 23 April about 425 miles west-south-west of Iceland by Liberator III serial FL923 of 120 Squadron, flown from Reykjavik by Flying Officer John K. Moffatt. The Liberator dropped four depth charges in the face of flak, whereupon the U-boat stopped and circled to port. Moffatt came back and dropped two more depth charges. The U-boat sank, leaving many men in the water, but none of her crew of fifty-four survived.

Ref: AIR 15/471

The Type VIIC *U-465* was built by Deutschewerke of Kiel and commissioned on 20 May 1942. It made three war cruises in the North Atlantic under the command of Kapitänleutnant Heinz Wolf, during which it did not achieve any sinkings. It was damaged on the third from an attack on 10 April 1943 by a Catalina of 210 Squadron flown from Pembroke Dock by Flight Lieutenant Frank Squire, but managed to reach St-Nazaire four days later. After repair, it left port again on 29 April 1943 for a fourth war cruise, but on 2 May was attacked by Sunderland III serial DV968 of 461 (RAAF) Squadron flown from Pembroke Dock by Flight Lieutenant E.C. Smith. This made two attacks, one of which is shown here, dropping four depth charges on each occasion. These straddled the U-boat and about fifteen men were seen jumping into the water on the second occasion. However, the U-boat was destroyed and there were no survivors from the crew of forty-eight.

Ref: CN 1/39

At 1018 hours on 2 May 1943 Whitley VII serial BD602 of 612 Squadron, flown by Sergeant J.L. Richards from Davidstow Moor in Cornwall, came across a U-boat heading north off La Rochelle. Richards attacked, but his depth charges undershot. An exchange of fire with machine-guns took place, the front gunner firing 200 rounds and the rear gunner firing 800 rounds. Hits were scored on the U-boat, which dived steeply. Nothing more was seen, although the Whitley remained in the area for two and a half hours.

Ref: ADM 199/1418

The Type IXB *U-109* was built by A.G. Weser of Bremen and commissioned on 5 December 1940. It had a successful career, sinking fourteen Allied merchant vessels in eight war cruises, while operating mainly from Lorient. It left this port on 28 April 1943 for another patrol in the North Atlantic, commanded by Oberleutnant zur See Joachim Schramm, but was located on 4 May 1943 north-east of the Azores by Liberator V serial FL955 of 86 Squadron, flown from Aldergrove in Northern Ireland by Pilot Officer J.C. Green on an escort to convoy HX236. Four depth charges straddled the U-boat a few seconds after this photograph was taken and the effect was lethal. Wreckage came to the surface and all fifty-two hands in the crew lost their lives.

Ref: AIR 15/471

```
     ADM(2)

     TO I D 8 G                          Z IP/ZTPGU/12249            274

     FROM N S


     5650 KC/S            TOO 0533          TOI 0425/5/5/43.

     FROM: MANKE

          SANK AN 8,000 TONNER AT 0424 AND A 6,000 TONNER AT $0448

     IN NAVAL GR ID SQUARE AJ 6517, BOTH SINKING IN LESS THAN A MINUTE.

     FIRED 1 'E' TORPEDO AND 2 T.3'S WITH IMPACT-FUZES.  STILL HAVE

     57 CUBIC METRES.

     ((WEATHER FOLLOWS)).

     1727/5/5/43 ++CEL/WAB+++
```

This signal was sent by Kapitänleutnant Rolf Mancke of the Type VIIC *U-358* on 3 May 1943, after he had sunk the British merchant ships *Bristol City* of 2,864 tons and *Wentworth* of 5,212 tons in the North Atlantic. The U-boat had been built by Flensburger Schiffbau and commissioned on 15 August 1942. It was on its second war cruise, having sunk another vessel on this second cruise. It made a third war cruise from St-Nazaire, during which it shot down a Catalina of 210 Squadron flown by Flying Officer G. Silva. It then left St-Nazaire once more, on 14 February 1944, but on 1 March when north-west of the Azores was depth-charged by the frigates HMS *Affleck, Garlies, Gore* and *Gould*. It succeeded in sinking HMS *Gould* but in turn was sunk by HMS *Affleck*, with the loss of fifty hands. Only one man was rescued.

Ref: DEFE 3/717

```
ADM (2)                                                    552

TO: I D 8 G      B                        ŻIP/ZTPGU/12513
FROM: N S


7647 KC/S              TOO 0501           TOI 0331/6/5/43


FROM: FOLKERS
MOST IMMEDIATE


     HAVE BEEN RAMMED.  AM UNABLE TO DIVE.  SQUARE AJ 8652.

     REQUEST ASSISTANCE, COURSE 90 DEGREES.


1728/9/5/43+++CEL/SMH
```

The Type IXC *U-125* was built by A.G. Weser of Bremen and commissioned on 3 March 1941. It made six war cruises, during which it sank sixteen merchant ships. Then it left Lorient on 13 April 1943, under the command of Kapitänleutnant Ulrich Folkers, and sank another merchant ship on 4 May. The end came a few minutes after this signal was sent on 6 May, when it was north-east of St John's in Newfoundland. It was forced to the surface by depth charges fired by the corvette HMS *Snowflake* and then sunk by gunfire and ramming, with the loss of all fifty-four crew members.

Ref: DEFE 3/717

At 1014 hours on 7 May 1943 Whitley VII serial BD680 of 612 Squadron, flown from Davidstow Moor in Cornwall by Warrant Officer G.F. McFarlane, was at 3,500 feet near Cape Ortegal on the north-west tip of Spain when a fully surfaced U-boat was spotted. McFarlane dived steeply and released a stick of six depth charges. One of these hung up but the remainder fell near the starboard bow of the U-boat. Another attack was made but the depth charges did not release since the bomb distributor was set incorrectly. The pilot was unaware of this and made an attack with machine-guns, but the U-boat dived and nothing further was seen. There is no record of any sinking.

Ref: CN 1/39

```
ADM(2)                                                    943

TO  I D 8 G                             ZIP/ZTPGU/13899

FROM N S

4412 KC/S              TOO 1017         TOI 1534/7/5/43

FROM: U 214

OFFIZIBR CYPHER

COMMANDING OFFICER SERIOUSLY WOUNDED IN AIRCRAFT ATTACK.

RETURN PASSAGE. QUERY: 'KERNBEISSER'? NAVAL GRID SQUARE B F 4474.

(DEPT NOTE: COMPLETE TEXT OF ZTPGU/12431)

0001/22/5/43     EE+++MRT+++
```

The Type VIID *U-214* was built by Germaniawerft of Kiel and commissioned on 1 November 1941. It made four war cruises in the North Atlantic, during which it sank three merchant vessels and damaged an auxiliary merchant cruiser. On 4 May 1943 it left Brest for a fifth cruise, commanded by Kapitänleutnant Günther Reeder, but two days later was attacked in the Bay of Biscay by Whitley V serial BD189 of No. 10 Operational Training Unit, flown from St Eval in Cornwall by Sergeant S.J. Barnett. The U-boat was not damaged but Reeder was among those wounded, resulting in this signal of 7 May 1943. *U-214* returned to Brest with casualties three days later. It was sunk on its eleventh war cruise, when under the command of Oberleutnant zur See Gerhard Conrad. It left Brest on 22 July 1944 to lay a mine barrage off Start Point near Plymouth but four days later was depth-charged by the frigate HMS *Cooke* and lost with all forty-eight crew members. By this time it had sunk a further merchant vessel and damaged another.

Ref: DEFE 3/718

```
ADM(1)                                                   197

TO  I D 8 G                            ZIP/ZTPGU/13192

FROM N S

3920 KC/S            TOO 0502          TOI 0334/12/5/43

FROM: (WAECHTER)

     RENDERED UNABLE TO DIVE BY DEPTH CHARGES IN NAVAL GRID

SQUARE CE 1687. AM BEING HUNTED BY DESTROYER.

0415/16/5/43 ++CEL/WAB++++
```

This signal was sent on 12 May 1943 from mid-Atlantic by the Type VIIC *U-223*, commanded by Oberleutnant zur See Karl-Jürg Wachter, after having been depth-charged and then by rammed by the destroyer HMS *Hesperus*. The U-boat had been built by Germaniawerft of Kiel and commissioned on 6 June 1942. It was on its second war cruise, having left St-Nazaire on 15 April 1943. Unable to dive, it was assisted by the Type VIICs *U-359* and *U-377*, and managed to return to St-Nazaire. After repair, it left again on 14 September 1943 and entered the Mediterranean. It was sunk on its sixth war cruise when north-east of Palermo in Sicily on 30 March 1944 by destroyers of the Royal Navy, with the loss of its commander Oberleutnant zur See Peter Gerlach and twenty-two hands. By this time it had sunk two merchant vessels and damaged the destroyer HMS *Cuckmere*. It had also sunk one of the destroyers which was hunting it on 30 March 1944, HMS *Laforey*.

Ref: DEFE 3/718

```
ADM(1)                                                              752
                                              ZIP/ZTPGU/12708
TO I D 8 G

FROM N S


11068 KC/S            TOO 1330            TOI 1151/12/5/43

MOST 'IMMEDIATE:

FROM: TEICHERT

     AM UNABLE TO DIVE. NAVAL GRID SQUARE BD 6646.  AIRCRAFT

IS MAXNXXNXNK  MAINTAINING CONTACT.  URGENTLY REQUEST ASSISTANCE.

10008 /14/5/43 ++EE/WAB++
```

This last message was sent on 12 May 1943 by the Type VIIC *U-456*, commanded by Kapitänleutnant Max-Martin Teichert, when in mid-Atlantic. The U-boat had been built by Deutschewerke of Kiel and commissioned on 18 September 1941. It had left Brest on 24 April 1943 for its eleventh war cruise, having sunk six merchant vessels and damaged another during its career, mostly in Arctic waters. The attack came from Liberator III serial FK229 of 86 Squadron, flown from Aldergrove in Northern Ireland by Flight Lieutenant John Wright, which dropped an acoustic homing torpedo known as a Mark 24 mine. The Liberator crew called up a destroyer escort from convoy HX237 but on its approach Teichert decided to attempt a dive. The U-boat sank and all forty-nine crew members were lost.

Ref: DEFE 3/717

The Type VIIC *U-266* was built by Bremer Vulkan of Vegesack and commissioned on 24 June 1942. On its first war cruise it sank one merchant vessel. On 14 April 1943 it left St-Nazaire for a second war cruise, under the command of Kapitänleutnant Ralf von Jessen, and sank three more merchant vessels in the North Atlantic. On 15 May 1943 it was spotted north of the Azores by Halifax II serial HR746 of 58 Squadron, flown from St Eval in Cornwall by the commanding officer, Wing Commander Wilfred E. Oulton, on an escort to convoy SC129. Oulton came out of the sun and dropped four depth charges which exploded under the U-boat, as shown here. The bows of *U-266* rose up out of the sea vertically before it went down with the loss of all forty-seven crew members.

Ref: AIR 15/471

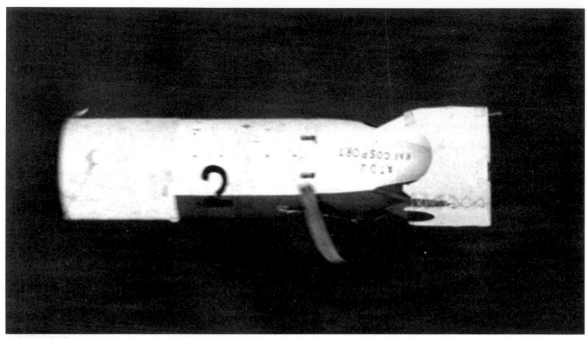

The acoustic homing torpedo, known by the cover name of the Mark 24 mine, was developed by US scientists and arrived in Britain in April 1943. It was first carried in the following month by the Liberators of 120 Squadron, based at Reykjavik, for anti-submarine work in mid-Atlantic. It remained a highly secret weapon throughout the rest of the war.

Ref: CN 1/5

```
ADM                                                                381

TO I D 8 0                                    ZIP/ZTPGU/15363

FROM N S
                                                       5
4412 KC/S              TOO 2357/17         TOI 1041/18/7/43

FROM : STAHL

        SHOT DOWN A/C AT 1400   IN NAVAL GRID SQUARE BF 4543. SHALL

BE AT ESCORT R/V AT 1500/19

0500/21/7/43+++ EGT/JR
```

This signal was sent from the Bay of Biscay on 18 May 1943 by the Type VIIC *U-648*, commanded by Oberleutnant zur See Peter Stahl, after having shot down Whitley serial R9438 of No. 10 Operational Training Unit flown from St Eval in Cornwall by Sergeant J.H. Castles. All crew members in the aircraft were killed. This U-boat had been built by Blohm & Voss of Hamburg and commissioned on 12 November 1942. It was on its first cruise, having left Kiel on 3 April 1943 for the North Atlantic. It sank no vessels on this cruise and arrived at Brest the day after this encounter.

DEFE 3/720

```
ADM (2)                                        191
TO I D 8 G                    ZIP/ZTPGU/14172
FROM N S

4600 KC/S          TOO: 1956        TOI: 2259/23/5/43

FROM: HUNGERSHAUSEN

  REPORT OF SURVIVORS FROM U 752: BOMBED BY CARRIER A/C
  AT 1210/23 AT PERISCOPE DEPTH.  INRUSH OF WATER INTO
  WARDROOM, UNABLE TO DIVE.  BLEW TANKS AND DROVE OFF
  3 FURTHER CARRIER A/C.  2 DESTROYERS CLOSED AND SUNK HER.
  C.O. AND EXECUTIVE OFFICER KILLED, ABOUT 15 RATINGS
  PICKED UP BY D/R, OF 10 PICKED UP BY ME WARRANT
  Q.M. WOLF  P.O. JACOBZIKS  P.O.SEEWALD  O.S. GOEDIKE
  HAVE BEEN SUCCESSFULLY GIVEN RESPIRATION.  NAMES OF
  ANY OTHERS REVIVED WILL BE REPORTED.

0505/24/5/43++EGT++DG
```

This signal was sent on 23 May 1943 by the Type VIIC *U-91*, commanded by Oberleutnant zur See Heinz Hungershausen, after picking up four survivors from *U-752*. The latter was also a Type VIIC, built by Kriegsmarinewerft of Wilhelmshaven and commissioned on 24 May 1941. It had made nine war cruises, during which it had sunk twelve vessels. It then left St-Nazaire on 22 April 1943 for a tenth cruise, under the command of Korvettenkapitän Karl-Ernst Schroeter. Its end came on 23 May 1943 when it was surprised on the surface about 670 miles south-east of Greenland by a Swordfish of 819 Squadron, Fleet Air Arm, flown from the escort carrier HMS *Archer* by Sub-Lieutenant Horrocks. This attacked with rockets which sank the U-boat, which was also strafed by a Martlet from the same carrier. The commander and twenty-nine of his men were killed, but twelve others were rescued by a destroyer, apart from the four survivors picked up by *U-91*.

Ref: DEFE 3/719

At 2158 hours on 27 May 1943 Liberator II letter T of 224 Squadron was returning to St Eval in Cornwall after escorting a convoy when contact was made with the Air to Surface Vessel radar about 400 miles west-south-west of Land's End. The aircraft, flown by Flight Sergeant J.S. Edwards, was above cloud at the time, but it homed on to the target while losing height from 2,500 feet to 500 feet. The rear and nose gunners spotted a U-boat on the surface through a break in the clouds, before it was lost to view. Edwards circled and descended to 50 feet, and the U-boat was spotted dead ahead on a westerly course. The Liberator went into the attack, with the gunners opening fire against return flak, but all six depth charges hung up. Edwards made another run and this time the depth charges were released, but they overshot astern of the U-boat. Contact was then lost in a fogbank, or the U-boat might have dived. It appeared to have been hit in the conning tower by machine-gun fire, while the Liberator received damage to the port inner engine and the hydraulics. Edwards landed back at St Eval at 0245 hours the following morning. No U-boat was lost in this area on that day.

Ref: ADM 199/1418

```
ADM(1)                                                        343

  TO I D 8 G                          ZIP/ZTPGU/14310

  FROM N S

  4412 KC/S              T O O 0207           TOI: 0020/30/5/43

  FROM: POPP

  MOST IMMEDIATE

    NAVAL GRID SQUARE BE 2858 SEVERE A/S BOMBS, ABILITY TO DIVE

  LIMITED TO 30 METRES, ALL A/A ARMAMENT KNOCKED OUT. REQUEST

  ESCORT, AM MOVING AWAY TO SOUTH.

  1753/4/6/43+EGT/PG
```

This signal was sent from the Type VIIC *U-552* on 30 May 1943 when far west of Ushant, after sustaining damage the day before. The U-boat had been built by Blohm & Voss of Hamburg and commissioned on 4 December 1940. It was on its twelfth war cruise, having left Brest on 4 April under the command of Kapitänleutnant Klaus Popp. The attacking aircraft was Liberator V serial FL984 of 59 Squadron flown from Aldergrove in Northern Ireland by Flying Officer H.A.L. 'Tim' Moran of the RAAF, which dropped two sticks of depth charges and machine-gunned the deck. The U-boat survived this attack and reached St-Nazaire on 13 June. It made three more cruises, in total sinking twenty-nine vessels and damaging five more. It then became a training boat and was scuttled off Wilhelmshaven on 2 May 1945.

Ref: DEFE 3/719

The Type VIIC *U-569* was built by Blohm & Voss of Hamburg and commissioned on 8 May 1941. After sinking three merchant vessels in nine war cruises, it left La Pallice on 19 April 1943 for another cruise, under the command of Oberleutnant zur See Hans Johannsen. It was found on the surface on 22 May 1943 about 600 miles south-east of Greenland by TBF-1 Avengers of VC-9 Squadron operating from the escort carrier USS *Bogue,* which was sailing with convoy ON184. The first to attack was Lieutenant (junior grade) W.F. Chamberlain, whose bombs straddled the target. Then Lieutenant (junior grade) H. Roberts in another Avenger continued the attack. The U-boat submerged but then resurfaced and was subjected to gunfire before finally sinking. Twenty-one of the crew were lost but twenty-five were rescued, including the commander.

Ref: ADM 199/1408

The Type VIIC *U-563* left Brest for its eighth war cruise on 29 May 1943, bound for the North Atlantic under the command of Oberleutnant zur See Gustav Borchardt. Still south-west of Brest two days later, it was attacked twice with depth charges by Halifax serial HR774 of 58 Squadron flown from St Eval in Cornwall by the commanding officer, Wing Commander Wilfred E. Oulton. This photograph was taken on the second attack. The U-boat was damaged but did not sink.

Ref: CN 1/39

The damaged Type VIIC *U-563* was evidently unable to submerge. It was then depth-charged, on the same day, by Sunderland III serial DV969 of 10 (RAAF) Squadron flown from Mount Batten in Devon by Flight Lieutenant Maxwell S. Mainprize. It began to sink but shortly afterwards was depth-charged twice by Sunderland III serial DD838 of 228 Squadron flown from Pembroke Dock by Flying Officer William M. French, taking this photograph on the second attack. The U-boat sank and about thirty men were seen in the water, but none of the crew of forty-nine survived.

Ref: CN 1/39

The Type VIIC *U-621* was built by Blohm & Voss of Hamburg and commissioned on 7 May 1942. After carrying out three war cruises in the North Atlantic, during which it sank four merchant vessels, it left Brest for the Azores area on 22 April 1943, commanded by Oberleutnant zur See Max Kruschka. On 31 May 1943, when returning from a cruise in which it sank another merchant vessel, it was attacked in the Bay of Biscay by a Liberator of 224 Squadron flown from St Eval in Cornwall by an American in the RAF, Pilot Officer Robert V. Sweeny. Two attacks were made, dropping six depth charges on each occasion. This photograph was taken immediately after the release of one of these sticks. The U-boat was damaged but managed to reach Brest five days later. (See also p. 194.)

Ref: ADM 199/1418

```
ADM (2)
                                                                      557
TO I D 8 G                              ZIP/ZTPGU/15524

FROM N S

5100 KC/S           TOO: 0014/7        TOI: 2335/6/6/43

FROM: BOEHME

    AIRCRAFT ATTACK IN SQUARE AE 8542 AT 1050/6/6 BY

    BOEING: BOMBS, FIRE FROM AIRCRAFT ARMAMENT.  DIVED AFTER

    THIRD RUN IN.  7 WOUNDED, 4 SERIOUSLY INCLUDING THE

    COMMANDING OFFICER, ONE MAN SHOT THROUGH THROAT AND NECK.

    WATERTIGHT STERN, BALLAST TANKS 1 AND 3 AND ALL BALLAST

    TANKS (FUEL) DEFECTIVE, BROAD OIL TRACE.  COURSE 200 DEGREES.

    REQUEST ASSISTANCE.  WIND SOUTHEAST 4, 68 CUBIC METRES,

    SERIAL NUMBERS UP TO 107 INTERCEPTED.

0818/28/7/43++EE++DG
```

The Type VIIC *U-450* was built by Schichau of Danzig and commissioned on 12 September 1942. It left Kiel for its first war cruise on 27 May 1943, under the command of Oberleutnant zur See Kurt Böhme, and headed for the North Atlantic. When south-east of Iceland on 6 June it was attacked by Fortress IIA serial FL458 of 220 Squadron, flown from Benbecula in the Outer Hebrides by Squadron Leader H. Warren. Depth charges were dropped and the U-boat was machine-gunned. It managed to reach Brest on 22 June, despite being badly damaged. It was eventually sunk on 10 March 1944 by destroyers of the Royal Navy and the US Navy when south-west of Anzio in Italy. Forty-two of the crew were rescued and taken prisoner, including Böhme.

Ref: DEFE 3/720

```
ADM(1)                                                              514
   TO I D 8 G                              ZIP/ZTPGU/14469

FROM N S

   (5425) KC/S           T O O 0527          TOI: 0344/9/6/43

FROM: MANSECK

   8 SHIP-BASED A/C DRIVEN OFF, 1 SHOT DOWN, 4 DAMAGED.    AM

REPAIRING  IN NAVAL  GRID SQUARE DF 9674. REQUEST  SURGEON.

   1419/11/6/43+CEL/PG
```

This signal was sent from the Type VIIC *U-758* on 9 June 1943 when it came under attack by Avengers from the escort carrier USS *Bogue*. The U-boat was built by Kriegsmarinewerft of Wilhelmshaven and commissioned on 5 May 1942. It was on its third war cruise, having left Bordeaux on 26 May 1943 under the command of Kapitänleutnant Helmut Manseck, when this attack took place off the Azores. It was the first U-boat to be fitted with a quadruple 20 mm gun and succeeded in shooting down one of the Avengers, although it was damaged and eleven of its crew were injured in the gun battle. It returned from this encounter and made four more war cruises. In the course of its career it sank one merchant ship and damaged another. It was decommissioned after being badly damaged during a raid by the US Eighth Air Force on Kiel on 11 March 1945.

Ref: DEFE 3/719

The Type XB *U-118* minelayer and auxiliary tanker was built by Germaniawerft of Kiel and commissioned on 6 December 1941. In eighteen months of active service, its mines sank seven vessels. Under the command of Korvettenkapitän Werner Czygan, it left Bordeaux on 25 May 1943 to refuel U-boats in the North Atlantic. On 12 June 1943 it was caught on the surface 520 miles south-west of the Azores by a TBF-1 Avenger flown by Lieutenant (junior grade) R.L. Stearms and an F4F-4 Wildcat flown by Lieutenant (junior grade) R.L. Johnson, both from VC-9 Squadron on the escort carrier USS *Bogue* commanded by Captain G.E. Short. Their attacks were followed by two more Avengers and two more Wildcats, until the U-boat was destroyed. Forty of the crew lost their lives, including Czygan, but fifteen were picked up to become prisoners.

Ref: ADM 199/1408

By the end of May 1943 the North Atlantic had become such a graveyard for U-boats that Admiral Karl Dönitz ordered the survivors to withdraw from these waters to the central Atlantic. Then, in an attempt to combat Coastal Command's anti-submarine operations, he ordered U-boats to cross the Bay of Biscay on the surface in daylight, sailing in groups to use their combined flak armament against attacking aircraft. At 1605 hours on 14 June 1943 a group of three U-boats was located about 80 miles north of the north-west tip of Spain by Whitley V serial BD289 of No. 10 Operational Training Unit, flown from St Eval by Sergeant K.G. McAlpine. An attack was made with depth charges and machine-gun fire, as shown here, but there is no record of any U-boat sunk in that area on that day.

Ref: CN 1/39

On 16 June 1943 Liberator V serial FL975 of 59 Squadron, flown by Flying Officer E.E. Allen from Aldergrove in Northern Ireland, came across three U-boats in vic formation about 320 miles south-west of Land's End. An attack was made on the centre U-boat with a stick of six depth charges, in the face of intense flak, but these overshot slightly. The rear gunner fired about 120 rounds at the U-boat, but enemy flak scored four hits on the aircraft, rendering most instruments useless. Nevertheless another attack was made, this time on the U-boat on the right of the vic, thirty seconds after it had submerged, but no results were seen. There are no records of a sinking or damage to a U-boat on this day.

Ref: ADM 199/1420

Whitley V serial EB399 of No. 10 Operational Training Unit, flown from St Eval by Pilot Officer R.H. Orr, attacked with depth charges and machine-gun fire a U-boat about 130 miles north of the north-west tip of Spain, at 1633 hours on 20 June 1943. Seven minutes later Whitley V serial LA814 of the same unit, flown by Flight Sergeant Harry Martin, was seen to crash in the sea when attacking the same U-boat. There were no survivors from the crew of six. No U-boats were reported sunk or damaged in this area on that day.

Ref: CN 1/39

```
ADM(1)                                                              29
   TO I D 8 G                              ZIP/ZTPGU/15026
FROM N S
   4412 KC/3              T O O 0810           TOI 0731/22/6/43
FROM:  VOWE
      HAVE BEATEN OFF 5 A/C AND PROBABLY SHOT DOWN ONE. DIESEL OIL
      TANK 7, STARBOARD HYDRAULIC PIPE AND STARBOARD OUTER EXHAUST
      CUT-OUT DAMAGED. ABLE SEAMAN BRUNNHAUSEN KILLED, BOATSWAIN'S
      MATES THIEL AND FISCHER AND ORDINARY SEAMAN POSCHMANN SERIOUSLY
      INJURED. SUB-LT. KNOKE SLIGHTLY INJURED. 0800 POSITION NAVAL
      GRID SQUARE BF 8229, COURSE 085 DEGREES, 10 KNOTS. STRONG AIR
2210/26/6/43+AGT/AM
```

The Type XVI supply U-boat *U-462*, commanded by Oberleutnant zur See Bruno Vowe, sent this signal on 22 June 1943 after having been attacked the day before in the Bay of Biscay. This 'milch cow' U-boat had been built by Deutschewerke of Kiel and commissioned on 5 March 1942. It was on its fifth war cruise, operating mainly as a fuel tanker, and had left Bordeaux only two days before this attack. The aircraft involved were four Mosquito NF11s of 151 and 456 Squadrons flown from Predannack in Cornwall, on patrol looking for enemy aircraft. They raked *U-462* with their cannon and machine-guns causing damage and casualties before returning without loss. The U-boat returned to Bordeaux on the following day. It was also forced to return with damage from its next cruise, after a Liberator of 224 Squadron delivered an attack on 2 July 1943. Its end came on 30 July 1943 in the North Atlantic when it was bombed by a Halifax II of 502 Squadron flown from Holmsley South in Hampshire by Flying Officer A. van Rossum and then finished off by depth charges from the Royal Navy. Only one crewman was killed, and the others were rescued to become prisoners.

Ref: DEFE 3/720

The Type IXD2 *U-200* was built by A.G. Weser of Bremen and commissioned on 22 December 1942. It left Bergen on 12 June 1943, under the command of Kapitänleutnant Heinrich Schonder, for its first war cruise in the North Atlantic. On 24 June 1943 it was located about 320 miles south-west of Iceland by Liberator I serial AM929 of 120 Squadron, flown from Reykjavik by Flight Lieutenant A.W. Fraser en route to escort convoy ONS11. The Liberator and the U-boat exchanged fire during the attack and the Liberator was hit. However, it dropped four depth charges which straddled the U-boat, as shown here. Oil, bubbles and bodies were seen to come to the surface, and all sixty-two men in the U-boat were killed. With the hydraulics damaged and one man wounded, Fraser made a skilful landing back at Reykjavik.

Ref: AIR 15/471

The Type IXC *U-518* was built by Deutschewerft of Hamburg and commissioned on 25 April 1942. It made two war cruises, during which it sank eight merchant vessels and damaged two more. It then left Lorient on 24 June 1943, under the command of Kapitänleutnant Friedrich-Wilhelm Wissmann, but three days later was spotted by Sunderland III serial W6005 of 201 Squadron flown from Castle Archdale in Northern Ireland by Flying Officer Brian E.H. Layne of the RNZAF. Two depth charges were dropped and the U-boat submerged. It reappeared a few minutes later and entered into a gun battle, as shown here, before submerging again. (See also p. 151.)

Ref: AIR 15/471

```
ADM(1)                                                        194
   TO I D 8 G                          ZIP/ZTPGU/15185
   FROM N S
   4412 KC/S          T O O 0155        TOI 0031/28/6/43
   FROM:  WISSMANN

     SEVERELY ████ BOMBED BY SUNDERLAND YESTERDAY AT 1240 IN NAVAL
     GRID SQUARE CG 1(2)13. CAN DIVE TO 60 METRES WITH LIMITATIONS,
     NOT ABLE TO CRASH DIVE. AM RETURNING. REQUEST ESCORT. POSITION
     IS CG 1232

   0744/5/7/43+EGT/AM
```

A signal sent by Kapitänleutnant Friedrich-Wilhelm Wissmann, the commander of the Type IXC *U-518*, the day after it was attacked by the Sunderland of 201 Squadron. It reached Bordeaux on 3 July, seriously damaged. It was sunk on its seventh war cruise, about 400 miles west-north-west of the Azores, on 22 April 1945, by the destroyers USS *Carter* and *Neal*. There were no survivors from the crew of fifty-six.

Ref: DEFE 3/720

```
ADM(2)                                                       567
   TO I D 8 G                          ZIP/ZTPGU/16509
   FROM N S
   4412 KC/S           TOO 2117        TOI 2208/6/7/43
   FROM:  SCHAUENBURG

   ON 5/7 ATTACKED BY CONSOLIDAED
   IN SQUARE BF 7832. ON RESURFACING ELMENREICH LOST,
   SEARCHED FOR IN VAIN. HAVE RESUMED RETURN PASSAGE WITH
   PFEFFER. SQUARE BF 8475.

   CC CONSOLIDATED   IN 1ST LINE
   1454/28/8/43  TZ/PMD
```

This signal was sent on 6 July 1943 by the Type IXC/40 *U-536* near Cape Finisterre in north-west Spain. The U-boat had been built by Deutschewerft of Hamburg and commissioned on 13 January 1943. It had left Kiel on 1 June 1943 on its first war cruise, operating as an auxiliary tanker under the command of Kapitänleutnant Rolf Schauenburg. It had witnessed an attack the day before in which the Type IXC/40 *U-535* was sunk by Liberator serial BZ751 of 53 Squadron, based at Thorney Island in Hampshire and flown by Flight Sergeant W. Anderson of the RNZAF. This U-boat, built by Deutschewerft of Hamburg and on its first war cruise under the command of Kapitänleutnant Helmut Elmenreich, was sunk with all fifty-five hands.

The other U-boat referred to in the signal was the Type IXC/40 *U-170*, built by Seebeckwerft of Bremerhaven and on its first war cruise under the command of Kapitänleutnant Günther Pfeffer. This had been damaged by the same Liberator but survived to return to Lorient on 9 September 1943 and then continued to serve for the remainder of the war.

The Type IXC/40 *U-536* survived this cruise but was sunk on its second. On the night of 19/20 November 1943, north-east of the Azores, it was sunk by the frigate HMS *Nene* and the corvettes HMCS *Calgary* and *Snowberry*. Thirty-eight of the crew were killed but seventeen were rescued, including Schauenberg.

Ref: DEFE 3/721

```
ADM (2)                                                        791
TO:  I D 8 G                    Z IP/ZTPGU/16709
FROM:  N S
9037 KC/S        T O O 2134        T O I 2119/7/7/43
FROM:  MAUS
```

1) FOLLOWING SUNK AT 0829 IN SQUARE FB 9396 FROM CONVOY 290

   DEGREES, 10 KNOTS: 1 FREIGHTER, 1 AMMUNITION STEAMSHIP

   OF 6,000 GRT., EACH. LEFT SINKING, ON FIRE. AT 0607 IN

   SQUARE FC 7179: 1 TANKER, 1 FREIGHTER OF 8,000 GRT., EACH.

   A FURTHER 'PI 2' HIT ON 7,000 TONNER. DIVED AT 0830 ON

   BEING ATTACKED WITH GUNFIRE.

2) DAY AIR WITH CONVOY, AT NIGHT ONLY ESCORTING VESSEL(S).

   INEXPERIENCED , SO FAR NO LOCATION.

3) 130 CUBIC METRES, 3 PLUS. 6 'EELS'. AM RELOADING.

   ALL NAVAL GRID SQUARES.

```
2053/1/9/43    TZ/ES+
```

The Type IXC/40 *U-185* was built by A.G. Weser of Bremen and commissioned on 13 June 1942. It made two war cruises during which it sank four Allied merchant vessels. It then left Bordeaux on 9 June 1943 under the command of Kapitänleutnant August Maus. Five days later it encountered the Type VIIC *U-564* in the Bay of Biscay, which had been damaged the day before by Sunderland III serial DV967 of 228 Squadron flown from Pembroke Dock by Flight Lieutenant L.B. Lee but had succeeded in shooting down the flying boat with the loss of the crew. This damaged U-boat was being attacked by Whitley V serial BD220 of No. 10 Operational Training Unit, flown from St Eval in Cornwall by Sergeant A.J. Benson, but the aircraft was hit by the combined fire from the two U-boats. It turned for home but was forced to ditch; all five crew members were picked up by a French fishing boat and taken into captivity. *U-564* sank with the loss of twenty-eight crew members, but eighteen men were rescued by *U-185*, including the commander, and transferred to two German destroyers.

Continuing its cruise, *U-185* sank five merchant vessels and damaged another, some of which are reported in this signal of 7 July 1943. But it did not return to port, as can be seen in a photograph taken on 24 August 1943. (See also p. 156.)

Ref: DEFE 3/721

```
ADM (2)                                             699
   TO: I D 8 G                    Z IP/ZTPGU/16625
   FROM: N S

   7082 KC/S         TOO 1758         TOI 2103/8/7/43
   FROM: STRELOW

      NAVAL GRID SQUARE CG 4886 AIRCRAFT ATTACK FROM
      GREAT HEIGHT BY HANDLEY-PAGE HAMPDEN. DEPTH-
      CHARGES. VENT 3 OUT OF ORDER, AM REPAIRING.
      51 CUBIC METRES.

   1142/31/8/43+++TZ/SMH
```

This message was sent from the Type VIIC *U-435* on 8 July 1943 when it was in serious difficulties. The U-boat was built by Schichau of Danzig and commissioned on 30 August 1941. It had already completed seven war cruises, five in the Arctic and two in the Atlantic, and sunk nine vessels and damaged two more. One of the vessels sunk was the minesweeper HMS *Leda* and another was the fighter catapult ship *Fidelity*. It left Brest on its ninth war patrol on 20 May 1943 under the command of Kapitänleutnant Siegfried Strelow and was returning from the Azores area when it was attacked off the coast of Portugal. The aircraft was not a Handley Page Hampden, a type that was never employed for this purpose, but a Wellington of 179 Squadron flown from Gibraltar by Flying Officer E.J. Fisher. It is evident that the lookouts on *U-435* did not spot its approach since there was no flak. Four depth charges were dropped from 50 feet and straddled the U-boat, which stopped and then went down bow first. It seems that the damage could not be repaired, for the U-boat was lost with all forty-eight hands.

Ref: DEFE 3/721

```
ADM (2)                                             540
   TO I D 8 G                     Z IP/ZTPGU/16484
   FROM N S

   5412 KC/S       T O O 0120/13      T O I 2350/12/7/43
   FROM: PAUCKSTADT

      BOMBED AGAIN IN SQUARE DU 12 . REQUEST 'METOX' OR
      EARLY R/V WITH BOAT ON RETURN PASSAGE . 55 CUBIC METRES
      (( WEATHER REPORT )). SQUARE DH 1773, COURSE NORTH , 6 KNOTS ,
      TRANSMITTER OUT OF ORDER UP TO NOW . ALLX NAVAL GRID SQUARES .

   1648/27/8/43 ++EE/EW
```

This signal was sent on 12 July 1943 by the commander of the Type IXD/40 *U-193*, Korvettenkapitän Hans Pauckstadt. This U-boat had been built by A.G. Weser of Bremen and commissioned on 10 December 1942. It was on its first war cruise, having left Kiel on 11 May 1943. On 6 July 1943 it was bombed when south-west of the Canary Islands, possibly by an aircraft from the RAF's West Africa Command, and two crewmen were wounded. It reached Bordeaux on 23 July. The end came on its fourth war cruise, after leaving Lorient on 23 April 1944 under the command of Oberleutnant zur See Dr Ulrich Abel. In the early hours of 28 April, when west of Nantes, it was depth-charged by a Wellington of 612 Squadron, fitted with a Leigh Light and flown from Chivenor in North Devon by Flying Officer C.G. Punter. There were no survivors from the crew of fifty-nine.

Ref: DEFE 3/721

The Type VIIC *U-558* was built by Blohm & Voss of Hamburg and commissioned on 20 February 1941. It made ten war cruises under its commander, Kapitänleutnant Günther Krech, during which it sank twenty-two merchant vessels, including an anti-submarine trawler, and damaged another. The final war cruise began when it left Brest on 8 May 1943. On its return voyage, it was attacked in the Bay of Biscay on 20 July 1943 by Liberator letter F of the 19th Squadron, 479th Antisubmarine Group, USAAF, flown from St Eval in Cornwall by First Lieutenant Charles F. Gallimeir. The U-boat put up intense flak, wounding one of the crew and damaging the port inner engine, but seven depth charges were dropped. More flak came up and the engine cut out. At this point Halifax serial DT642 of 58 Squadron took over the attack, flown from Holmsley South in Hampshire by Flight Lieutenant Godfrey Sawtell. This exchanged gunfire and dropped eight depth charges, as shown here. The U-boat sank, leaving about thirty men in the water. Five of these got into a dinghy, including Krech, and were picked up on 25 July by the destroyer HMCS *Athabaskan*. Forty-five others were lost. It transpired that *U-558* was already sinking as a result of the first attack, with chlorine gas filling the hull.

Ref: AIR 15/471

```
ADM     (3)
TO:   I D 8 G                          ZIP/ZTPGU/16711
                                                            793
FROM:   N S

6792 KC/S            T O O   0713      T O I  0606/21/7/43

FROM:  U 662

  1) AT 1840 IN SQUARE EP 8552 STICK OF BOMBS FROM CATALINA A

     HAIR'S-BREADTH AHEAD OF BOW. AFTER 1 HOUR GUN DUEL IT

     TURNED AWAY. THEN I DIVED. PERMANENT DEFECTS: 'METOX'.

  2) PURSUIT OF STEAMSHIP REPORTED BROKEN OFF WHEN MOON ROSE.

  3) REQUEST 2 CM. AMMUNITION URGENTLY. CATALINA USED UP 1,600

     RXXXRXXX ROUNDS. STILL 2,000 LEFT. SUPPLY TOO SMALL.

     ALSO 'METOX'.

  4) SQUARE EP 8911 ALL NAVAL GRID SQUARES. 90 CUBIC METRES.

     ((WEATHER REPORT)).

  2145/1/9/43   TZ/AHM+++
```

This signal was sent by the Type VIIC *U-662* on 21 July 1943 when about 240 miles north of the mouth of the river Amazon. It was on its fourth war cruise, having left St-Nazaire on 26 June 1943 under the command of Kapitänleutnant Eberhard Müller. The attack on 21 July came from a Catalina of VP-94 Squadron, US Navy, flown by Lieutenant (junior grade) R.H. Rowland. The U-boat eventually sank with the loss of forty-four crew members, but three were rescued to become prisoners, including Müller.

Ref: DEFE 3/721

The Type XIV *U-459* was built by Deutschewerke of Kiel and commissioned on 15 November 1942. It was one of the tankers known as 'milch cows' and carried out five refuelling operations for other U-boats in the Atlantic. It left Bordeaux on 22 July 1943, commanded by Korvettenkapitän Georg von Wilamowitz-Möllendorf, for its sixth refuelling operation. Two days later, while in the Bay of Biscay, it was caught on the surface by a Wellington of 172 Squadron flown from Chivenor in North Devon by Pilot Officer W.H.T. Jennings. The U-boat stayed on the surface to fight the Wellington. This was hit during its attack and crashed into the U-boat, killing all men in the crew except the rear gunner, Sergeant A.A. Turner, who managed to get into an inflated dinghy. The U-boat was also damaged and was circling, down by the stern and out of control, when a Wellington of 547 Squadron arrived from Davidstow Moor in Cornwall, flown by Flying Officer J. Whyte, and took this photograph. Whyte made another attack with depth charges on the stricken U-boat and the crew began to abandon ship. Nineteen of the crew lost their lives but thirty-seven were rescued by the Polish destroyer *Orkan*, as well as Sergeant Turner.

Ref: ADM 199/1419

```
    ADM (2)                                                    35

    TO:  I D 8 G                        ZIP/ZTPGU/16025

    FROM:  N S

    4412 KC/S

                 T O O  1800/28/7/43    B' FDL

  AM BEING ATTACKED BY AN A/C. MY POSITION IS SQUARE BF 47.

        UEU (U.404)

  1316/15/8/43   CEL/ES+
```

The Type VIIC *U-404* was built by Danzigerwerft and commissioned on 6 August 1941. It made six successful war cruises, sinking thirteen merchant ships, damaging two more, and sinking a destroyer. On 24 July 1943 it left St-Nazaire on a seventh cruise, bound for the North Atlantic under the command of Oberleutnant zur See Adolf Schönberg. This signal was sent on 28 July 1943 when it was near Cape Ortegal on the north-west tip of Spain. Three aircraft were involved in the attack. The first was a B-24 Liberator of 4 Squadron, USAAF, flown from St Eval in Cornwall by Major McElroy. This was followed by another Liberator from the same squadron, flown by First Lieutenant Arthur Hammar; this Liberator was damaged by flak but returned safely. Lastly, Flying Officer R.V. Sweeny in a Liberator of the RAF's 224 Squadron from St Eval delivered the *coup de grâce*; one of the engines in this Liberator was set on fire by flak but it also returned safely. The U-boat sank with the loss of all fifty-one crew members.

Ref: DEFE 3/721

```
.ADM (2)                                                    28

TO:  I D 8 G                          ZIP/ZTPGU/16020 .

FROM:  N S

4412 KC/S
                    T O O 1015/30/7/ 3    B' QOF

AM BEING SHADOWED X BY 2 ENEMY A/C.

QOB   (U.461)

1324/15/8/43   CEL/ES+
```

The Type XIV *U-461* was built by Deutschewerke of Kiel and commissioned on 30 January 1942. Its main function was that of a tanker refuelling other U-boats. It left Bordeaux on 27 July 1943 on its sixth war cruise, bound for the North Atlantic under the command of Korvettenkapitän Wolf-Harro Stiebler, and sent this message three days later when north-west of Spain. Shortly afterwards, when it was attempting to refuel the Type XIV *U-462* and the Type IXC *U-504*, an RAF Halifax and a US Liberator attempted to attack but were driven off by the combined fire of the three U-boats. Then Sunderland serial W6077 of 461 (RAAF) Squadron arrived, flown from Pembroke Dock by Flight Lieutenant Dudley Marrows. The Sunderland attacked and straddled *U-461* with seven depth charges, which sank with the loss of fifty-three of its crew. Fifteen were rescued, including Stiebler. The Sunderland was hit by flak but managed to return safely.

Ref: DEFE 3/721

Opposite Top: Kapitänleutnant Horst Höltring sent this signal on 31 July 1943, after his *U-604* had been attacked in mid-Atlantic during the previous day. The U-boat was a Type VIIC, built by Blohm & Voss of Hamburg and commissioned on 8 January 1942. It had left Brest on 24 June 1943 for its sixth war cruise, having sunk six ships during its previous cruises, including a passenger liner. The attacking aircraft was a Liberator of VB-129 Squadron, US Navy, and the attack resulted in the deaths of the first watch officer and the boatswain. The U-boat never returned to port, for when north-west of the Ascension Islands on 11 August 1943 it was damaged further by Liberators of VB-107 and VB-129 Squadrons of the US Navy, as well as the destroyer USS *Moffett*. The U-boat was scuttled on 24 August after the crew was taken off by *U-172* and *U-185*, but Höltring shot himself. (See also p. 165.)

Ref: DEFE 3/720

Opposite Bottom: This signal of 4 August 1943 sent by Captain U-boat West would have met with no response. It was sent to Kapitänleutnant Alexander von Zitzewitz, the commander of the *U-706*. This U-boat had been built by Stülcken Sohn of Hamburg and commissioned on 16 March 1942. It had made four war cruises and sunk three merchant vessels. On 2 August 1943, off Cape Ortegal in Spain, it had been attacked and sunk by a Hampden of 415 (RCAF) Squadron flown from Thorney Island in Sussex by Squadron Leader C.G. Ruttan, as well as a B-24 Liberator of 4 Squadron, USAAF, flown by First Lieutenant J.L. Hamilton from St Eval in Cornwall. Only four men in the U-boat survived, picked up by the frigate HMS *Waveney*, but these did not include the commander.

The request concerned the Type VIIC *U-454*, built by Deutschewerke of Kiel and commissioned on 24 July 1941. This had made eleven war cruises and sunk the destroyer HMS *Matabele* as well as damaging two merchant vessels. It had left St-Nazaire on 26 July 1943 for its twelfth cruise, commanded by Kapitänleutnant Burkhard Hackländer, and damaged another merchant vessel. However, in the Bay of Biscay on 1 August it had been sunk by Sunderland III serial W4020 of 10 (RAAF) Squadron, flown from Mount Batten in Devon by Flight Lieutenant K.G. Fry. The Sunderland had been shot down. The sloop HMS *Kite* had rescued six men from the Sunderland and fourteen from the U-boat, including the commander.

Ref: DEFE 3/721

```
ADM(1)                                                    699
TO I D 8 G                              ZIR/ZTPGU/15664
FROM N S
4180 KC/S              TOO 0108        TOI 0137/31/7/43
FROM: HOELTRING
SQUARE F J 91 SURPRISED BY LOCKHEED. COW SHOT THROUGH JAWBONE
AND NECK, BOATSWAIN LURZ SHOT THROUGH STOMACH. C.O. AND 1 RATING
SLIGHTLY WOUNDED. A/C SET ON FIRE, 2 WELL PLACED DEPTH CHARGES.
URGENTLY REQUEST SURGEON'S ASSISTANCE. RETURN PASSAGE, 80 CBM,
ALL EELS, TRADES WEATHER.
1538/1/8/43     EGT+++MRT+++
```

```
ADM(1)                                                    101
TO I D 8 G                              ZIP/ZTPGU/16084
FROM N S
4412 KC/S             TOO 1021         TOI 0915/4/8/43
FROM: CAPTAIN (U/B) WEST
    WHEN SENDING PASSAGE REPORT, ZITZEWITZ IS ALSO TO REPORT
WHERE AND IN WHAT CIRCUMSTANCES HACKLAENDER WAS LOST.

2006/16/8/43 ++EE/WAB+++
```

The Type IXB *U-106* was built by A.G. Weser of Bremen and commissioned on 24 September 1940. It carried out nine war cruises, in the North Atlantic and off the American coast, in which it sank twenty-two merchant vessels and damaged three more. During its seventh cruise it was damaged on 27 July 1942 by a Wellington of 311 (Czech) Squadron from Beaulieu in Hampshire but was fortunate enough to reach Lorient for repairs. It left Lorient on 28 July 1943 for its tenth cruise, under the command of Oberleutnant zur See Wolf-Dietrich Damerow, but its luck ran out on 2 August 1943 when north-west of Cape Ortegal in Spain. Wellington XII of 407 (RCAF) Squadron, flown from Chivenor in North Devon by Wing Commander J.C. Archer (as shown here), delivered this attack. *U-106* was damaged and forced to head back on the surface for Lorient. (See also p. 159.)

Ref: ADM 199/2060

```
ADM (2)
                                                            277
   TO: I D 8 G                    Z IP/ZTPGU/16250
   FROM: N S

   7770 KC/S          T O O 1107      T O I 0945/2/8/43

   SHORT S IGNALS FROM MXB U 106:
       URGENTLY REQURX REQUEST ASS ISTANCE BY A IRCRAFT IN
        NAVAL GR ID SQUARE BE 6940.  BOAT IS UNABLE TO D IVE.
        SER IAL NO.77, 78 AND 80 HEREBY DEALT W ITH.
   (DEPT. NOTE: SER IAL NOS. 77, 78 AND 80 HAVE T O O 0959/2,
    1004/2, 1014/2 RESPECT IVELY).

   0746/21/8/43+++EE/MH +++++
```

This signal was sent by the Type IXB *U-106* while en route to Lorient on 2 August 1943.

Ref: DEFE 2/721

The ordeal of the Type IXB *U-106* continued when two more aircraft were sent out. These were Sunderland III serial JM708 of 228 Squadron, flown from Pembroke Dock by Flying Officer Reader D. Hanbury, and Sunderland III serial DV968 of 461 (RAAF) Squadron flown from the same base by Flight Lieutenant I.A.F. 'Chick' Clarke. Both aircraft exchanged gunfire with the U-boat and then dropped depth charges, as shown by this photograph taken from the Sunderland of 228 Squadron. Damerow ordered his men to abandon the U-boat shortly before it blew up and left debris and bodies in the water. Twenty-five men were killed but thirty-seven were picked up by the German torpedo boats *T-22, T-24* and *T-25*. Damerow was one of those rescued but he was badly wounded and taken to hospital. He died of his wounds on 21 May 1944.

Ref: ADM 199/2060

```
    ADM (2)                                                        123
   TO: I D 8 G                        ZIP/ZTPGU/16105

   FROM: N S

   9948 KC/S         T O O 2016         T O I 1938/3/8/43

   FROM: U 196


   XXQXX9XXQX

   FROM NORTHBOUND CONVOY OF 3 SHIPS AND 4 D/RS AND ESCORTS

   IN NAVAL GRID SQUARE LT 8582  SANK 10,000 TONNER AND

   SECOND 10,000 TONNER DISAPPEARED FROM SIGHT IN FLAMES.

  )AFTER INTERNAL EXPLOSIONS SINKING PROBABLE.

   0415/17/8/43++++EGT/MH ++++
```

They Type IXD2 *U-196* was built by A.G. Weser of Bremen and commissioned on 11 September 1942. It left Kiel on 13 March 1943 for its first war cruise, bound for the waters off South Africa, under the command of Korvettenkapitän Eitel-Friedrich Kentrat. This signal was sent on 3 August 1943 when near Madagascar. In fact, it had sunk the British merchant ship *City of Oran* of 7,323 tons on the previous day. The U-boat reached Bordeaux on 23 October 1943. It set off on 16 March 1944 for a war cruise in the Indian Ocean, commanded by Oberleutnant zur See Werner Striegler. It was eventually sunk in the Sunda Strait around the end of November 1944 from unknown causes, with the loss of all sixty-five hands.

Ref: DEFE 3/721

```
ADM   A(1)                                                     81
TO:   I D 8 G                          ZIP/ZTPGU/16065
FROM:  N S

9948 KC/S              T O O   2245        T O I  2124/4/8/43

FROM: LUETH

1) EARLY TODAY 'DALFRAM' SUNK IN KG 8555 .COURSE 040 DEGREES FROM
   LOURENCO TO MEDITERRANEAN VIA KG 5870.  YESTERDAY THERE IN
   MORNING HALF-LIGHT OUTWARD BOUND SHIP COURSE 210 DEGREES.  WAS
   PICKED UP BY D/RS SEARCHLIGHT, HYDROPHONE HUNT ONLY.  AT NOON
   INWARD BOUND SHIP ON COURSE 020 DEGREES.
2) KR 14 TO 55 TO 90 AND KG 72.  BOTH HARBOURS N.T.R. EXCEPT ON 18/7.
   A FAST STEAMSHIP IN KR 1390 FOLLOWED FOR 16 HOURS WITHOUT
   SUCCESS COURSE 010 DEGREES.  ALL NAVAL GRID SQUARES.
3) 272 CBM 4 'A' TORPEDOES, 'E' TORPEDO.  CYPHER KEGS ONLY UNTIL 1/10.

0908/16/8/43   AGT/AHM++++
```

Above: This signal was sent on 4 August 1943 from the Type IXD2 *U-181*, commanded by Korvettenkapitän Wolfgang Lüth while operating in the Indian Ocean. The U-boat, built by A.G. Weser of Bremen and commissioned on 9 May 1942, had left Bordeaux on 23 March 1943 on its second war cruise. The British merchant vessel *Dalfram* of 4,558 tons was on a voyage from Lorenço Marques and Durban to Aden and Alexandria, carrying 6,821 tons of coal. She became the twentieth vessel sunk by *U-181*. The U-boat ace Wolfgang Lüth had already been awarded the Knights Cross with Oakleaves, Swords and Diamonds. He survived the war, after sinking forty-seven ships totalling 221,981 tons, including a submarine, but was killed accidentally a few days afterwards. (See also p. 228.)

Ref: DEFE 3/721

Opposite Top: This dramatic message was sent by *U-66* on 4 August 1943. This U-boat was a Type IXC, built by A.G. Weser of Bremen and commissioned on 2 January 1941. It was on its ninth war cruise, having previously sunk twenty-seven merchant vessels and damaged three more. It had left Lorient on 27 April 1943, under the command of Kapitänleutnant Friedrich Markworth, and had already sunk two more vessels and damaged another before being attacked in mid-Atlantic by an Avenger and a Wildcat from the escort carrier USS *Card* on 3 August. Three crewmen were killed and eight seriously wounded, including Markworth, but the U-boat did not sink. (See also p. 203.)

Ref: DEFE 3/721

Opposite Bottom: The Type XB *U-117* was a large minelayer which also served in the role of a supply boat to operational U-boats in distant waters. Built by Germaniawerft of Kiel, it was commissioned on 25 October 1941 and spent twenty-two months on active service. It then left Bordeaux on 22 July 1943, commanded by Korvettenkapitän Hans-Werner Neumann, and came to the rescue of the damaged Type IXC *U-66* on 6 August 1943, about 330 miles west of the Azores. Oberleutnant zur See Frerks went aboard to take over command from the wounded Markworth. On the following day the two U-boats were spotted together on the surface by a TBF-1 Avenger of VC-1 Squadron flown from the escort carrier USS *Card* by Lieutenant (junior grade) A.H. Sallenger. He dived down against intense flak and dropped two depth charges with 25 feet settings as well as a mine with a contact fuse, as shown here. This was followed by attacks from two more Avengers and two F4F-4 Wildcats. *U-117* was destroyed, probably by a homing torpedo dropped by one of the Wildcats. There were no survivors from the crew of sixty-two.

Ref: ADM 199/1408

```
ADM(1)                                                    115
TO  I D 8 G                          ZIP/ZTPGU/16097
FROM N S
4963 KC/S            TOO 0513              TOI 0355/4/8/43
FROM: MARKWORTH

     AT 2130 ATTACKED BY 2 FIGHTERS OUT OF THE SUN. BOMBS AND
FIRE FROM AIRCRAFT ARMAMENT. HEAVY CASUALTIES. COMMANDING OFFICER
ABDOMINAL PLUG SHOT (('STECKSCHUSS')). PARTIALLY ABLE TO DIVE.
QUERY: HANDING OVER OF SERIOUSLY WOUNDED MIDSHIPMAN PFAFF IN THE
AZORES. AM IN NAVAL GRID SQUARE CD 8298.

2158/16/8/43 ++EE/WAB+++
```

```
!?" (1)

TC: I D 8 G                          ZIP/ZTPGU/16281

FROM: N S                                                    308

10310 KC/S            T O O 1335      T O I 1219/8/8/43

TO:  U 614 FOR BOATSWAIN'S MATE ALFRED WOLLBRANDT

     IN RECOGNITION OF YOUR SERVICES ASX A PETTY OFFICER OF THE

  SEAMAN BRANCH IN A U-BOAT, I CONFER ON YOU IN THE NAME OF THE

  FUEHRER AND C. IN C. ARMED FORCES THE GERMAN CROSS IN GOLDX.

                    DOENITZ.

     SINCERE CONGRATULATIONS

          CAPTAIN (U/B) WESTXX.

  0916/21/8/43+++EE/FA
```

This congratulatory signal was sent to the Type VIIC *U-614* on 8 August 1943. Unknown to Karl Dönitz (who had been promoted to Grossadmiral on 30 January 1943), the U-boat had already been sunk. Built by Blohm & Voss of Hamburg, it had been commissioned on 19 March 1942 and made two war cruises, during which it had sunk a merchant vessel and damaged another. Its last war cruise had begun on 25 July 1943 when it left St-Nazaire under the command of Kapitänleutnant Wolfgang Sträter. Four days later, in the Bay of Biscay, it had been depth-charged by a Wellington of 172 Squadron flown from Chivenor in North Devon by the commanding officer, Wing Commander Rowland G. Musson. The U-boat had sunk, leaving a spreading oil patch and men in the water, some waving to the Wellington. However, nothing could be done to save them and all forty-nine crew members had lost their lives.

Ref: DEFE 3/721

```
  ADM(1)                                                    144

  TO I D 8 G                          SIP/ZTPGU/16125

  FROM N S

  6792 KC/S            TOO 0432        TOI 0356/10/8/43

  FROM: MARKWORTH

   KEPT UNDER WATER AT THE RENDEZVOUS BY HUNTING DESTROYERS AND A/C .

  PASSAGE NORTHWARD IMPOSSIBLE IN VIEW OF THE BOATS' $ CONDITION.

  PROPOSE AROZ UNTIL A MORE FAVOURABLE MOMENT. SURGEON CONSIDERS IT

  URGENT THAT THE COMMANDING OFFICER AND MIDSHIPMAN SHOULD BE

  DISEMBARKED SOON. 25 CUBIC METRES, 13 DAYS , NAVAL GRID SQUARE

  CE 1439.

   2108/17/8/43/CEL/MS++
```

The crippled Type IXC *U-66* sent this signal on 10 August 1943, having escaped further damage from aircraft of the escort carrier USS *Card*. Despite this gloomy forecast, it succeeded in reaching Lorient on 1 September 1943, where the wounded personnel received medical attention and repairs to the U-boat began.

Ref: DEFE 3/721

```
ADM (1)
                                                    16295
TO: I D 8 G                          ZIP/ZTPGU/QYWOT      324
FROM: N S
9037 KC/S            T O O 0318         T O I 0655/9/8/43
FROM: FRANKE
        WAS ATTACKED AT 1010 BEFORE STARTING TO TAKE OVER BY 2
CARRIER A/C. BOMBS AND M/G FIRE: DRIVEN OFF. FIRST A/C MADE
OFF IN FLAMES AND PROBABLY CRASHED: SECOND A/C SHOT DOWN.
GRAEF DIVED. DIVING TANKS 2 AND 4 HOLED. A/C HUNT CONTINUES
OWING TO OIL TRACE. HUNT WITH D/CS BEFORE DARK. VENTILATION
KONYRAKXX EXTRACT TRUNK SPLIT. AWAITING ORDERS. NAVAL GRID SQUARE
CD 3479.  CAN RECEIVE ONLY ON V/LF 'AMERICA 2' SERVICE.
CC SERIAL NO ZIP/ZTPGU/16295
    LINE 5 GRP 4  TRACE
1145/21/8/43+++EGT/EA
```

This signal was sent by the Type VIIC *U-664* on 9 August 1943. The U-boat had been built by Howaldtswerke of Hamburg and commissioned on 17 June 1942. It made four war cruises, during which it sank two merchant ships. It then left Brest on 21 June 1943 for a fifth war cruise, under the command of Kapitänleutnant Adolf Graef. On 8 August 1943 it was at a rendezvous west of the Azores with the Type VIICs *U-760* and *U-262* when it was attacked by a Grumman F4F-4 Wildcat and a Grumman TBF-1 Avenger from the Composite Squadron on the escort carrier USS *Card,* commanded by Captain A.J. Isbell. The combined fire from *U-664* and *U-262* brought down both aircraft and the U-boats escaped immediate damage.

Ref: DEFE 2/721

The *U-664* met its end later on 9 August 1943 when attacked by three more aircraft from the carrier USS *Card.* This took place in clear weather under broken cloud. The first was a Grumman TBF-1 Avenger, flown by Lieutenant (junior grade) G.G. Hogan, which dropped two 500 lb depth bombs with contact fuses in two separate attacks. Between these attacks Lieutenant N.D. Hodson in his Grumman F4F-4 Wildcat raked the U-boat with gunfire. Then Lieutenant (junior grade) J.C. Forney dropped another depth bomb from his TBF-1 Avenger. He refrained from dropping the other when he saw the crew abandoning the U-boat. Eight of the crew were killed but forty-four were picked up and taken prisoner by one of the destroyer escorts. Kapitänleutnant Adolf Graef was one of the survivors. The swordfish emblem on the conning tower of the U-boat was that of the 9th Flotilla at Brest.

Ref: ADM 199/1408

```
ADMC 3)                                                    228
    TO I D 8 G                          ZIP/ZTPGU:16208
    FROM N S


    13570 KC/S           TOO 2031           TOI  1912/17/8/43

    FROM: BARTELS

    HAVE JUST SUNK THE 'EMPIRE STANLEY' IN NAVAL GRID SQUARE KQ 6676,

    COURSE 050 DEGREES. VESSEL USED HER W/T . THE REPORTED LARGE TANKER

    WAS THE ' PEGASUS' WHICH WAS SUNK. QUERY. NEW RENDEZVOUS.

    7 'A' TORPEDOES, 265 CUBIC METRES.

    2256/20/8/43/CEL/MS++
```

This signal was sent from the Type IXD2 *U-197* on 17 August 1943. The U-boat was built by A.G. Weser of Bremen and commissioned on 10 October 1942. It left Kiel on 3 April 1943 under the command of Korvettenkapitän Robert Bartels, bound for the Indian Ocean. It sank the Dutch *Benakat* of 4,763 tons and the Swedish *Pegasus* of 9,583 tons, as well as damaging the American *William Ellery* of 7,181 tons, before sinking the British *Empire Stanley* of 6,921 tons. However, this run of successes came to an end on 20 August 1943 when it was about 240 miles south of Madagascar. It was located by Catalina IB serial FP126 of 259 Squadron, flown from St Lucia in Natal by Flight Lieutenant Lionel O. Barnett, and was attacked with six depth charges as well as raked with machine-gun fire. The U-boat remained on the surface, trailing oil. The Catalina radioed Durban control and another RAF aircraft was alerted. This was Catalina IB serial FP313 of 265 Squadron, based at Mombasa but operating from Tulear in Madagascar. It was already on patrol, flown by Flying Officer C. Ernest Robin, who arrived and made two passes at the manoeuvring U-boat before dropping his depth charges on the third. One of these landed on the deck and three others nearby. The U-boat went to the bottom, taking with it its entire crew of sixty-seven.

Ref: DEFE 3/721

The next episode in the eventful career of *U-185* took place on 11 August 1943 when it shot down a Liberator of VB-107 Squadron, while rescuing survivors from the Type VIIC *U-604*, which had been crippled by this Liberator and an American destroyer. The end came on 24 August 1943, as shown here. It was about 800 miles south-west of the Azores when it was bombed by a TBF-1 Avenger flown by Lieutenant R.P. Williams and strafed by an F4F Wildcat flown by Lieutenant M.G. O'Neill, both from VC-13 Squadron on the escort carrier USS *Core* commanded by Captain N.B. Greer. Twenty-nine men from *U-185* and fourteen from *U-604* died in this attack, and two more died among the survivors picked up by the USS *Core.* Kapitänleutnant August Maus was among those who survived to become prisoners of war.

Ref: ADM 199/1408

```
ADM (2)

    TO: I D 8 G                            ZIP/ZTPGU/16430

    FROM: N S                                                      483

    10310 KC/S          TTO 1610          TOI 1505/12/7/43

    FROM: WEBER

         VIOLENT BATTERY EXPLOSION IN FORWARD BATTERY. 3

         SERIOUSLY INJURED. 1 OOW DANGEROUSLY ILL.

         POSITION NAVAL GRID SQUARE BE 8442 1938 W 4415 N.

         REQUEST SURGEON URGENTLY.   CANNOT DIVE.

    CC LINE 3 'SQUARE BE 8452'

    2131/25/8/43+++EGT/SMH
```

The Type VIIC *U-709* was built by Stülcken Sohn of Hamburg and commissioned on 12 August 1942. It left Brest on 5 July 1943 on its third war cruise, under the command of Oberleutnant zur See Karl-Otto Weber, but suffered the explosion reported in this signal seven days later. Two crewmen were killed and one wounded, but it managed to return to Brest. The last cruise began on 25 January 1944, when it left Lorient under the command of Oberleutnant zur See der Reserve Rudolf Ites. It was sunk on 1 March 1944 about 600 miles north of the Azores by the American destroyers *Bostwick, Bronstein* and *Thomas,* and all fifty-two crew members were killed. It sank no ships during five war cruises.

Ref: DEFE 3/721

The Type VIIC *U-617* was built by Blohm & Voss of Hamburg and commissioned on 9 April 1942. It made seven successful war cruises, six of which were in the Mediterranean, under the command of Kapitänleutnant Albrecht Brandi, during which it sank ten vessels. One of these was the fast minelayer HMS *Welshman*, which had brought a succession of supplies to the beleaguered fortress of Malta. *U-617* left Toulon on 28 August 1943 for its eighth war cruise and sank the destroyer HMS *Puckeridge* on 8 September. However, on 12 September it was depth-charged by two Leigh Light Wellingtons of 179 Squadron, flown from North Camp in Gibraltar by Squadron Leader D.B. Hodgkinson and Pilot Officer W.H. Brunini, and was so badly damaged that Brandi was forced to beach it near Cape Forcas in Spanish Morocco. It was then attacked with bombs and rockets by Hudsons of 48 and 233 Squadrons from Gibraltar, as shown here.

Ref: AIR 27/472

The stranded Type VIIC *U-617* was further attacked by Swordfish of the Fleet Air Arm and shelled by the minesweeper *Wollongong* of the Royal Australian Navy as well as the trawler HMS *Haarlem*. The crew of the U-boat had destroyed all important material and moved inland.

Ref: AIR 15/471

```
ADM     (2)

TO:     I D 8 G                              Z IP/ZTPGU/17368

FROM:   N S                                                    394

10310 KC/S              T O O   1937        T O I   1759/27/9/43

BRANDI OBSERVED DURING AIR ATTACK ROCKET PROJECTILES WHICH

SCREAMED AND WHISTLED TERRIFICALLY LOUDLY.  THE ATTACK WAS

CARRIED OUT BY LOW-FLYING TWIN-ENGINED A/C.

1318/29/9/43   AGT/AHM++++
```

Kapitänleutnant Albrecht Brandi and his crew were interned by the Spanish. While being held in the officers' camp near Cadiz, Brandi managed to send this description of the rocket attacks by the Hudsons on his stranded U-boat. He eventually escaped from internment and made his way back to Germany, where he survived the war.

Ref: DEFE 2/722

In September 1943 a new device with three tubes in tandem, each throwing a charge weighing 350 lb for over 700 yards, came into action with the Royal Navy. The weight restricted its use to destroyers, frigates and sloops. It was not until 31 July 1944 that it made its first kill, when fired from the sloop HMS *Starling* and the frigate HMS *Loch Killin* about 50 miles west-south-west of the Scillies. The victim was the long-serving and hitherto highly successful Type VIIC *U-333,* built by Nordseewerke of Emden and commissioned on 25 August 1941. This was on its tenth war cruise, under the command of Kapitänleutnant Hans Fiedler, having left La Pallice on 23 July. There were no survivors from the crew of forty-five. (See also p. 178.)

Ref: ADM 199/2060

In the early evening of 16 September 1943 seventy-two B-17 Flying Fortresses of the US Eighth Air Force bombed the port area of La Pallice and the nearby Lalou airfield of La Rochelle, dropping 717 general-purpose bombs of 500 lb. There was no fighter escort and one aircraft was lost. This photograph shows a heavy concentration of bomb bursts on the port area. There was at least one hit on the lock gate, approximately five hits on the new locks under construction, eight hits on No. 1 basin, six on a fuel station, one on a Sperrbrecher (a mine-exploding and flak ship), and other hits on warehouses, commercial buildings, the railway station, an electrical sub-station and flak positions. There were also twenty bomb bursts on the airfield and two direct hits on a hangar.

Ref: AIR 40/466

```
ADM (1)                                                    94

    TO: I D 8 G                        ZIP/ZTPGU/17088

    FROM: N S

    10805 KC/S              TOO 1425          TOI 1539/21/9/43

    FROM: PURKHOLD

        REFERENCE SHOT AT DESTROYER AT 0000:

        AFTER BEING PASSED OVER AND SERIES OF DEPTH-CHARGES,

        PROPELLER NOISES SILENCED.  THEN SINGLE HEAVY

        EXPLOSION AFTER TOTAL RUNNING TIME OF 9 MINUTES.

        THEREAFTER NOTHING MORE.  QUERY:  HIT POSSIBLE?

    CC LINE R 'EXPLOSION'

    1948/24/9/43++++EE/SMH
```

This signal was sent on 21 September 1943 by the commander of the Type VIIC *U-260*, Kapitänleutnant Hubertus Purkhold. His U-boat had been built by Bremer Vulkan of Kiel and commissioned on 14 April 1942. It was on its fourth war cruise in the North Atlantic, having left St-Nazaire on 25 August 1943. In fact, none of its torpedoes scored hits, on this occasion or on any of its subsequent six war cruises. The last cruise began when it left Horten in Norway on 18 February 1945, under the command of Oberleutnant zur See Klaus Becker. It struck a mine in the Irish Sea on 14 March 1945 and the crew scuttled it off Galley Head in Eire. They then reached the shore in their dinghies and were interned.

Ref: DEFE 3/722

```
ADM (2)                                                    229

    TO: I D 8 G                        ZIP/ZTPGU/17219

    FROM: N S

    10805 KC/S            T O O 1011      T O I 1035/21/9/43

    FROM: RENDTEL

        AT 0001, STARSHELLS IN AK 2936 AND AT 0100 2 DESTROYERS

    WERE THERE, HOVE-TO, PRESUMABLY TO TURN ON THE BASIS OF A

    HYDROPHONE BEARING. FIRED A ''T 5'' AT A DESTROYER AT 0127.

    HEAVY EXPLOSION AND SINKING NOISES AFTER 6 MINUTES 10 SECONDS.

    NO DEPTH CHARGES. HYDROPHONE AND DEPTH CHARGE PURSUIT BY

    HUNTING GROUP FROM 0300. 90 CUBIC METRES.

    (DEPT. NOTE: THE ORIGINAL GERMAN IS DEVOID OF PUNCTUATION.)

    1620/24/9/43++CEL/FA
```

This signal was sent by Kapitänleutnant Horst Rendtel on 21 September 1943 when he was in command of the *U-641* south-west of Iceland. This U-boat was built by Blohm & Voss of Hamburg and commissioned on 24 September 1942. It was on its third war cruise, having left St-Nazaire on 4 September 1943. It returned safely from this cruise and set off again from St-Nazaire on 11 December 1943. The end came on 19 January 1944 when it was sunk in the North Atlantic by the corvette HMS *Violet*, with the loss of all fifty crew members. It sank no vessels during any of its war cruises.

Ref: DEFE 3/722

```
ADM (2)

TO I D 8 G                              ZIP/ZTPGU/17301          320

FROM N S

10310 KC/S              TOO: 1126        TOI: 1356/24/9/43

FROM: POESCHEL

1) AT 2005/23 IN AJ 9622  HALIFAX OUT OF THE CLOUDS WITH

   BOMBS AND CANNON, NO LOCATION.

2) 1 MAN SLIGHTLY WOUNDED, 1 WOUNDED IN ARM, 1 IN LEG.

   ARTERY ENDANGERED.  RQ REQUIRE MEDICAL ASSISTANCE.

3) EXHAUST CONDUIT, VENTILATION INLET AND EXTRACT TRUNK,

   OUTBOARD, PORT SIDE SHOT TO PIECES.

4) AM MOVING AWAY SOUTHEAST TO REPAIR, 50 CBM, ALL EELS.

0656/26/9/43++EGT+DG
```

This signal was sent on 24 September 1943 by the commander of the Type VIIC *U-422*, Oberleutnant zur See Wolfgang Poeschel, when east of Newfoundland. The U-boat had been built by Danzigerwerft and commissioned on 10 February 1943, and had left Bergen on 8 September 1943 for its first war cruise. The attacking aircraft on 23 September was not a Halifax but a Liberator of 10 (RCAF) Squadron from Canada. The U-boat survived this attack but on 4 October it was attacked and damaged by twelve aircraft from VC-9 Squadron of the escort carrier USS *Card*, during an attempt to refuel from the Type XIV *U-460* about 250 miles north of the Azores. The supply U-boat, commanded by Kapitänleutnant Ebe Schnoor, was sunk with all sixty-two hands during this attack. Later the same day *U-422* was located by a Wildcat flown by Ensign J.B. Horn and then sunk by a 'Fido' homing torpedo dropped by an Avenger flown by Lieutenant S.B. Holt, both from USS *Card.* There were no survivors from the crew of forty-nine.

Ref: DEFE 3/722

An X-Craft of the Royal Navy, surfaced and running on main engine. These midget submarines were 51 feet long and weighed about 30 tons. A diesel engine of 42-brake horsepower gave a maximum speed of 6½ knots on the surface while a 25 horsepower electric motor gave a maximum speed of 5 knots submerged. They had a maximum range of about 1,500 miles on the surface at 4 knots. Their armament was two 1-ton explosives carried on each side of the hull. The crew consisted of three officers and an engine room artificer.

Ref: ADM 199/888

The submarine HMS *Thrasher* towing the X-Craft *X5*, commanded by Lieutenant H. Henty-Creer, leaving Loch Cairnbawn in north-west Scotland on 11 September 1943. This X-Craft was lost on the final approach to Kaa fjord on 21/22 September, from unknown reasons but possibly enemy gunfire.

Ref: ADM 199/888

The battleship *Tirpitz* in Kaa fjord on 23 September 1943, protected by torpedo booms and netting. The previous day she had been seriously damaged by X-Craft of the Royal Navy.

Ref: ADM 199/888

Kaa fjord on 28 September 1943, showing the huge oil slick spreading seaward from the damaged battleship *Tirpitz*.

Ref: ADM 199/888

171

```
ADM   1                                                              654

TO ! D 8 G                              ZIP/ZTPGU:17608

FROM N S

4412 KC/S

          TC O 2155/8/10/43 B' PTK

AM IB BEING ATTACKED BY AN A/C SQUARE BF 8230.

               UQS (U 373)


0504/9/10/43/CEL/MS+++
```

This signal, sent by the Type VIIC *U-373* in the evening of 8 October 1943 while in the Bay of Biscay, indicates that it was being attacked by an aircraft equipped with a Leigh Light. The U-boat had been built by Howaldtswerke of Kiel and commissioned on 19 May 1941. It was on its tenth war cruise, having sunk three merchant vessels during its previous cruises, and had left La Pallice six days before, bound for the North Atlantic under the command of Kapitänleutnant Paul-Karl Loeser. It survived this cruise, although it sank no ships, and returned to La Pallice on 26 November 1943. (See also p. 189.)

Ref: DEFE 3/722

The Type VIIC *U-762* was built by Kriegsmarinewerft of Wilhelmshaven and commissioned on 30 January 1943. It left Bergen on 28 September 1943 for its first war cruise, under the command of Kapitänleutnant Wolfgang Hille, to operate in the North Atlantic. On 8 October it was located about 250 miles south-west of Iceland by Liberator III serial FK225 of 120 Squadron, flown from Reykjavik by Warrant Officer Bryan W. Turnbull of the RNZAF. Turnbull attacked with one 500 lb and three 250 lb depth charges, as shown here, causing damage and casualties. The U-boat made for Brest, from where it left on 28 December 1943 for its second war cruise, under the command of Oberleutnant zur See Walter Pietschmann. It was depth-charged and sunk on 8 February 1944 by the sloops HMS *Starling*, *Woodpecker* and *Wildgoose* about 320 miles west of Land's End, with the loss of all fifty-one crew members.

Ref: AIR 15/471

Top: The Type VIIC *U-643* was built by Blohm & Voss of Hamburg and commissioned on 8 October 1942. It left Bergen on 14 September 1943 for its first war cruise, under the command of Kapitänleutnant Hans-Harald Speidel, heading for the North Atlantic. Some 450 miles south of Iceland on 8 October it came under machine-gun fire from Liberator III serial FL930 of 86 Squadron flown by Flight Lieutenant J. Wright from Ballykelly in Northern Ireland, which had already dropped all its depth charges on another U-boat. Then two more aircraft arrived, both from Reykjavik. These were Liberator V serial FL954 of 86 Squadron flown by Flying Officer C.W. Burcher, and Liberator III serial FK233 of 120 Squadron flown by Flying Officer D.C.L. Webber. The combined attack with depth charges caused an explosion in the U-boat and it started sinking. The crew began to stream out of the conning tower, as shown in this photograph. Thirty of the men were lost but twenty-one were rescued by the destroyer HMS *Orwell*, including Speidel.

Ref: AIR 15/471

Right: The destroyer HMS *Orwell* picking up survivors from *U-643* on 8 October 1943. The photograph was taken from the Liberator of 120 Squadron flown by Flying Officer Denis C.L. Webber.

Ref: ADM 199/1415

```
ADM (2)

TO: I D 8 G                    ZIP/ZTPGU/17613          659

FROM: N S

5110 KC/S              T O O 0248        T O I 0108/9/10/43

FROM: U 91

    MISSED A DESTROYER WITH A ''T.5'' AT 2340 IN NAVAL GRID

SQUARE AL BXX 5112 AND WAS THEN DEPTH-CHARGED BY 2 DESTROYERS. NO

HYDROPHONE BEARINGS ON THE CONVOY.

0526/9/10/43++CEL/FA
```

The Type VIIC *U-91* was built by Flenderwerft of Lübeck and commissioned on 28 January 1942. This signal of 9 October 1943 was sent during its fifth war cruise, after leaving Brest on 21 September 1943 under the command of Kapitänleutnant Heinz Hungershausen. It had sunk six merchant vessels during its previous war cruises. There were no successes on this cruise and it returned safely to Brest. It left again on 25 January 1944 but exactly a month later, some 630 miles north of the Azores, it was depth-charged and sunk by the frigates HMS *Affleck, Gould, Gore* and *Garlies*. Thirty-six of the crew were lost but sixteen were rescued by the Royal Navy, including Hungershausen.

Ref: DEFE 3/722

```
ADM (3)

TO: I D 8 G                    ZIP/ZTPGU/17978
                                                        1969
FROM: N S

10825 KC/S            T O O 1916/16/10/43     B' QOF

AM BEING ATTACKED BY AN A/C. SQUARE AK 2690.

        HJR (U.470)

1124/17/10/43    CEL/ES+
```

This final signal was sent by *U-470* on 16 October 1943, some 380 miles south-west of Eire. It was a Type VIIC, built by Deutschewerke of Kiel and commissioned on 7 January 1943. It left Bergen on 29 October 1943 on its first war cruise, commanded by Oberleutnant zur See Günther Grave. The first attack came from a Liberator of 120 Squadron, flown from Reykjavik by a Canadian, Flight Lieutenant Harold F. Kerrigan, which dropped four depth charges in spite of being damaged by intense flak. Then another Liberator of 120 Squadron arrived, flown by Flight Lieutenant Barry E. Peck, which made two attacks on the damaged U-boat. Finally, a Liberator of 59 Squadron arrived from Ballykelly in Northern Ireland, flown by Pilot Officer W.G. Loney of the RAAF, and this finished off the U-boat. Loney's aircraft was also hit, but the crew managed to get back to Ballykelly. Only two crewmen from *U-470* were rescued by an escort vessel from the convoy. Forty-six others were lost, including the commander.

Ref: DEFE 3/722

```
ADM (3)

TO:  I D 8 G                          ZIP/ZTPGU/17977          ˝  1959

FROM:  N S


10825 KC/S

              T O O 1739/16/10/43    B' JTD


    AM BEING ATTACKED BY AN A/C. SQUARE AL 1749.

         GAO (U.964)
```

This was the last signal sent by *U-964*, on 16 October 1943. It was a Type VIIC U-boat, built by Blohm & Voss of Hamburg and commissioned on 18 February 1943. It left Bergen on 5 October 1943 for its first war cruise, commanded by Oberleutnant zur See Emmo Hummerjohann, but was caught on the surface in mid-Atlantic by a Liberator III of 86 Squadron, flown from Ballykelly in Northern Ireland by Pilot Officer George D. Gamble. The first attack was made with three depth charges, in the face of intense flak. Another attack was made in the evening twilight and three remaining depth charges straddled the U-boat. Smoke arose and it sank, leaving about thirty-five men in dinghies or in the water. Five of these were rescued later by the Type VIIC *U-231* but forty-seven others were lost, including Hummerjohann.

Ref: DEFE 3/722

```
ADM (1)                                                        1027

  TO I D 8 G                          ZIP/ZTPGU/17945

  FROM N S

  7910 KC/S

               T O O 1120/16/10/43    B' BHL

  AM BEING ATTACKED BY AN A/C . MY POSITION IS SQUARE AL 2514

        BHS  ( U.540 .)


  0934/17/10/43 +++CEL/EE
```

The Type IXC/40 *U-540* was built by Deutschewerft of Hamburg and commissioned on 10 March 1943. It left Bergen on 4 October 1943 for its first war cruise under the command of Kapitänleutnant Lorenz Kasch, but was attacked on 16 October when west of Eire by Liberator V serial FL984 of 59 Squadron flown from Ballykelly in Northern Ireland by Pilot Officer W.J. Thomas. It survived this attack but its ordeal continued the following day. (See also p. 176.)

Ref: DEFE 3/722

On the following day the Type IXC/40 *U-540* was attacked by two more Liberators from Reykjavik in Iceland. These were Liberator V serial BZ712 of 59 Squadron, flown by Lieutenant Eric Knowles, and Liberator I serial AM929 of 120 Squadron, flown by Warrant Officer Bryan W. Turnbull of the RNZAF. Knowles made two attacks and on the second the depth charges were seen to straddle the U-boat. Turnbull also made two attacks, one of which is shown here. The U-boat was destroyed with the loss of all fifty-five crew members.

Ref: ADM 199/1415

Liberator I serial AM929 of 120 Squadron, flown by Warrant Officer Bryan W. Turnbull of the RNZAF during the sinking of the Type IXC/40 *U-540* on 17 October 1943.

Ref: AIR 15/472

The Type IXD-2 *U-848* was built by A.G. Weser of Bremen and commissioned on 20 February 1943. It left Kiel on 18 September 1943 bound for the Indian Ocean under the command of Korvettenkapitän Wilhelm Rollmann, and sank a merchant vessel fourteen days later. On 5 November 1943, about 250 miles west-south-west of Ascension Island in the South Atlantic, it was depth-charged by four Liberators of VP-107 Squadron, USN, and two more from the 1st Composite Squadron, USAAF. The U-boat was sunk with the loss of sixty-two of the crew after a lengthy battle. One crew member was picked up the following day, but later died.

Ref: AIR 15/471

```
ADM( 3)                                                              55
    TO I D 8  G                       ZIP/ZTPGU/19046
    FROM N S

    6290 KC/S
        0825/9/11/43  B' LXK

    AM BEING ATTACKED BY AIRCRAFT

            ZXZ  ( U 707 )
    0451/11/11/43++EE++PG
```

The Type VIIC *U-707* was built by Stülcken Sohn of Hamburg and commissioned on 1 July 1942. It made two war cruises under the command of Oberleutnant zur See Günther Gretschel, during which it sank one merchant ship and damaged another. The last cruise began when it left Bordeaux on 12 October 1943, bound for the area of the Azores. This final signal was sent on 9 November 1943 when it was under attack about 300 miles east of the Azores by Fortress IIA serial FL459 of 220 Squadron, flown from Lagens in the Azores by Flight Lieutenant Roderick P. Drummond. Four depth charges were dropped during an exchange of gunfire, and three more during a second attack. The U-boat sank, leaving men in the sea. A K-type dinghy was dropped to them, but none of the crew of fifty-one survived.

Ref: DEFE 3/724

```
      D
    ADM(2)                                                              465
    TO I D 8 G                                    ZIP/ZTPGU/19422
    FROM N S
    4020 KC/S                  TOO 1930          TOI 1915/20/11/43
    FROM: BABERG'S U/BOAT
     JUST NOW ON POSITION, SHORTLY AFTER NAXOS LOCATION, WAS
    ATTACKED BY A FOUR ENGINED A/C WHICH WENT INTO THE DRINK
    IN FLAMES. CONSIDER LINE HAS BEEN RECOGNISED.
    1517/21/11/43       CEL+++MRT+++
```

This signal was sent on 20 November 1943 by the commander of the Type VIIC *U-618*, Kapitänleutnant Kurt Baberg, after shooting down Leigh Light Liberator V serial BZ916 of 53 Squadron flown from Beaulieu in Hampshire by Squadron Leader K.A. Aldridge. The RAF crew lost their lives. This U-boat was built by Blohm & Voss of Hamburg and commissioned on 16 April 1942. It was on its fifth war cruise, having left St-Nazaire nine days before bound for the North Atlantic. Its end came on 14 August 1944, after leaving Brest bound for La Pallice under the command of Oberleutnant zur See Erich Faust. It was first depth-charged and badly damaged by Liberator VI serial EW302 of 53 Squadron, also equipped with a Leigh Light and flown from Beaulieu by Flight Lieutenant Gilbert G. Potier. Then it was finished off by the frigates HMS *Duckworth* and *Essington,* with the loss of all sixty-one on board. By this time it had completed eight war cruises and sunk three merchant vessels.

Ref: DEFE 3/724

```
    ADM  3
      TO I D 8 G                                                        414
      FROM N S                              ZIP/ZTPGU:19372
      4020 KC/S              TOO 0601                TOI 0538/20/11/43
      FROM: CREMER
      SUBMERGED DAY ATTACK, PERISCOPE DEPTH AIRCRAFT BOMBS, RAMMED BY K
      DESTROYER, EXTREMELY HEAVILY DEPTH- CHARGED, REDUCED FLOATING AND XXX
      DIVING EFFICIENCY, SHORT WAVE WORKING. PIENING ROUTE, NAVAL GRID
      SQUARE CF 5193.
       1046/20/11/43/EE/MS+++
```

This signal of 20 November 1943 was sent by Kapitänleutnant Peter-Erich Cremer, the commander of the Type VIIC *U-333*, after being rammed two days before by the frigate HMS *Exe,* followed by nine hours of depth-charging. The position was roughly halfway between the Azores and the coast of Portugal. The U-boat had been built by Nordseewerke of Emden and commissioned on 25 August 1941. It was on its eighth war cruise, having left La Pallice on 21 October 1943. During its career it had sunk nine merchant vessels and damaged another. It had also shot down a Wellington of 172 Squadron. Despite the damage on this occasion, *U-333* managed to limp back to La Pallice by 1 December. (See also p. 209.)

Ref: DEFE 3/724

```
ADM (3)                                                              566
TO I D 8 G                              ZIP/ZTPGU/19516
FROM N S
5600 KC/S
              (TOI :- 0617/23/11/43  B' VV.)
      DAMAGED BY DEPTH CHARGES, AM MOVING OFF TO REPAIR.
                            UEB  (U 515)
   0910/23/11/43+++CEL+++DG
```

Kapitänleutnant Werner Henke, the commander of the Type IXC *U-515*, sent this signal on 23 November 1943 after a long attack with depth charges by the sloop HMS *Chanticleer*. This U-boat had been built by Deutschewerft of Hamburg and commissioned on 21 February 1942. It was on its fifth war cruise, having left St-Nazaire on 9 November 1943 to operate off West Africa. It survived this encounter but its end came after leaving Lorient on 30 March 1944, once more bound for West Africa. On 9 April 1944 it was depth-charged to the surface by Avengers and Wildcats of VC-58 Squadron from the escort carrier USS *Guadalcanal*, when north-west of Maderia. By this time Henke was a Korvettenkapitän, his *U-515* was on its sixth war cruise and had sunk a total of twenty-three vessels and damaged four more. Fifteen of his crew lost their lives but he and forty-three others were rescued by US destroyers to become prisoners. Henke was shot and killed on 15 June 1944 when attempting to escape from a US PoW camp.

Ref: DEFE 3/724

```
ADM (3)                                                          827
TO: I D 8 G                            ZIP/ZTPGU/19759
FROM: N S
5710 KC/S             TOO 1859           TOI 1832/28/11/43
FROM: HEPP

  1)  NAVAL GRID SQUARE CF 6544 ONE A/C CRASHED AT 2212.  PRESUME
      IT WAS SHOT DOWN BY BREMEN.   HAVE TAKEN W/T OPERATOR AND
      SECOND PILOT ON BOARD.
  2)  SAW AN A/C CRASH AT 0451 IN SQUARE CR 6222.  PRESUME IT WAS
      SHOT DOWN BY FRANKE.
  3)  NAVAL GRID SQUARE CF 3883 AT 1042 'T5' ON CORVETTE INCLINATION
      150 RANGE 5000.   EXPLOSION AFTER 13 MINUTES 25 SECONDS.
      NO FURTHER HYDROPHONE BEARINGS.   THEN SECOND CORVETTE AND
      D/R(S) MADE OFF.   NO D/CS.
  4)  CONVOY'S POSITION AT 0930 NAVAL GRID SQUARE CF 3882, COURSE
```

This signal was sent on 28 November 1943 by the commander of the Type VIIC *U-238*, Kapitänleutnant Horst Hepp, after rescuing two survivors of a Wellington VIII of 172 Squadron equipped with a Leigh Light and flown from Chivenor in North Devon. The aircraft had been shot down west of Spain by the Type VIIC *U-764* on the previous day. The Type VIIC *U-238* was built by Germaniawerft and commissioned on 20 February 1943. It was on its second war cruise when this incident occurred, having left Brest on 11 November 1943. On the following day it was damaged by Avengers from the escort carrier USS *Bogue*, with two crewmen killed and five wounded, and was forced to return to Brest. By this time it had sunk four merchant ships and damaged another. Its end came on 9 February 1944 when it was depth-charged about 270 miles west of Ireland by the sloops HMS *Kite*, *Magpie* and *Starling*. There were no survivors from the crew of fifty.

Ref: DEFE 3/724

```
        ADM (1)                                              149
        TO:  I D 8 G                    ZIP/ZTPGU/20145
        FROM:  N S
        ALL ATLANTIC U/B FREQUENCIES        T O I 1723/5/12/43
                    T O O 1743
        ADMONITORY W/T MESSAGE NO.66
              THERE ARE STILL BOATS WHICH DIVE WHEN AIRCRAFT ATTACK, AT
        THE MOMENT AT WHICH THE AIRCRAFT FLIES OVER THE BOAT. THIS IS
        WRONG AND FATALLY DANGEROUS. EVEN THE LARGEST AIRCRAFT AND FLYING-
        BOATS ARE BACK AGAIN FOR A NEW ATTACK AFTER A MINUTE. IN THIS TIME
        NO BOAT CAN REACH PROTECTIVE DEPTH, PARTICULARLY IF MANY MEN WERE
        ON THE BRIDGE FOR FLAK DEFENCE.
        1728/14/12/43   TZ/ES+
```

Advice sent on 5 December 1943 to all U-boats from U-boat Headquarters in Kiel.

Ref: DEFE 3/725

A rare wartime photograph of the Colossus computer at Bletchley Park, with young ladies of the Women's Royal Naval Service. It became operational in December 1943 and was used to break the cypher of the German High Command before D-Day. This was the world's first electronic programmable computer.

Author's collection

CHAPTER SIX

Defeat of the U-Boats

By the beginning of January 1944 losses at sea had reduced the U-boat Arm to 168 operational boats. This was only about two-thirds of its strength at its peak nine months previously, despite a continuous flow of replacements. However, a total of 268 newly built U-boats were undergoing trials during the month. The colossal bombing campaign by RAF Bomber Command and the US Eighth Air Force had done little to limit U-boat production. Although great swathes of residential districts in Kiel, Wilhelmshaven, Bremen, Vegesack and Hamburg had been destroyed, the effect on manufacturing areas and dockyards had been far less severe. Many more U-boats were being built than in the earlier years of the war.

Many of the best commanders and crews in the U-boat Arm had been lost, although there were plenty of newcomers to take their places. Most of these were volunteers but some were drafted from other branches of the Kriegsmarine. The trainees first underwent a three-month course during which discipline was the key ingredient. Then they were split up to train in their specialist trades, which took varying lengths of time. A few were trained as commanders, first watch officers or engineering officers. Others became helmsmen, diesel mechanics, electro mechanics, torpedo mechanics or cooks, etc. Some duties in a U-boat were common to several men, such as keeping lookout or steering. After qualification, a few were sent to join operational U-boats as apprentices, but the majority were posted to the newly built boats for familiarisation and further training. Again, the length of training time depended on each function. All knew that they would experience very cramped and uncomfortable conditions on their war cruises.

Some of these newcomers may have guessed that they would probably meet the fate of many of their predecessors, although most of them probably believed that they would somehow survive the war. The truth was that the majority would end their young lives entombed in shattered hulls somewhere on the bottom of the sea, although a few of the luckier ones would be picked up by the Allies and spend most of the rest of the war in PoW camps. The U-boat Arm was operating with reduced numbers of operational boats and by then was without its Italian allies. Its war was being fought in great areas of the world's oceans and seas – the North Atlantic, the South Atlantic, the Arctic Ocean, the Mediterranean and the Indian Ocean, with a handful of boats in the distant waters of the Far East. However, the men were buoyed up with the hope that new developments would enable them to regain some advantage over an increasingly powerful enemy.

The ideal would have been a U-boat that could remain submerged throughout its war cruise, and indeed such a boat had already been designed by Professor Hellmuth Walter in combination with Germaniawerft of Kiel. Known as a 'Type V boat', it consisted of two hulls, one on top of the other. The top hull contained a turbine engine and the crew with their controls, while the lower hull was simply a huge fuel tank containing concentrated hydrogen peroxide. Such a boat could travel underwater at the extraordinary speed of 30 knots, faster than most Allied escort vessels, but it was impractical for two main reasons. One was that there were inadequate facilities in Germany to provide the enormous quantities of fuel required, while the other was that the Type V boat could be produced at only about half the rate of conventional U-boats.

Although the project to manufacture the Type V boat was abandoned, there was a simple adaptation that could be produced rapidly. This was the 'Schnorkel' breathing tube, which was fitted to conventional U-boats and came into service in early 1944. There was nothing new in the concept of an underwater breathing tube, for one had been designed centuries before by Leonardo da Vinci, although this was intended to be attached to a diving suit in which a man would walk across the Venetian sea bed and cause underwater damage to any Turkish galleys which invaded the port. Various efforts had been made in more recent times to fit a ventilation tube to submarines, culminating in a development by the Royal Netherlands Navy before the Second World War. With the destruction of so many of their boats in 1943, the method was approved as a defensive measure by the U-boat Arm in the summer of that year. In essence, it was devised as a simple retractable tube with a ballcock valve to prevent water from being washed into the boat.

In use, the Schnorkel could enable U-boats to avoid enemy warships and aircraft, as well as allowing them to remain underwater to recharge their batteries or sometimes during submerged attacks on vessels, but it had serious disadvantages. The underwater speed was reduced and movement within the boat had to be limited to avoid upsetting the trim. Exhaust fumes restricted the vision of those within the boat, while these fumes could be spotted by keen-eyed crew members of Allied aircraft. If waves happened to close the cut-off valve, the diesel engines sucked up the available air within the boat, so that the crew began to suffocate and then suffered agonies with their eardrums when air rushed in again. Long periods underwater also created foul conditions, since food waste and the contents of toilets could not be disposed of so readily. The invention did not seem to provide the expected protection, and indeed the first boat to attempt a war cruise with it, the Type VIIC *U-264*, was sunk in the North Atlantic on 19 February 1944.

In the event, the massacre of the U-boats continued into 1944. They sank only thirteen merchant vessels totalling about 18,500 tons in January, from an overall total of 123,500 tons lost by the Allies. In return, fourteen U-boats were sunk, almost all in the North Atlantic, where they sank only five of the thirteen merchant vessels lost. By this time the Allied shipbuilding programme had forged ahead, reaching a total of about 32 million gross tons since the beginning of the war, with the rate of production far exceeding the rate of sinkings.

February was even worse for the U-boats. Despite sinking eighteen merchant ships totalling about 93,000 tons from Allied losses of 117,000 tons, they lost twenty of their

```
ADM(1)                                                            1034

  TO I D 8 G                              ZIP/ZTPGU/20977

FROM N S

  4075 KC/S              T O O 2105                TOI 2120/7/1/44

FROM:  BAHR

  1)  AT 1711 NAVAL GRID SQUARE BE 7655 A/S GROUP OF 3 D/RS.

      SANK ONE OF THEM WITH A 3-FAN

  2)  ON EACH OF 24/12 AND 2/1 A 'T 5' MISS ON CRUISER OR DESTROYER,

      BOTH INCLINATION 140, 'TRIER'

  3)  24/12 LT. DOHRMANN KILLED BY GUNFIRE.

  4)  3.7 CM KNOCKED OUT, BRAKE FLUID HAS RUN. 56 CBM, STILL

      5 GOOD EELS

  (DEPT. NOTE: FOR 'TRIER' = ENEMY SPEED TOO LOW, SEE

          ZTPGU/17146, 1422/21/9)
```

The Type VIIC *U-305* was built by Flenderwerft of Lübeck and commissioned on 17 September 1942. It made three war cruises under the command of Kapitänleutnant Rudolf Bahr, during which it sank two merchant vessels and the destroyer HMCS *St Croix,* as well as damaging another merchant vessel. It also received damage on two of these cruises but returned safely to Brest on both occasions. It left Brest once more on 8 December 1943 and on 7 January 1944 sent this signal after receiving further damage. Its end came ten days later on this war cruise when about 420 miles west-south-west of Eire, after depth-charging from the destroyer HMS *Wanderer* and the frigate HMS *Glenarm.* There were no survivors from the crew of fifty-one.

Ref: DEFE 3/725

own number, primarily in the North Atlantic campaign. In March they sank twenty-three merchant ships totalling about 123,000 tons from the 158,000 tons lost by the Allies, but twenty-three U-boats went down to attacks by aircraft and escort vessels. Three of these U-boats were lost attacking Arctic convoys but once again most of them were destroyed by escort vessels and aircraft in the North Atlantic.

By the end of March the battleship *Tirpitz* was seaworthy again, following repairs to the damage inflicted on her by the X-craft of the Royal Navy on 22 September 1943. Enigma decrypts revealed that she was about to put to sea from Kaa fjord for trials in the adjoining waters of Alten fjord. This timing coincided with the running of two Russian convoys, the eastbound JW57 and the westbound RA57, giving the Admiralty the opportunity to launch a huge airborne attack from warships which sailed under the guise of protecting the convoys. These were the fleet carriers HMS *Victorious* and HMS *Furious,* accompanied by three escort carriers.

```
ADM (3)                                                              832
TO: I D 8 G                              ZIP/ZTPGU/20786

FROM: N S

4412 KCÅS               TOO 0532              TOI 0519/4/1/44

FROM: BENKER

    C.O. AND 1 MAN OVERBOARD DURING ATTACK BY A/C ON 2/1.  C.O.

    WAS NOT FOUND AGAIN.

0745/4/1/44++++CEL/SMH
```

The Type VIIC *U-625* was built by Blohm & Voss of Hamburg and commissioned on 4 June 1942. It carried out eight war cruises in the Arctic, under the command of Kapitänleutnant Hans Benker, during which it sank three British and two Soviet merchant vessels, and damaged another Soviet vessel. It then left Trondheim on 15 November 1943 to operate in the North Atlantic. On 2 January 1944 it was attacked by two Liberators of 224 Squadron flown from St Eval in Cornwall. During an attack by the Liberator flown by Flying Officer E. Allen, the commanding officer and another man were blown overboard and not seen again. The U-boat arrived at Brest four days later under the temporary command of Oberleutnant zur See Kurt Sureth.

Ref: DEFE 3/725

The attack was launched in the early morning of 3 April by two waves of Fairey Barracuda bombers, some of which carried a single 1,600 lb armour-piercing bomb while others carried three 600 lb anti-submarine bombs. Their fighter escorts consisted of Supermarine Seafires, Vought Corsairs, Grumman Wildcats and Hellcats, which were given the additional task of raking the gun positions and deck of the battleship. The attack achieved complete surprise when *Tirpitz* was weighing anchor. She was hit by fourteen bombs, some of which penetrated the upper armoured deck and burst below, but none penetrated the lower 8 inch armoured deck. The crew suffered 122 dead and 336 wounded, and the battleship was so badly damaged that she was out of action for three more months. Two Barracudas failed to return.

The earlier attack on *Tirpitz* by the X-craft midget submarines of the Royal Navy had shocked the Kriegsmarine and resulted in the formation of the *Kleinkampfverbande (K-Verband)* or 'Small Battle Unit Command'. Its main purpose was to combat Allied vessels in any invasion force crossing the narrow waters of the English Channel. The simplest of the units which formed part of the new command were manned torpedoes. One of these, which entered service in March 1944, was named *Neger* (Nigger). It was fitted with rudimentary controls and could travel only on the surface for short distances. Another was *Marder* (Pine Marten), which was similar to *Neger* but included a diving tank and a pump for compressed air. This entered service in June 1944. The *K-Verband* was also equipped with *Linsen* (Lentil) motor boats, which operated in units consisting of one control boat and two carrying explosive charges. The explosive boats were steered by pilots who jumped out after directing them against targets, and then hoped to be picked up by the control boats. The chances of the pilots surviving attacks in all these vessels were rated as no more than 50 per cent and all the crews were volunteers for what became suicide missions.

In addition, midget submarines were rapidly designed and put into production. One of these was *Hecht* (Pike), also known as the Type XXVIIA, which began to enter operational service in May 1944. This was a three-man submarine, capable of travelling underwater as well as on the surface, and armed with a single torpedo. The *Biber* (Beaver) was a one-man submarine which could also operate both on the surface and submerged, and carried a single torpedo. It began to enter operational service in June 1944. A version with a shorter range, designed solely for coastal work, was the *Molch* (Salamander), which entered service at around the same time. Yet another was *Seehund* (Seal) or the Type XXVIIB, with a crew of two and capable of carrying two torpedoes, but this did not begin entering service until November 1944.

On their roughly one-to-one basis of sinkings against losses, the ocean-going U-boats were not justifying their existence. However, replacements continued to arrive steadily and by the beginning of April 1944 the operational strength stood at 166, with 278 more undergoing training and trials. The inexperienced crews were being prepared almost like lambs for the slaughter. U-boats sank only nine merchant ships totalling 62,000 tons in April, from the 82,000 tons lost by the Allies, but nineteen of their own number were sunk.

The ratio of successes against losses became even worse for the U-boat Arm in May. This was one of its worst months of the war, for only four merchant vessels totalling 24,500 tons were sunk, while twenty-two U-boats were picked off and went to the bottom of the sea. No area was safe for the U-boats, except perhaps the Baltic – but even there one was lost in a collision in May.

The anticipated invasion of Europe by the Western Allies began on 6 June, when airborne troops dropped inland and spearheads of seaborne forces stormed the beaches of Normandy, escorted by Allied warships and covered by an overwhelming number of Allied aircraft. The German defences were caught off guard by forecasts of unfavourable weather issued by their own meteorologists. Even then, the location of this invasion was believed to be an Allied diversionary tactic by Hitler and the Wehrmacht, who were fooled by Allied deception measures. They continued to believe for several weeks that the main thrust would be made across the narrows of the English Channel to the Pas de Calais.

Dönitz was on leave with his family at Badenweiler, a holiday resort in the Black Forest, when D-Day began. Alerted by telephone, he hastened back to his headquarters near Berlin to chair a conference on the situation. Meanwhile the commander of Marinegruppe West, Vizeadmiral Theodor Krancke, issued his orders. Thirty-six U-boats in the Biscay bases and twenty-two in Norwegian ports had been put on full alert. Five others from France already heading for the North Atlantic were recalled and seven dispatched from Norway were to await new orders. Seventeen based at Brest were then ordered to attack the western flank of the Allied invasion force and all set course on D-Day. Nineteen others based at Lorient, St-Nazaire and La Pallice were ordered to form a patrol line in the Bay of Biscay, for it was believed from Allied deception measures that other landings would be made on the western coast of France.

Movement of German surface vessels also took place, but none of the heavier warships was available to assist in repelling an invasion from the west. The pocket battleships *Admiral von Scheer* and *Lützow* were engaged in the Baltic, as were the heavy cruisers *Admiral Hipper* and *Prinz Eugen,* where their main tasks were in support of the German armies facing the advance of the Red Army. The crews of the few surface vessels available were enjoined to attack the enemy 'regardless of cost' and they did their best with very limited results. Four torpedo boats (the size of small destroyers) left Le Havre and sank a Norwegian destroyer before slipping back into port. Three destroyers in the Gironde were ordered to the English Channel but they were intercepted on D-Day near Belle Ile by Beaufighters of Coastal Command and two were so badly damaged that all three put into Brest while repairs were carried out. Eighteen Schnellboote (known as E-boats by the British) were available to attack the eastern flank of the invasion force. After an abortive attempt during daylight, when no torpedo hits were scored, these began to operate at night.

The U-boats were hunted remorselessly by aircraft of Coastal Command. They sank two on D-Day plus one, two on the following day, one on the next day, and another on the day after that. It was another miserable month for the U-boat Arm, for twenty-five boats were lost in all waters and their only achievements were the sinking of eleven merchant vessels amounting to about 58,000 tons, from a total of 104,000 tons lost by the Allies.

The 'human torpedoes' suffered huge losses during the early weeks of the invasion. They were transported by road to ports near the Normandy beaches. Bletchley Park was aware of their location but could not forecast the days of attack. Twenty-six of the *Neger* class set off on 5 July. Two suffered mechanical problems and fifteen others were lost to Allied gunfire or other hazards. The other nine managed to sink two minesweepers. Twenty-one others left on 7 July and sank a minesweeper as well as damaging a cruiser, but all of these were sunk by surface vessels or aircraft.

Those of the *Marder* human torpedo class and the *Linsen* motor boats did not begin attacking until the night of 2/3 August, when fifty-eight of the former and twenty-two of the latter were dispatched against Allied shipping off the Normandy coast near Courseuilles-sur-Mer. The *Marder* began the attack and one managed to hit a cruiser with a torpedo. Then a major engagement took place, in which they sank a destroyer, a minesweeper and a Liberty ship but forty-one of the attackers were eventually sunk. The *Linsen* then joined in the attack, sinking a minesweeper, a motor launch and a landing craft, for the loss of fourteen of their own number. Twenty-eight *Linsen* were sent out on 8/9 August but they sank no ships and twenty were lost.

Yet another attack took place on 16/17 August when forty-two of the *Marder* set off for the eastern flank of the Allied invasion fleet. They sank a barrage balloon vessel but lost twenty-six of their own number. The midget submarines failed to make any effective attack in these waters before the Allied advances overran the French ports from which they could operate. This type of attack on the invasion area, by either 'human torpedoes', motor launches or midget submarines, became impossible by the end of August.

Meanwhile, replacements built up the number of operational ocean-going U-boats to 188 by the beginning of July, with 246 more undergoing training and trials, but their achievements continued at a dismal level during July. They sank only twelve merchant ships totalling 63,500 tons, but lost twenty-three of their own number. Aircraft were the main cause of these losses, which included three destroyed during a heavy raid on Kiel by RAF Bomber Command.

The Western Allies planned another seaborne landing in August, this time on the southern coast of France, under the codename operation Dragoon. Ten U-boats were still operating in the Mediterranean, from the bases of Toulon in France or Pola in Yugoslavia. Their main targets were the convoys which brought supplies and reinforcements to the Allied troops fighting their way up the peninsula of Italy, or which were passing through the Mediterranean to the Suez Canal and thence to the Allied forces in India. The Allies decided to eliminate these U-boats by utilising the immense Allied air and sea superiority in an operation which was aptly named 'Swamp'. So many of these Allied forces were available that it was possible to pursue a U-boat so intensively that it was likely to be spotted when it was eventually forced to surface.

B-Dienst had correctly forecast that an Allied landing would take place in the south of France although the exact location and date were not known. As a preliminary, the Allies made heavy raids against the German-held ports of Toulon, Genoa and Trieste, resulting in the sinking of many merchant ships and small warships. On 6 August the US Fifteenth Air Force raided Toulon once more and succeeded in destroying four U-boats, all of which had been damaged in a previous raid, and further damaging a fifth. The Allied landings took place on 15 August with French and American divisions and were successful everywhere. The Germans had no option but to to scuttle or blow up three of the remaining U-boats, all of which had been damaged previously. Only three U-boats remained in the Mediterranean, all based at Pola.

Three days after the landings in the south of France, Hitler ordered the U-boats in Brest, Lorient, St-Nazaire, La Pallice, La Rochelle and the Gironde to evacuate their ports and to head round the north of Britain to Norwegian waters. It was clear that these French ports would soon become unusable with the advance of the Allies from the north and the south. The move was also accelerated by the knowledge that the RAF was by then capable of breaching the immensely thick roofs of the U-boat shelters. On 12 August Lancasters of Bomber Command dropped the new 12,000 lb 'Tallboy' bombs on the shelters at Brest, penetrating part of the roof. Eight U-boats which were unfit for the journey to Norwegian ports were either scuttled or scrapped. The French ports were not to be evacuated by ground personnel, who were ordered to defend them as 'fortresses' against the Allied troops.

Apart from the seven U-boats destroyed in the Mediterranean and the eight scuttled in French ports, twenty-one others were lost during August for various reasons, mainly sunk by air attack while on war cruises. The U-boat Arm succeeded in sinking eighteen merchant vessels amounting to about 99,000 tons during this month, from a total of 118,500 tons lost by the Allies, but it was continuing to fight a losing battle. By this time new shipbuilding of merchant vessels in America and Britain had reached about 38 million gross tons since the beginning of the war, whereas total sinkings had amounted to about

23 million tons, of which about 14.5 million tons had been sunk by U-boats. Moreover, further production was proceeding at an accelerated pace, whereas the pace of sinkings was declining sharply.

The decline of the U-boats continued into September, for they sank only seven merchant vessels amounting to 43,000 tons, apart from which the Allies lost only one vessel which struck a mine. The slaughter of the U-boats continued, for they lost twenty-one of their number during the month. Three of these were scuttled after being transported in sections from the Baltic to the Black Sea, where they were reassembled. The advance of the Red Army threatened to cut them off. The three remaining U-boats in the Mediterranean were also destroyed, one sunk by destroyers north of Crete and the other two during an American bombing raid on Salamis in Greece, where they were sheltering. Henceforth, the U-boat Arm could operate only from bases in Norway. It was reduced to 144 operational boats by the end of the month, with 260 more undergoing training and trials.

The giant battleship *Tirpitz* was badly damaged again on 15 September. On this occasion the attacking force consisted of twenty-eight Avro Lancasters of RAF Bomber Command operating from North Russia. Twenty-one of them were carrying the huge Tallboy bomb. The bombers arrived in daylight over Kaa fjord, flying between 6,500 and 10,000 feet, and achieved initial surprise. One of the Tallboy bombs scored a direct hit and blew a great hole in the bows and the side. Other bombs scored near misses and caused further damage. German marine engineers concluded that repairs would take about another nine months. A month later, after work on her engines, she steamed about 200 miles south-west to Tromsö to act in a new role as a flak battery.

October brought no improvement in the circumstances for the U-boat Arm. Although replacements were still pouring through the system, the number of operational boats had been reduced to 141, with 260 under training and trials. Eleven U-boats were sent from Norway to operate off the west coast of Britain, in waters such as the English Channel, the Bristol Channel and the North Channel. Four others were dispatched to waters off Newfoundland and another off Gibraltar, but the achievements of the entire U-boat fleet were limited to the sinking of only one merchant vessel of about 7,000 tons during October, while three other Allied vessels were sunk from mines. In return, eleven U-boats were lost, four of them in a raid by RAF Bomber Command on the pens at Bergen and another during a similar raid on Wilhelmshaven.

November was little better for this hard-pressed service, for the U-boats sank only seven merchant vessels totalling about 29,500 tons from an overall figure of 38,000 tons lost by the Allies from all causes. However, the number of U-boats sunk fell to eight, perhaps indicating that the commanders were becoming more skilled with the use of schnorkels and evasion techniques. The inshore campaign in waters off the west coast of Britain was causing some difficulty for the Admiralty, for there were insufficient anti-submarine vessels to hunt in these waters. The U-boats seldom appeared on the surface during daylight and were difficult to detect by Asdic when submerged among offshore rocks. RAF Coastal Command hunted for them, but often fruitlessly in daylight hours.

November was the month which saw the end of the battleship *Tirpitz*, partly because her new location brought her within the range of RAF Lancaster bombers operating from

```
ADM  3

  TO I D 8 G                                    808

  FROM N S                          ZIP/ZTPGU/20763

  XRRQWX

  4412 KC/S

               TOO 2059/3/1/44 B' HBL

  AM BEING ATTACKED BY AN AIRCRAFT. AM UNABLE TO DIVE.

  SQUARE BF 5741.

               UQS (U.373)

  0402/4/1/44/CEL/MS+++
```

The Type VIIC *U-373* left La Pallice on 1 January 1944 for its eleventh war cruise, under the command of Oberleutnant zur See Detlef von Lehsten. Two days later it was attacked by Wellington XIV serial MP756 of 612 Squadron flown from Chivenor in North Devon by the commanding officer, Wing Commander John B. Russell, as well as by a Liberator of 224 Squadron flown from St Eval in Cornwall by Flying Officer Harold R. Pacey of the RCAF. The attacks resulted in this signal of 3 January 1944. It returned damaged to La Pallice on the following day, when two unexploded depth charges were found in the foredeck casing. After repair, it left La Pallice on 7 June 1944 under the same commander, bound for the invasion area. It was attacked and sunk on the following day by another Liberator of 224 Squadron flown from St Eval by Flight Lieutenant Kenneth C. Moore of the RCAF, using a Leigh Light. Six crew members lost their lives but forty-seven were picked up by French fishermen, including von Lehsten.

Ref: DEFE 3/725

Scotland. Twenty-nine of these took off from Lossiemouth on the night of 11/12 November and arrived individually over their target during daylight. The battleship received direct hits from at least two Tallboy bombs and then suffered a huge internal explosion. She capsized and came to rest upside down at the bottom of the fjord, killing 1,204 men from her crew of about 1,900. This action removed a major threat to the Arctic convoys, which henceforth experienced only spasmodic attacks from U-boats.

It must have been obvious to Dönitz that his U-boats were fighting a losing battle in the Atlantic and elsewhere, and yet he continued to throw all available resources into the conflict. Senior officers in the Wehrmacht nurtured the belief that their country possessed a technical superiority capable of producing 'wonder weapons' that would enable them to gain ultimate victory. Examples were the V-1 flying bomb, the V-2 long-range rocket and the Messerschmitt Me262 jet aircraft. Within the Kriegsmarine, it was the new 'electro-boats'. These were being built as a compromise for the Walter Type V boat which had been considered impracticable. An engineer on this project, Heinrich Heep, had recommended that the lower of the two tanks, originally intended to hold concentrated hydrogen peroxide, should be utilised to contain diesel/electric motors. This would treble the capacity of the motors in existing boats, provide faster surface and submerged speeds, and enable the boat to dive to greater depths. Two versions were being built, the Type XXI to replace the conventional ocean-going boats and the smaller Type XXIII for coastal operations. Production was in the hands of the Reich Minister for Armaments, Albert Speer, who had inaugurated a system of prefabricating sections in thirteen dispersed factories, capable of being transported along canals to final assembly lines. This reduced the man-hours utilised on building the conventional boats, and production was in full flow. Enigma decrypts revealed this programme to the Allies, who estimated that some of these new and dangerous U-boats would enter operational service in early 1945.

December brought the usual winter storms which reduced activities in the high seas, but the ocean-going U-boats sank nine merchant ships totalling about 58,500 tons in the month, from a total of almost 135,000 tons lost by the Allies. They lost thirteen of their own number, two of which were destroyed during a raid on Hamburg by the US Eighth Air Force.

Despite these unfavourable results for the U-boat Arm, there was some evidence in December that its commanders were becoming more adept at avoiding detection by the use of the schnorkel, which was by then fitted with a radar device for identifying the approach of aircraft. The Admiralty was also viewing the imminent appearance of the electro-boats with concern, aware from decrypts and air reconnaissance that numbers had been built, were working up to operational efficiency and would soon be sent on war cruises. On the last day of the year the US Eighth Air Force was diverted from its main task of destroying the German synthetic oil plants to an attack on the assembly yards at Hamburg, and the bombers succeeded in destroying two Type XXIs and badly damaging others.

Another worry for the Admiralty concerned the decrypts, for the U-boat Arm was making increasing use of the *Sonderschlüsel* (Special Key) system in which the Enigma keys were different for individual U-boats. Bletchley Park was unable to decrypt these and thus the departure times, locations and return times of some U-boats were not known to the Admiralty.

Despite these ominous developments on the high seas, by January 1945 the Wehrmacht faced an impossible military situation and the prospect of inevitable defeat. The centres of most German cities lay in ruins from concentrated air bombardment, the Luftwaffe had been reduced to a fraction of its former strength, Anglo-American armies had broken through the 'Western Wall' and were advancing into German territory, while great Russian armies had overrun East Prussia and were pouring through Poland towards Berlin itself. Yet it seems that Dönitz believed in miracles and was convinced that his new electro-boats could deal a decisive blow against the Western Allies.

The Kriegsmarine was also presented with an enormous operation in the Baltic in this period, for it had become necessary to begin evacuating civilians and military personnel from the eastern provinces, away from the advancing Russian forces. All available warships and merchant ships were pressed into service for this purpose, even including some U-boats. The pocket battleships *Lützow* and *Admiral Scheer* and the heavy cruiser *Prinz Eugen* attempted to cover this operation by bombarding the forward positions of the Red Army.

On the Western Front the first day of the New Year began with an attack by seventeen *Seehunde* Type XXVIIB midget submarines of *K-Verband*, which set out from Ijmuiden in the Netherlands to hunt for Allied shipping in the Outer Scheldt bound for Antwerp. This port had been captured by the British 11th Armoured Division on 4 September 1944. Its docks were almost undamaged and had become an important means of supply for the British and Canadian forces in the northern sector of operations. Dönitz had set great store on this operation, but he was to be disappointed. The two-man submarines succeeded in sinking one small trawler but only two returned to base. Some of those missing were destroyed by gunfire but others had run ashore and become stranded. Further attacks by small attack craft on shipping off the coasts of Kent and Belgium were completely unsuccessful. Their losses during the month amounted to ten *Seehunde,* ten *Biber* one-man submarines and seven *Linsen* motor boats.

The strength of the operational ocean-going U-boats in January stood at 144, with 260 more undergoing training and trials. These sank eleven merchant vessels amounting to about 58,000 tons during the month, from a total of 104,000 tons lost by the Allies. Mines accounted for much of the remainder. Fourteen U-boats were lost, with another raid on Hamburg by the US Eighth Air Force destroying three more Type XXIs and damaging nine others. These massive air attacks also caused huge damage to dock and assembly facilities, bringing the production of the electro-boats almost to a halt.

The small battle units of *K-Verband* fared somewhat better in February, sinking one tank landing ship and a cable ship, as well as damaging a tanker, but they lost four *Seehunde* and three *Linsen,* as well as six *Molch* or *Biber* one-man submarines. The month brought no improvement in the situation for the major U-boat Arm. A new coastal Type XXIII electro-boat which had sailed from Horten in Norway on 29 January attacked a convoy off Newcastle-on-Tyne, without success, and then returned to base. Another Type XXIII was lost in a collision in the Baltic. The U-boat Arm accounted for fifteen merchant vessels totalling about 65,000 tons, within an overall total of 110,000 tons lost by the Allies during the month, but it lost twenty-two of its ocean-going boats. The expected carnage from the new electro-boats had not occurred, owing primarily to delays in production and damage to the assembly facilities. The war was drawing to its inevitable close, with defeat for Germany.

During March U-boats sank thirteen merchant vessels totalling about 65,000 tons but suffered the enormous loss of thirty-two of their own number. Thirteen of these were destroyed by the US Eighth Air Force during concentrated raids on Wilhelmshaven, Bremen and Hamburg at the end of the month. These losses included only two Type XXI electro-boats and once again the assembly programme for these vessels was seriously impaired. The midget submarines and motor boats continued their suicide missions during the month, sinking three merchant vessels at the expense of huge losses. Nine *Seehunde* and twenty-seven *Linsen* were lost, as well as forty-two *Biber* or *Molch.* Fourteen of the *Biber* were destroyed by an accidental explosion while in harbour at Rotterdam.

April was the last full month of the war. By this time the newly trained crews with their ocean-going U-boats had built up numbers to as many as 166, with 263 others following behind within the system. The new arrivals joined in the fruitless task of overcoming an increasingly powerful enemy at sea. The U-boat Arm sank thirteen merchant vessels totalling almost 72,000 tons during the month, from an overall total of 104,500 tons lost by the Allies, but suffered its worst monthly losses of the entire war. No fewer than fifty-five ocean-going U-boats were destroyed, twenty of them as a result of massive air strikes by the US Eighth Air Force and RAF Bomber Command on Kiel and Hamburg. Others were sunk by cannon-firing de Havilland Mosquitos of RAF Coastal Command while en route from Germany to bases in Norway. The only Type XXI electro-boat to embark on a war cruise, *U-2511,* was scheduled to leave Bergen on 17 April but its departure was delayed by a damaged periscope and it encountered no enemy forces before being ordered to surrender. If this type had been available in earlier months, it could have had a profound influence on the course of the war at sea.

The small vessels of *K-Verband* also attempted to make an impact on the enemy in April, laying mines and making torpedo attacks. Two *Seehunde* sank one small tanker and a large merchant ship in waters off Dover, but the group lost twelve *Seehunde,* nine *Biber* and seventeen *Linsen* in the month, from attacks by aircraft and warships. The operations of this ill-starred group then came to an end.

With the Russian forces on the outskirts of Berlin, Hitler committed suicide on 30 April. The Deputy Führer was Reichsminister Herman Goering but Hitler had bypassed him and appointed his staunchest supporter, Grossadmiral Karl Dönitz, as his successor. It was evident to Dönitz that the military situation had become completely hopeless and that he should capitulate immediately, but he delayed for a few days to complete, so far as possible, the evacuation of troops and civilians from the eastern provinces. On 4 May he advised U-boat commanders that they were to scuttle or destroy their boats on receipt of the codeword 'Regenbogen'. Meanwhile, he appointed Generaladmiral Hans von Friedeburg to take his place as commander-in-chief of the Kriegsmarine and also authorised him to surrender to Field Marshal Sir Bernard Montgomery at his headquarters on Luneburg Heath. The proposal to scuttle U-boats was not authorised by the Allies and could not be implemented. Instead, all U-boat commanders were ordered to fly black surrender flags and begin their journeys home. The surrender became effective at one minute past midnight on 8 May but the terms were transmitted to all German forces, including U-boats at sea, during 4 May.

Not all U-boat commanders received the messages immediately and some engagements took place. In the first seven days of the month twenty-eight more U-boats were sunk, primarily from air attack in the areas of Kiel Bay and the Kattegat, while U-boats sank three merchant vessels totalling about 10,000 tons. It is estimated that by the end of the war the Kriegsmarine had evacuated about two million troops and civilians via the Baltic, of whom about 20,000 were lost at sea, in what must be regarded as its biggest operation of the war.

The Allies lost approximately 21.5 million gross tons of merchant shipping from all causes during the war, although their massive rebuilding programme produced over 45 million gross tons during this period. It is calculated that U-boats sank 2,927 merchant vessels amounting to almost 15 million gross tons of the total lost, as well as 175 Allied warships totalling about 243,000 tons. The records also show that 1,110 ocean-going U-boats were dispatched on war cruises. Almost 800 of these were destroyed at sea, from air bombardment in docks, or from causes which cannot be determined. The U-boat Arm came close to winning the Battle of the Atlantic during 1942 but was defeated by Allied skill, determination and improved weaponry, with the decryption of Enigma signals playing a major part in the conflict.

On 8 January 1944 the Coastal Command Development Unit reported that successful trials had been carried out at night with a Mark III Low Level Bombsight installed in a Wellington XII fitted with a Leigh Light. It was recommended that this bombsight should be fitted in the nose of all Leigh Light squadrons in replacement for the front gun, and that depth charges should in future be dropped by the searchlight operator instead of the pilot.

Ref: AIR 65/68

The Type VIIC *U-426* was built by Danzigerwerft and commissioned on 12 May 1943. It made its first war cruise in the North Atlantic and sank one merchant vessel. On 3 January 1944 it left Brest for another cruise under its commander, Kapitänleutnant Christian Reich, but five days later was spotted about 400 miles west of St-Nazaire by Sunderland III serial EK586 of 10 (RAAF) Squadron flown from Mount Batten in Devon by Flying Officer J.F. Roberts. Six depth charges were dropped, straddling the stern of the U-boat. The bows rose and some of the crew began to clamber out of the conning tower. They were left in the water after the U-boat sank, but there were no survivors from the crew of fifty-one.

Ref: AIR 27/153

```
     ADM(1)

       TO I D 8 G                                    ZIP/ZTPGU/21192

     FROM N S

       4412 KC/S              TOO 1950            TOI 2110/14/1/44
     FROM: KRUSCHKA

         RETURN PASSAGE OWING THE DROPPING OUT OF PERSONNEL AND

     MATERIAL DEFECTS AS A RESULT OF AIRCRAFT ATTACK. ORDINARY SEAMAN

     THOMAS KILLED, 6 MEN WOUNDED. SQUARE BE 55.

     0629/15/1/44++ EE/WAB+++
```

The Type VIIC *U-621* was repaired and carried out another war cruise, in the Bay of Biscay. It left Brest for a sixth war cruise on 6 January 1944, still under the command of Oberleutnant zur See Max Kruschka, but on 13 January was attacked by Liberator GR V serial FL990 flown from Ballykelly in Northern Ireland by Flying Officer Wes G. Loney of the RAAF. Ordinary Seaman Thomas was killed and six others wounded by depth charges and strafing attacks, as noted here. Kruschka decided to return to Brest, arriving on 23 January. The U-boat made another war cruise under him. Command was then taken over by Oberleutnant zur See Hermann Stockmann, who sank an American tank landing craft and a British infantry landing craft, as well as damaging a merchant vessel, after the initial D-Day landings. *U-621* finally met its end on 18 August 1944, when sailing from Brest to La Pallice, from depth charges fired from the destroyers HMCS *Ottawa*, *Kootenay* and *Chaudière*. There were no survivors from the crew of fifty-six.

Ref: DEFE 3/726

The Type VIIC *U-271* was built by Bremer Vulkan of Vegesack and commissioned on 23 September 1942. It completed two war cruises in the North Atlantic without sinking any vessels and in mid-1943 its flak armament was increased in order to combat Allied aircraft. On 12 January 1944 it left Brest for the North Atlantic, commanded by Kapitänleutnant Curt Barleben. On 28 January it was spotted by a PB4Y-1 Liberator of VPB-103 Squadron of the US Navy, flown by Lieutenant C.A. Enloe, when about 210 miles west of Blacksod Bay in the north-west of Eire. This American squadron was under the operational control of the RAF's No. 19 Group, and the aircraft was escorting convoy ON221. Enloe approached out of the sun and dropped a stick of depth charges, while his gunners exchanged fire with the U-boat. The depth charges straddled the target, which lost forward movement and began to sink, filling the surrounding water with air bubbles. It was lost with all fifty-one hands.

Ref: AIR 15/472

```
ADM(2)                                                    45

  TO: I D 8 G                    ZIP/ZTPGU/22038

  FROM: N S


  7700 KC/S        T O O 1144           T O I 1054/11/2/44


  TO: MANNESMANN, SIEDER, KRANKENHAGEN, SCHWEBKE

  THE FIRST BOAT TO ARRIVE IS TO TAKE OVER THE CREW AND

  THEN SINK U.545. REPORT EXECUTION IMMEDIATELY BY SHORT SIGNAL.

  BOATS ARE THEN TO SUBMERGE AND MOVE OFF ON A COURSE OF 250

  DEGREES. FURTHER ORDERS WILL FOLLOW. IF TWO BOATS ARRIVE

  SIMULTANEOUSLY, THEY ARE TO DIVIDE THE CREW BETWEEN THEM.


  0544/12/2/44+CEL/MH+
```

This order of 11 February 1944 was intended to effect the rescue of the crew of the Type IXC/40 U-boat *U-545*, commanded by Kapitänleutnant Gert Mannesmann. This U-boat was built by Deutschewerft of Hamburg and commissioned on 19 May 1943. It was on its first war cruise, having left Kiel on 9 December 1943 to operate in the North Altantic. It had already damaged one merchant vessel. However, in the evening of 10 February 1944 a Wellington VIII of 612 Squadron, flown by Pilot Officer Max H. Paynter of the RAAF from Limavady in Northern Ireland, had spotted the U-boat west of the Outer Hebrides and straddled it with a stick of depth charges. One man had been killed and the U-boat crippled.

Ref: DEFE 3/727

```
ADM (1)              DEFE 3/727                46

  TO: I D 8 G                    ZIP/ZTPGU/22039

  FRM : N S


  9350 KC/S          T O O 1152      T O I 1109/11/2/44


  FROM: SCHWEBCKE


  NAVAL GRID SQUARE AM 1527. AM TAKING OFF MANNESMANN'S CREW AND

  WILL THEN BEGIN RETURN PASSAGE.

  0443/12/2/44 CEL/JG
```

The Type VIIC *U-714*, commanded by Oberleutnant zur See Hans-Joachim Schwebcke, on its third war cruise, reached the stricken *U-545* later on 11 February 1944 and rescued all the remaining fifty-six members of the crew. It brought them to St-Nazaire four days later.

Ref: DEFE 3/727

On 14 February 1944 the Coastal Command Development Unit experimented with night photography on the submarine HMS *Umbra*. A Wellington XII fitted with a Leigh Light dropped three bakelite bombs from 40 feet, spaced at 80 feet, while a 'Sea Search' camera illuminated the target. The photograph was taken through a mirror by an American K24 camera with a 7 inch lens.

Ref: AIR 65/77

```
ADM (3)                                                          241

  TO I D 8 G                          ZIP/ZTPGU/22224

 FROM N S


 15650 KC/S          T O O 1110          TOI 1051/14/2/44

 TO:  EICK

     FROM 20/2 A JAPANESE SUBMARINE WILL OPERATE IN THE SAME

     OPERATIONAL AREA FOR ABOUT 40 DAYS. ATTACK ON ⓍX SUBMARINES

     IS FORBIDDEN UNLESS WITH ENEMY SEA OR AIR ESCORT

 ⓍⓍⓍⓍⓍⓍ
 1414/15/2/44+EE/AM
```

This signal was sent on 14 February 1944 to Kapitänleutnant Alfred Eick, the commander of the Type IXC *U-510*. This U-boat was built by Deutschewerft of Hamburg and commissioned on 25 November 1941. It made four war cruises in the Atlantic and then, on 3 November 1943, left Lorient to operate in the Indian Ocean. It was eventually based in Penang and then Jakarta. During its career it sank fourteen merchant vessels and damaged eight more. It returned to St-Nazaire on 23 April 1945 and surrendered at the end of the war.

Ref: DEFE 3/727

```
  ADM(2)                                                        411

    TO  I D 8 G                              Z IP/ZTPGU/22382

    FROM  N S

ALL  ATLANTIC U/B          TOO 0039/19          TOI 2359/18/2/44

    FREQUENCIES

     IN THE GULF OF GAETA ON 18/2 FENSKI SANK AN 'AURORA' CLASS

    CRUISER, COURSE NETTUNO.

     CC: PLS READ FREQ. AS ALL ATLANTIC ETC

    0515/19/2/44    EGT+++MPS+++
```

This signal was sent to all Atlantic U-boats following information received from the Type VIIC *U-410*, commanded by Oberleutnant zur See Horst-Arno Fenski. On 18 February 1944 it had sunk HMS *Penelope* in the Gulf of Gaeta in Italy. This was one of the cruiser escorts for supply vessels reaching the Anglo-American forces which on 22 January had begun landing on the beaches at Anzio. This U-boat had been built by Danzigerwerft and commissioned on 23 February 1943. It had completed three war cruises in the Atlantic and had then left Lorient on 26 April 1943 to operate from La Spezia and Toulon. During its career it sank seven merchant vessels and damaged another, in addition to HMS *Penelope* and an American Landing Ship (Tank). It was finally destroyed on 11 March 1944 during a bombing attack by the USAAF on the docks of Toulon, one crew member being killed.

Ref: DEFE 3/727

The Type VIIC *U-601* was built by Blohm & Voss and commissioned on 18 December 1941. It made ten war cruises in the Arctic region, during which it sank three Soviet merchant vessels. It left Hammerfest in Norway on 14 February 1944 for an eleventh war cruise, under the command of Kapitänleutnant Otto Hansen. It was attacked on 25 February 1944 about 250 miles west of North Cape by Catalina letter M of the RAF's 210 Squadron, flown from Sullom Voe in the Shetlands by Squadron Leader Frank J. French. The U-boat fired on the Catalina, which attacked towards its starboard quarter. The Catalina dropped two depth charges and then circled, seeing survivors in the water. Visibility was then lost in a snowstorm. All fifty-one men on board the U-boat lost their lives.

Ref: AIR 15/472

The Type VIIC *U-625* left Brest on 29 February 1944, commanded by Oberleutnant zur See Siegfried Straub, for another war cruise in the North Atlantic. On 10 March 1944, in combination with the Type VII *U-741*, it shot down Wellington XIV serial HF311 of 407 (RCAF) Squadron, flown by Pilot Officer E.M. O'Donnell from Chivenor in North Devon. Its luck ran out later the same day when it was picked up by Sunderland III serial EK591 of 422 (RCAF) Squadron from Castle Archdale in Northern Ireland, under the captaincy of Flight Lieutenant Sidney W. Butler. The U-boat was straddled with a stick of six depth charges. The Sunderland was hit in an exchange of gunfire but was able to continue operating. The U-boat crash-dived but resurfaced and signalled 'Fine bombish' to the Sunderland. It then sank for the last time. Some men were seen in dinghies but all fifty-three crew members lost their lives.

Ref: AIR 15/472

Survivors from the Type VIIC *U-625* sunk on 10 March 1944. They were about 380 miles west of Eire and none could be rescued.

Ref: AIR 15/472

```
ADM(1)                                                    18
   TO I D 8 G                          ZIP/ZTPGU/23014
   FROM N S

   3920 KC/S              TOO: 0628      TOI: 0609/13/3/44

   FROM: BRAUEL

      AT 2150/11/3 IN AL 8438 AN A/C WITH SEARCHLIGHT AND

      NAXOS LOAXXXX LOCATION, APPROACHING ATHWARTSHIPS AT LOW

      LEVEL, CRASHED 1500 METRES AWAY BEFORE FIRE WAS OPENED.

   1007/13/3/44+++CEL++DG
```

The Type VIIC *U-256* was built by Bremer Vulkan of Vegesack and commissioned on 18 December 1941. It left Kiel on 28 July 1942 for its first war cruise in the North Atlantic, commanded by Kapitänleutnant Odo Loewe, but on 24 August was depth-charged and damaged by the corvette HMS *Potentilla* and the destroyer HMS *Viscount*. Seven days later it was attacked and nearly sunk by two Whitleys, one of 502 Squadron flown from St Eval by Flying Officer Edward B. Brooks and the other of 51 Squadron flown from Chivenor by Flight Lieutenant E.O. Tandy. It reached Lorient so badly damaged that it was nearly scrapped but instead was converted into a 'flak trap boat'. On 11 March 1944, during its third war cruise under the command of Oberleutnant zur See Wilhelm Brauel, Wellington XIV serial HF311 of 407 (RCAF) Squadron flown from Limavady in Northern Ireland by Flying Officer E.M. O'Donnell crashed when making a night attack with a Leigh Light, as described here. There were no survivors. The U-boat surrendered at the end of the war.

Ref: DEFE 3/728

```
ADM(2)                                                    135
   TO I D 8 G                          ZIP/ZTPGU/23124
   FROM N S

   3804 KC/S              TOO 0306       TOI 0412/17/3/44

   FROM: BRANS

   FIRE FROM 2 FIGHTER BOMBERS AT 1930 IN NAVAL GRID SQUARE EH 3811.
   SLIGHT DAMAGE. 9 SEAMEN ARE CASUALTIES, 5 SERIOUSLY WOUNDED,
   COMMANDING OFFICER SLIGHTLY. AM GOING TO HERWARTZ. 195 CUBIC
   METRES.

   0938/17/3/44++ EE/WAB+++
```

The Type IXC/40 *U-801* was built by Seebeckwerft of Bremerhaven and commissioned on 24 March 1943. It made its first war cruise from Kiel on 6 November 1943 under the command of Kapitänleutnant Hans-Joachim Brans and returned to Lorient. It left this port on 26 February 1944, bound for the South Atlantic, but when 300 miles west of the Cape Verde Islands on 17 March was attacked by Avengers of VC-6 Squadron from the escort carrier USS *Block Island*, as shown here. The destroyers USS *Corry* and *Bronstein* then finished off the U-boat with depth charges. Ten men were killed, including Brans, but forty-seven were rescued to become prisoners.

Ref: DEFE 3/728

The Type VIIC *U-342* was built by Nordseewerke of Kiel and commissioned on 12 January 1943. It left Bergen for its first war cruise on 3 April 1944, under the command of Oberleutnant zur See Albert Hossenfelder, but when 330 miles south-south-west of Iceland fourteen days later was attacked by Canso 'S' 9767 of 162 (RCAF) Squadron flown from Reykjavik by Flying Officer Thomas C. Cooke. The U-boat and the Canso exchanged gunfire on the run-in and then three depth charges were dropped. One exploded close to the U-boat, which sank leaving wreckage. There were no survivors from the crew of fifty-one.

Ref: AIR 15/472

```
ADM(4)

TO I D 8  G                    ZIP/ZTPGU/24386                    410

FROM N S


10300 KC/S          T O O 1626        TOI: 1520/20/4/44


1)  HERWARTZ SANK NEBRASKA (8300 GRT.) IN NAVAL GRID SQUARE FL

    9171 ON 8/4 AND WAS ATTACKED BY AIRCRAFT IN NAVAL GRID

    SQUARE FT 1447 ON 10/4 AND WAS SEVERELY DEPTH-CHARGED.

2)  THE ATTENTION OF ALL BOATS IS ONCE AGAIN CALLED TO SERIAL ORDER

    NO 13, ACCORDING TO WHICH 'MONSUN' AND TRANSPORT BOATS ARE TO

    PROCEED SUBMERGED BY DAY AS FAR AS APPROXIMATELY 15 DEGREES

    SOUTH. THE ONLY EXCEPTION IS IN CASES OF ENEMY SIGHTINGS.

    SIMILARLT ON RETURN PASSAGE.

23332/20/4/44+EE++PG
```

The Type IXC/40 *U-843* was built by A.G. Weser of Bremen and commissioned on 24 March 1943. After its first war cruise, under the command of Kapitänleutnant Oscar Herwartz, it was sent from Lorient on 19 February 1944 to operate in the Indian Ocean and as a blockade runner from the Far East. On 8 April it sank the British steamship SS *Nebraska* of 8,261 tons in the South Atlantic, as shown here. Its end came on 9 April 1945 when returning from Batavia with materials for the German war industry. It was nearing the Kattegat when it was sunk by rockets fired from Mosquito A of 235 Squadron flown from Banff in Banffshire by Flying Officer A.J. Randall. Twelve men were rescued but forty-four were killed, including Herwartz.

Ref: DEFE 3/729

During a convoy to Russia on 2 May 1944 two Swordfish biplanes of the Fleet Air Arm's 842 Squadron operated from the escort carrier HMS *Fencer* and sank two U-boats. One of these was the Type VIIC *U-674*, built by Howaldtswerke of Hamburg and commissioned on 15 June 1943; this had left Narvik on 17 April 1944 on its third war cruise, commanded by Oberleutnant zur See Harald Muhs. The other was the type VIIC *U-959*, built by Blohm & Voss of Hamburg and commissioned on 21 January 1943; this had left Narvik on 22 April 1944 on its second war cruise, commanded by Oberleutnant zur See Martin Duppel.

The operations took place about 360 miles west of the Lofoten Islands. One U-boat was attacked in the early morning with rocket projectiles and the other in the afternoon with a stick of three depth charges, as shown in these photographs. All forty-nine crew members were lost in *U-674* and all fifty-three in *U-959*.

Ref: ADM 199/206

```
ADM 2                                                          893

   TO  I  D  8  G                      Z IP/ZTPGU/24841

   FROM N S

   13570 KC/S

                    0818/2/5/44 B' LZM


   AM BEING ATTACKED BY AN A/C IN SQUARE MP 97

              BQO (U 852)
```

The Type IXD2 *U-852* was built by A.G. Weser of Bremen and commissioned on 15 June 1943. It left Kiel on 18 January 1944 to operate in the Indian Ocean under the command of Kapitänleutnant Heinz-Wilhelm Eck. It sank two merchant vessels, one of which was the Greek SS *Peleus* of 4,695 tons. Eck ordered his men to machine-gun and throw hand grenades at the survivors, but three of these lived to tell the tale. From 1 to 3 May 1944, when patrolling the approaches to the Red Sea, *U-852* was attacked by five Wellington XIIIs of 621 Squadron and one of 8 Squadron, all based at Khormaksar in Aden but operating from various airfields. Seven Germans were killed in these attacks and the U-boat was so badly damaged that Eck was forced to beach it on the coast of Somalia near Cape Garafui and blow it up. Fifty-nine survivors were taken prisoner. After the war Eck and two of his crew were convicted of their crimes and executed.

Ref: DEFE 3/729

The Type IXD2 *U-852* beached on the coast of Somalia near Cape Garafui after the attacks by Wellingtons of 8 and 621 Squadrons between 1 and 3 May 1944.

Ref: ADM 199/2061

```
ADM(2)                                                          918

TO  I D 8 G                              ZIP/ZTPGU/24857

FROM N S

4412 KC/S

              0407/3/5/44  B' MMZ

     AM BEING ATTACKED BY AIRCRAFT IN SQUARE BF 8111.

                              REXXXXX RCD (U. 846)
```

The Type IXC/40 *U-846* was built by A.G. Weser of Bremen and commissioned on 29 May 1943. It made its first war cruise in the North Atlantic under the command of Oberleutnant der Reserve Berthold Hashagen and arrived at Lorient on 3 March 1944. It left Lorient for a second cruise on 29 April 1944. On 2 May 1944 it shot down a Halifax of 58 Squadron, flown from St Davids in Pembrokeshire by Flight Lieutenant D.E. Taylor. The end came two days later during the early morning when it was north of Cape Ortegal in Spain. The attacking aircraft was Wellington XIV serial HF134 of 407 (RCAF) Squadron, flown from Limavady in Northern Ireland by Flight Lieutenant L.J. Bateman. Although the Wellington was equipped with a Leigh Light, this was not switched on since the U-boat was clearly visible in the moonlight. Six depth charges were dropped and *U-846* sank with all fifty-seven hands.

Ref: DEFE 3/729

```
ADM(1)                                                        1018

TO  I D 8 G.                            ZIP/ZTPGU/24940

FROM N S

4790 KC/S

              0621/6/5/44  B' CAE

     AM BEING ATTACKED BY SURFACE FORCES' IN SQUARE EH 2546.

                        QWI  (U 66)
```

After the damage received on 4 August 1943 was repaired, the Type IXC *U-66* left Lorient on 16 January 1944 for its tenth war cruise, under the command of Kapitänleutnant Gerhard Seehausen, to operate off West Africa. It sank four more merchant vessels, but when on its return journey and west of the Cape Verde Islands on 6 May 1944 it was attacked by Avenger and Wildcat aircraft of VC-55 Squadron from the escort carrier USS *Block Island,* as reported in this signal. One of the Avengers, flown by Lieutenant (junior grade) J.J. Sellars, caused such damage that the U-boat was unable to dive. It was then rammed by the destroyer USS *Buckley* and also boarded before sinking. Twenty-four of the crew were killed, including Seehausen, but thirty-six were rescued to become prisoners.

Ref: DEFE 3/729

```
    ADM (2)                                                        994

    TO:  I D 8 G                        Z IP/ZTPGU/24919

    FROM: N S

    3800 KC/S

               T O O 0225/6/5/44  B' NPD

    AM BEING ATTACKED BY AN A/C, SQUARE AK 9377.

                    JZM (U.765)
```

The Type VIIC *U-765* was built by Kriegsmarinewerft of Wilhelmshaven and commissioned on 19 June 1943. It left Bergen on 3 April 1944 for its first war cruise in the North Atlantic under the command of Oberleutnant der Reserve Werner Wendt. Exactly a month later it sank the destroyer escort USS *Donnell*. However, its end came on 6 May 1944 when it was located by Swordfish of 825 Squadron, Fleet Air Arm, from the escort carrier HMS *Vindex*, resulting in this signal. After submerging, it was forced to the surface by the frigates HMS *Aylmer*, *Bickerton* and *Bligh*, and finally destroyed. Eleven men were rescued but thirty-seven were lost, including Wendt.

Ref: DEFE 7/72

```
      ADM (2)

        TO:  I D 8 G                     Z IP/ZTPGU/25319      353

      FROM: N S


      6265 KC/S              TOO 0821         TOI 0717/19/5/44

      FROM: B.D.U. OPS
      TO:   3RD U/B FLOTILLA
      SECRET 4040 A5

          PREVIOUS REF. 2ND NAVAL WAR STAFF, B.D.U. OPS SECRET 8645 A 5

          OF 22/8/43.

          U 572 (KUMMETAT) IS REPORTED MISSING, 2 STARS, WITH EFFECT

          FROM 6/8/43.  NO FRESH NEWS.   MUST BE PRESUMED A TOTAL LOSS.

      1156/19/5/44+++++EGT/SMH
```

The Type VIIC *U-572* was built by Blohm & Voss of Hamburg and commissioned on 29 May 1941. It made eight war cruises, in the North Atlantic and off West Africa, during which it sank six merchant vessels and damaged another. Its final cruise came when it left La Pallice on 2 June 1943 under the command of Oberleutnant zur See Heinz Kummetat, bound for the Caribbean. After sinking a small merchant vessel, it was bombed on 3 August 1943 when about 420 miles east of Trinidad by a Mariner P-6 of VP-205 Squadron, flown by Lieutenant (junior grade) C.C. Cox. The U-boat was sunk with all forty-seven crew members, but the Mariner did not return. The loss of *U-572* was not reported until this signal of 19 May 1944.

Ref: DEFE 3/730

```
ADM (1)                                                    570
TO: I D 8 G                    ZIP/ ZTPGU/25512
FROM: N S

3795 KC/S

              0001/25/5/44 B'OOD

((AM BEING ATTACKED BY A/C )),SQUARE BF 5459.

      HMX (U736)

2205/25/5/44  AGT/MU
```

The Type VIIC *U-736* was built by Schichau of Danzig and commissioned on 16 January 1943. It left Bergen on 1 April 1944 for its first war cruise in the North Atlantic under the command of Oberleutnant der Reserve Reinhard Reff. On its return passage through the Bay of Biscay it may have been attacked during the night of 24/25 May by a Wellington of 612 Squadron flown by a Canadian, Flying Officer K.H. Davies. This Wellington did not return to its base at Chivenor in North Devon. However, the U-boat was certainly attacked after midnight by a Leigh Light Liberator of 224 Squadron from St Eval in Cornwall, which dropped depth charges and caused considerable damage. The U-boat managed to reach Brest and underwent repairs. It did not leave until 5 August and on the following day, near Belle Ile, was sunk by the sloop HMS *Starling* and the frigate HMS *Loch Killin*. Twenty-eight crew members were killed but nineteen were rescued, including the commander.

Ref: DEFE 3/730

One of the escort carriers which accompanied convoys across the Atlantic and to Russia, HMS *Biter*, photographed from a Swordfish that had just taken off. Two Wildcat fighters are on the flight deck.

Ref: ADM 199/2061

```
ADM (3)

TO I D 8 G                              ZIP/ZTPGU/25879        987
FROM N S


5580 KC/S        T O O 2319/6/0025/0111/7
                 T O I 2218/2319/6/0020/7/6/44

TO: ALL COMMANDING OFFICERS AT SEA

THE ENEMY HAS BEGUN THE INVASION OF EUROPE AND THE WAR HAS

THEREBY ENTERED ITS DECISIVE PHASE.  A SUCCESSFUL LANDING

BY THE ANGLO-AMERICANS WOULD MEAN FOR US THE LOSS OF LARGE

AREAS VITAL TO OUR WAR ECONOMY AND WOULD ALSO BE AN IMMEDIATE

THREAT TO OUR MOST IMPORTANT INDUSTRIAL AREAS, WITHOUT WHICH THE

WAR COULD NOT BE CONTINUED.  THE ENEMY IS AT HIS WEAKEST AT THE

MOMENT OF THE LANDING ITSELF.  IN THIS EARLY STAGE EVERYTHING MUST

BE CONCENTRATED ON DRIVING HIM BACK AND INFLICTING LOSSES WHICH

WILL FINALLY ROB HIM OF ALL DESIRE TO ATTEMPT FURTHER LANDINGS.

ONLY THEN WILL IT BE POSSIBLE TO DIVERT TO THE EASTERN FRONT THE

FORCES WHICH ARE AT PRESENT LACKING THERE.

END OF PAGE ONE
```

```
ADM (3)                    PAGE TWO         ZIP/ZTPGU/25879      988
?======                    ========         =================

U-BOAT MEN:

UPON YOU ALSO DEPENDS NOW, MORE THAN AT ANY OTHER TIME, THE FUTURE

OF OUR GERMAN PEOPLE.  I THEREFORE DEMAND FROM YOU ALL-OUT OPERATION

WITHOUT ANY THOUGHT TO THE PRECAUTIONARY MEASURES WHICH WOULD

OTHERWISE OBTAIN.  EVERY ENEMY VESSEL CONCERNED IN THE LANDING IS

TO BE ATTACKED UNDER FULL OPERATION EVEN AT THE RISK OF LOSING YOUR

OWN BOAT.  EVERY MAN AND EVERY WEAPON DESTROYED BEFORE THE LANDING,

DECREASES THE ENEMY'S PROSPECTS OF SUCCESS.  FOR THIS I KNOW THAT

I CAN RELY ON YOU, MY U-BOAT MEN, WHO HAVE PROVED YOUR WORTH IN

THE BITTEREST BATTLES.

                    YOUR C. IN C. OF THE NAVY AND B.D.U.
```

The exhortation from Grossadmiral Karl Dönitz to all those serving in the Kriegsmarine. It was issued on 7 June 1944, the day after D-Day.

Ref: DEFE 3/730

```
ADM (2)                                                    996

TO:  I D 8 G                    Z IP/ZTPGU/25887

FROM:  N S

3920 KC/S

              ((0732))/7/6/44 B'LXK

AM BEING ATTACKED BY AN AIRCRAFT IN SQUARE BF 9132.

IWS (U 212)

0833/7/6/44 EE/ES+
```

The Type VIIC *U-212* was built by Germaniawerft of Kiel and commissioned on 25 April 1942. It made ten war cruises under the command of Kapitänleutnant Helmut Vogler, nine of which were from Narvik in the Arctic Ocean and the other from La Pallice, but sank no vessels. It then left La Pallice on D-Day 6 June 1944 for the North Atlantic, but on the following day was attacked in the Bay of Biscay by two Mosquito XVIIIs (Tsetses) of 248 Squadron from Portreath in Cornwall. These were serial MM425 flown by Flying Officer Douglas J. Turner and serial NT225 flown by a Canadian, Flying Officer A.J.L. Bonnett. The U-boat was hit and damaged by several of the 6-pounder shells fired by the 57mm Molin guns with which the Tsetses were equipped, resulting in this signal.

Ref: DEFE 3/730

```
ADM(2)                                                    1054

TO I D 8 G                     Z IP/ZTPGU/25937

FROM N S

3920 KC/S          TOO 2223        TOI 2050/7/6/44

FROM: VOGLER

AS A RESULT OF FIRE FROM AIRCRAFT ARMAMENT FUEL TANK ('BUNKER')

4 PORT AND REGULATING FUEL TANK PORT HIT. PORT MAIN EXHAUST

BLOWING VALVE CANNOT BE OPENED. ((ONLY)) POSSIBLE TO

'SCHNORCHEL' WITH STARBOARD DIESEL. AM IN SQUARE B F 9122.

0746/8/6/44        EE+++MPS+++
```

The Type VIIC *U-212* suffered such severe damage that it sent this signal later on the same day, 7 June 1944. Nevertheless, it managed to limp back to La Pallice, where it arrived two days later to begin undergoing repairs. Its end came on 21 July 1944 after depth-charging by the frigates HMS *Curzon* and *Ekins,* when south-west of Beachy Head. It was sunk with the loss of all forty-nine hands.

Ref: DEFE 3/730

```
ADM (2)                                              996
TO:  I D 8 G                    Z IP/ZTPGU/25887
FROM:  N S

3920 KC/S

         ((0732))/7/6/44 B'LXK

AM BEING ATTACKED BY AN AIRCRAFT IN SQUARE BF 9132.

IWS (U 212)

0833/7/6/44 EE/ES+
```

The Type VIIC *U-413* was built by Danzigerwerft of Danzig and commissioned on 3 June 1942. It made six war cruises, mostly in the North Atlantic, during which it sank three merchant vessels and the destroyer HMS *Warwick*. It then left Brest on 6 June 1944 under the command of Oberleutnant zur See Dietrich Sachse but in the approaches to the English Channel in the early moonlit hours of 8 June was located by a Halifax of 502 Squadron flown from Brawdy in Pembrokeshire by Flying Officer J. Spurgeon. Four bombs were dropped, causing damage, but the Halifax was also hit and forced to turn back; it landed at Predannack in Cornwall. The U-boat managed to reach Brest and underwent repairs. It left again on 2 August and sank another merchant vessel on 18 August, but was sunk itself on the following day when south-south-west of Beachy Head by the destroyers HMS *Forester*, *Vidette* and *Wensleydale*. There were no survivors from the crew of forty-five.

Ref: DEFE 3/730

```
ADM(2)                                              1054
TO I D 8 G                     Z IP/ZTPGU/25937
FROM N S

3920 KC/S           TOO 2223        TOI 2050/7/6/44

FROM: VOGLER

AS A RESULT OF FIRE FROM AIRCRAFT ARMAMENT FUEL TANK ('BUNKER')

4 PORT AND REGULATING FUEL TANK PORT HIT. PORT MAIN EXHAUST

BLOWING VALVE CANNOT BE OPENED. ((ONLY)) POSSIBLE TO

'SCHNORCHEL' WITH STARBOARD DIESEL. AM IN SQUARE B F 9122.

0746/8/6/44      EE+++MPS+++
```

The Type VIIC *U-821* was built by Oderwerke of Stettin and commissioned on 11 October 1943. It left Bergen on 19 March 1944 for its first war cruise in the North Atlantic, commanded by Oberleutnant zur See Ulrich Knackfuss, and then arrived in Brest without having sunk any vessels. It was one of the U-boats ordered to attack the western flank of the Allied invasion fleet, and left Brest on 6 June 1944. At midday on 10 June it was spotted west of Ushant by four Mosquito FB VIs of 248 Squadron from Portreath in Cornwall, led by Flight Lieutenant Stanley G. Nunn, which attacked until their ammunition was exhausted. The attack was then taken up by Liberator GR VI serial EV943 of 206 Squadron, flown from St Eval in Cornwall by Lieutenant Alexander D.S. Dundas, which dropped two sticks of depth charges. The U-boat sank, leaving an oil slick and survivors in the water. Some of the latter were picked up by a German motor launch, but this was in combat with six other Mosquitos of 248 Squadron later in the afternoon. Only one German sailor survived this encounter.

Ref: AIR 15/472

```
ADM (2)                                                    996

  TO:  I D 8 G                    Z IP/ZTPGU/25887

  FROM:  N S

  3920 KC/S

              ((0732))/7/6/44 B'LXK

  AM BEING ATTACKED BY AN AIRCRAFT IN SQUARE BF 9132.

  IWS (U 212)

  0833/7/6/44 EE/ES+
```

This signal was sent on 11 June 1944 by Kapitänleutnant Peter-Erich Cremer, the commander of the Type VIIC *U-333*, after being attacked in the early morning by a Sunderland of 10 (RAAF) Squadron flown from Mount Batten in Devon by Flight Lieutenant H.A. McGregor. It survived this attack but then another took place, in the late evening of the same day, by Sunderland III serial ML880 of 228 Squadron flown from Pembroke Dock by Flight Lieutenant M.E. Slaughter of the RCAF. *U-333* managed to shoot this flying boat down into the the sea. The U-boat had left La Pallice on 6 June 1944 for the approaches to the English Channel, and returned damaged to this port the day after these attacks. After repair, it left La Pallice on 23 July 1944, commanded by Kapitänleutnant Hans Feidler and bound once more for the English Channel. The end came on 31 July 1944, when about 50 miles west-south-west of the Scillies. It was depth-charged by the sloop HMS *Starling* and the frigate HMS *Loch Killin*, and went down with all forty-five crew members.

Ref: DEFE 3/731

Survivors from the Type VIIC *U-715* about 100 miles east-south-east of the Faroes, photographed on 14 June 1944 by Sunderland III serial DV992 of 330 (Norwegian) Squadron flown by Lieutenant Devold from Sullom Voe in the Shetlands. This U-boat had been built by Stülcken Sohn of Hamburg and commissioned on 17 March 1943. It left Stavanger on 8 June 1944 on its first war cruise, bound for the North Atlantic under the command of Kapitänleutnant Helmut Röttger, but was attacked on 13 June by Canso serial 9816 of 162 (RCAF) Squadron flown from Wick in Caithness by Wing Commander St G.W. Chapman. The U-boat was sunk but the Canso was hit by flak and ditched on the way back to base. A lifeboat and Lindholme dinghies were dropped to the RCAF crew by Warwicks but three men died before the remaining five were picked up by an air-sea rescue launch. Sixteen men from the U-boat were also rescued but thirty-six lost their lives, including the commander.

Ref: AIR 15/472

```
ADM (3)                                                     599

TO I D 8 G                              ZIP/ZTPGU/26528

FROM N S

5425 KC/S              TOO: 2120        TOI: 1927/16/6/44

MOST IMMEDIATE

  FIEDLER IS SINKING IN NAVAL GRID SQUARE AF 8787

  AFTER AIR ATTACK.  BOATS WITHIN A 60- MILE RADIUS

  ARE TO GO TO HIS ASSISTANCE.

2317/16/6/44++AGT++DG
```

The Type VIIC/41 *U-998* was built by Blohm & Voss of Hamburg and commissioned on 7 October 1943. It left Kiel on 12 June 1944 for its first war cruise, headed for the Arctic under the command of Kapitänleutnant Hans Fiedler, but was attacked four days later, when about 75 miles north-west of Bergen, by Mosquito VI serial HP864 of 333 (Norwegian) Squadron flown from Leuchars in Fife by Lieutenant E.U. Johanssen. The U-boat did not sink, as this signal suggests, and managed to reach Bergen on the following day. However, it was so badly damaged that it had to be withdrawn from service.

Ref: DEFE 3/731

```
ADM (1)                                                    671

TO: I D 8 G                            ZIP/ZTPGU/26594

FROM: N S

3920 KC/S

              TOO: 0050/18/6/44 B'NLT

  AM BEING ATTACKED BY AN A/C. SQUARE BF 2448.

        CLC (U.988)

  0201/18/6/44        CEL/JG
```

The Type VIIC *U-988* was built by Blohm & Voss of Hamburg and commissioned on 15 July 1943. It left Marviken on 22 May 1944 for its first war cruise, under the command of Oberleutnant zur See Erich Dobberstein, and headed for the English Channel, but in the early hours of 18 June was sunk with all fifty hands about 40 miles north of Ushant. It is believed that this U-boat may have been attacked by Wellington XIV serial HF331 of 304 (Polish) Squadron, flown from Chivenor in North Devon by Flight Lieutenant L. Antoniewicz.

Ref: DEFE 3/731

```
TO: I D 8 G                    ZIP/ZTPGU/26636

FROM: N S
                                                        717
4420 KC/S

        TOO: 0005/19/6/44 B'PND


AM BEING ATTACKED BY AN A/C, SQUARE AL 9392.

     EFZ (U.971)
```

The Type VIIC *U-971* was built by Blohm & Voss of Hamburg and commissioned on 1 April 1943. It left Marviken on 8 June 1944 for its first war cruise, under the command of Oberleutnant zur See Walter Zepplien, and headed for the English Channel. At 2235 hours on 19 June it was spotted west of Eire by Wellington XIV serial HF286 of 407 (RCAF) Squadron, equipped with a Leigh Light and flown from Chivenor in North Devon by Flying Officer F.H. Foster. The U-boat was damaged but sent this signal and continued its journey. However, on 24 June it was further damaged by a Liberator V of 311 (Czech) Squadron flown from Predannack in Cornwall by Flying Officer Jan Vella. It then received more attacks with depth charges by the destroyers HMS *Eskimo* and *Haida*. It came to the surface and was scuttled. One man was killed but fifty-two of the crew were picked up by the destroyers.

Ref: DEFE 3/731

```
ADM (2)

  TO I D 8   G            ZIP/ZTPGU/26663

  FROM N S

  8842 KC/S         T O O 0407/20/6/44 B'KSD

  AM BEGINNING RETURN PASSAGE. HAVE SUKXXSUKX SUFFERED

  SEVERE KXSUKX CASUALTIES. SQUARE BE 7413.


        IYO (U.853)

  0503/20/6/44 CEL/MW
```

The Type IXC/40 *U-853* was built by A.G. Weser of Bremen and commissioned on 25 June 1943. It left Bergen on 29 April 1944 for the North Atlantic, under the command of Kapitänleutnant Helmut Sommer, and survived attacks on 25 May by Swordfish from the carriers HMS *Ancylus* and *MacKendrick*. More attacks followed on 17 June by aircraft from the carrier USS *Croatan*, as recorded in this signal, but it managed to reach Lorient on 4 July. After returning to Norway, it left Stavanger on 23 February 1945, under the command of Oberleutnant zur See Helmut Frömsdorf, and sank two merchant vessels. It was sunk on 6 May 1945 by the destroyers USS *Atherton* and *Ericsson*, together with the frigate USS *Moberly*, with the loss of all fifty-five crew members.

Ref: DEFE 3/731

This U-boat was attacked north-east of the Shetlands on 20 June 1944 by Liberator III serial FK231 of 86 Squadron, flown from Tain in Ross-shire by Flying Officer E.D. Moffit of the RAAF. Three attacks were made and eight depth charges were dropped, while gunfire was exchanged. It was the Type VIIC *U-743*, built by Schichau of Danzig and commissioned on 15 May 1943. It had left Kiel on 15 June 1944 for its first patrol, under the command of Oberleutnant zur See Helmut Kandizor, and was so badly damaged that it had to put into Bergen. After repair, it left on 21 August but was sunk on 9 September by the frigate HMS *Helmsdale* and the corvette HMS *Portchester Castle*, with the loss of all fifty crew members.

Ref: AIR 15/472

The Type VIIC/41 *U-317* was built by Flenderwerft of Lübeck and commissioned on 23 October 1943. It left Egersund on 21 June 1944 for its first patrol, under the command of Oberleutnant der Reserve Peter Rahlff. North-east of the Shetlands on 26 June it was attacked by Liberator III serial FL916 of 86 Squadron, flown from Tain in Ross-shire by Flight Lieutenant Geoffrey W.T. Parker. Two sticks of depth charges were dropped on separate attacks and on the second occasion the U-boat rolled over and sank. Men were seen in the water but there were no survivors. The Liberator was hit by return fire but Parker managed to land safely at Stornaway in the Hebrides.

Ref: AIR 15/472

```
ADM(2)                                                          326
TO ID8G                              ZIP/ZTPGU/27273
FROM NS
7770 KC/S       TO.O. 2059/30/6/44   B'FRV
AM BEING ATTACKED BY AN A/C SQUARE AF 4872
PDO (U. 478)
2222/30/6/44     CEL/IH
```

The Type VIIC *U-478* was built by Deutschewerke of Kiel and commissioned on 8 September 1943. It left Kiel on 25 June 1944, bound for the North Atlantic on its first war cruise, under the command of Oberleutnant zur See Rudolf Rademacher. Five days later it was attacked off Norway by a Canso of 162 (RCAF) Squadron flown by Flight Lieutenant R.E. McBride, based at Wick in Caithness. This guided in a Liberator III of 86 Squadron flown by Flying Officer N.E.M. Smith from Tain in Ross-shire. The U-boat was sunk with all fifty-one hands.

Ref: DEFE 3/732

After its entry into RAF service in March 1941, the Consolidated Catalina eventually equipped twenty-four RAF and Commonwealth squadrons. It served in such areas as the Indian Ocean as well as the Atlantic.

Two captains of Catalinas were awarded the Victoria Cross, the first of which was posthumous. On 24 June 1944 Flying Officer David E. Hornell of 162 (RCAF) Squadron flew from Wick and attacked the Type IXC/40 *U-1225* commanded by Oberleutnant zur See Ernst Sauerburg north-west of Bergen, and sank it with all hands. But the aircraft was hit and ditched. The crew got into two dinghies but it was almost a day before they were rescued by a high-speed launch and Hornell died of exposure.

On 17 July 1944 Flying Officer John A. Cruickshank of 210 Squadron at Sullom Voe made two attacks on the Type VIIC/41 *U-347* commanded by Oberleutnant der Reserve Johann de Buhr, when west of the Lofoten Islands, and sank it with all hands. The Catalina was hit during the second attack: the navigator was killed and Cruickshank was one of three wounded. However, he managed to continue the second attack and then, together with the co-pilot Flight Sergeant John Garnett, nursed the machine on a very lengthy flight back to base.

Author's collection

The Type VIIC *U-243* was built by Germaniawerft of Kiel and commissioned on 2 October 1943. It left Bergen on 15 June 1944 under the command of Kapitänleutnant Hans Märtens, heading for the coast of France and then the English Channel, to attack the western flank of the Allied invasion force. In the early afternoon of 8 July it was spotted west of St-Nazaire by Sunderland III serial W4030 of 10 (RAAF) Squadron, flown from Mount Batten in Devon by Flying Officer W.B. Tilley. Six depth charges were dropped and there was an exchange of fire with machine-guns. The U-boat was obviously in difficulties when Sunderland III serial JM684 of 10 (RAAF) Squadron arrived, flown by Flight Lieutenant R.E. Cargeeg, as well as a Liberator of VP-105 Squadron, USAAF. Both these dropped depth charges, but they fell short. The U-boat sank from the first attack, together with ten of the crew, but thirty-nine men were rescued by the destroyer HMCS *Restigouche*. Among the latter was Märtens but he died of his wounds.

Ref: AIR 37/1231

```
ADM (3)                                                    138
TO: I D 8 G                          ZIP/ZTPGU/28109
FROM: N S

403 KC/S
                  2149/17/7/44   B' PDU

    AM BEING ATTACKED BY AN A/C IN SQUARE AB 8750.

                                        WQO (U 361)
0052/18/7/44+++AGT/SMH
```

The Type VIIC *U-361* was built by Flensburger Schiffbau and commissioned on 18 December 1942. Under the command of Kapitänleutnant Hans Seidel, it made two war cruises in the Arctic and then left Narvik for a third on 27 June 1944. When nearing Narvik on its return, it was attacked on 17 July by Liberator serial FK233 of 86 Squadron flown from Tain in Ross-shire by Pilot Officer Michael G. Moseley. The Liberator came under fire and was hit, but six depth charges were dropped. The U-boat managed to get off this signal before it sank with the loss of all fifty-two hands.

Ref: DEFE 3/733

```
ADM (3)                                                    137
TO: I D 8 G                          ZIP/ZTPGU/28108
FROM: N S

5665 KC/S
                  1638/17/7/44   B' HGQ

    AM BEING ATTACKED BY AN A/C IN SQUARE AN 2481.

                                        IMW (U 994)
0054/18/7/44+++AGT/SMH
```

The Type VIIC *U-994* was built by Blohm & Voss of Hamburg and commissioned on 2 September 1943. It left Kiel on 22 June 1944 for its first patrol, under the command of Oberleutnant der Reserve Volker Melzer. Off southern Norway on 17 July it was attacked by Mosquito VI serial HF710 of 333 (Norwegian) Squadron flown from Sumburgh in the Shetlands by Lieutenant R. Leitle. The pilot opened fire with his four cannon and four machine-guns before dropping two depth charges. The U-boat was damaged and five crew members were wounded, but it managed to reach Bergen on the same day. After repair it made one more cruise in the Arctic, and then surrendered at Trondheim in May 1945.

Ref: DEFE 3/733

```
    ADM (2)
                                                                       171
    TO  I D 8 G                        Z IP/ZTPGU/28139
    FROM N S

    5665 KC/S              TOO: 1204        TOI: 1214/18/7/44

    FROM: DIETRICH'S U/BOAT

      DROVE OFF A STIRLING IN SQUARE AN 3528.  ONE DEAD, THREE

      SERIOUSLY AND FOUR SLIGHTLY WOUNDED.  BOAT WAS ATTACKED WITH

      2 BOMBS.    AM PUTTING INTO KRISTIANSAND WITH ESCORT.

    CC 4TH AND 5TH GRPS 'STIRLING IN'

    1854/18/7/44++++CEL++DG
```

The Type VIIC *U-286* was built by Bremer Vulkan of Vegesack and commissioned on 5 June 1943. It left Flekkefj on 5 July 1944 for its first war cruise in the Arctic, under the command of Oberleutnant zur See Willi Dietrich. On 18 July when near Egeroy it was attacked, not by a Stirling but by Mosquito VI serial HP858 of 333 (Norwegian) Squadron flown from Sumburgh in the Shetlands by Flight Sergeant W.D. Livock, resulting in these casualties. The U-boat reached Kristiansand South on the following day. It then made two more war cruises in the Arctic, sinking two Soviet vessels but was sunk on its fourth war cruise. The sinking was believed to have occurred on 29 April 1945 off the Kola inlet by the frigates HMS *Anguilla, Cotton* and *Loch Shin*. It was lost with all fifty-one hands.

Ref: DEFE 3/733

```
    ADM  2                                                             188
    TO  I D 8 G                            Z IP/ZTPGU:28155
    FROM N S

    4245 KC/S            T O O 2213        T O I 2044/18/7/44

    FROM: WESTPHALEN

    HAVE SHOT DOWN A LIBERATOR IN SQUARE AB 8959, 7 DEPTH-

    CHARGES, NO DAMAGE, RUN- IN FROM 180 DEGREES.

    0023/19/7/44/EE/.MS++++
```

The Type VIIC *U-968* was built by Blohm & Voss of Hamburg and commissioned on 18 March 1943. It made a war cruise in the Arctic, under the command of Oberleutnant zur See Otto Westphalen, and then left Narvik on 17 July 1944 for another. On the following day it was spotted by Liberator III serial FL930 of 86 Squadron flown by Flight Lieutenant W.F.J. Harwood from Tain in Ross-shire, which made two attacks under fire and dropped eight depth charges. Despite this report, the Liberator was not hit and returned safely, but the U-boat was damaged and forced to return. It made five more war cruises in the Arctic, sinking four vessels and damaging three others, before surrendering at Trondheim on 16 May 1945.

Ref: DEFE 3/732

```
(5)                                                         319
   TO: I D 8 G                    ZIP/ ZTPGU/28270
   FROM: N S

   7905 KC/S           T O O 1444        T O I 1452/20/7/44

   FROM: DUNKELBERG

   TO:   KRK  CAPTAIN (U/B) NORWAY


   7 DEPTH CHARGES FROM A LIBERATOR AT 1920 IN AB 8436. DAMAGED.

   VRETURN PASSAGE TO ANDFJORD. AM IN AB 8523.


   CC FIRST WORD LAST LINE TO READ    RETURN


   2236/20/7/44 CEL/MU
```

The Type VIIC *U-716* was built by Stülcken Sohn of Hamburg and commissioned on 15 April 1943. It made four war cruises in the Arctic under the command of Oberleutnant zur See Hans Dunkelberg and then left Bergen on 14 June 1944 for a fifth cruise. On 19 July it was attacked by Liberator V serial FL985 of 59 Squadron flown from Tain in Ross-shire by Flying Officer R.C. Penning, as shown by this signal, and forced to return to Bergen in a damaged state. The Liberator dropped eight depth charges in two attacks in the evening of 19 July, according to RAF records, although this signal is dated 20 July. (See also p. 235.)

Ref: DEFE 3/733

```
ADM  4                                                     540
   TO I D 8 G                    ZIP/ZTPCU:28470
   FROM N S

   4245 KC/S           T O O 1333        T O I 1217/23/7/44

   FROM: UNVERZAGT

   REQUEST AMBULANCE FOR 2 WOUNDED. AM PROCEEDING

   THROUGH THE SKERRIES, SPEED 16 KNOTS.

   2002/23/7/44/CEL/MS+++
```

The Type VIIC *U-965* was built by Blohm & Voss of Hamburg and commissioned on 25 February 1943. It made a war cruise to the Arctic under the command of Kapitänleutnant Klaus Ohling and then, on 23 June 1944, left Bogenbucht for another under the command of Oberleutant zur See Günther Unverzagt. On 22 July, when nearing port on its return, it was attacked by an aircraft which has not been identified, resulting in two wounded, one of whom died. It reached Narvik on the day this signal was sent. The U-boat made four more war cruises in the Arctic but was sunk by the frigate HMS *Conn* on its fifth, when near Cape Wrath on 27 March 1945, and lost with all fifty-one crew members.

Ref: DEFE 3/733

```
    ADM  (3)                                                    736
    TO: I D 8 G                    ZIP/ZTPGU/28644
    FROM: N S


    7885 KC/S        TOO : 2353        TOI : 2233/27/7/44

        FROM: STELLMACHER

        TO:   13TH U/B FLOTILLA

        LOW LEVEL ATTACK BY LIBERATOR, 6 BOMBS.

        SLIGHT DAMAGE CAUSED BY A/C ARMAMENT.

        SHALL BE AT HALTEN AT 0200. REQUEST ESCORT.
```

The Type IXC/40 *U-865* was built by A.G. Weser of Bremen and commissioned on 25 October 1943. It left Kiel on 20 June 1944 for its first war cruise, under the command of Oberleutnant der Reserve Dietrich Stellmacher, but was forced to put into Trondheim on 5 July with defects. It was fitted with a Schnorkel and left this port on 27 July, but on the same day was attacked by a Liberator of 86 Squadron from Tain in Ross-shire flown by Flying Officer G.G. Gates. Six depth charges were dropped but these overshot. There was an exchange of gunfire, in which the conning tower was hit and two engines of the Liberator were set on fire. These fires were put out and the Liberator returned safely. The U-boat returned once more to Trondheim for further repairs and sailed again on 8 September. It was lost about a week later, possibly from striking a mine south-east of Iceland. There were no survivors from the crew of fifty-nine.

Ref: DEFE 3/733

```
    ADM  (3)                                                    436
    TO: I D 8 G                    ZIP/ ZTPGU/29383
    FROM: N S


    5885 KC/S        T O O 0950        T O I 0839/10/8/44

    FROM: U/B  BASE LORIENT

    TO:   CAPTAIN U/B WEST

    EMERGENCY              NO 1080 FT

    U 270 (SCHREIBER) LEAVES LORIENT AT 2200/10

    1408/10/8/44 EGT/MU
```

This is an example of the very useful information decrypted by the Allies. The Type VIIC *U-270* was built by Bremer Vulkan of Vegesack and commissioned on 5 September 1942. It made five war cruises, all in the North Atlantic, and was damaged on four occasions. It duly left Lorient on 10 August 1944 under the command of Oberleutnant zur See Heinrich Schreiber, taking important personnel to the safer area of La Pallice. It was constantly harried by aircraft, culminating in an attack shortly after midnight on 11/12 August when Sunderland III serial ML735 of 461 (RAAF) Squadron arrived from Pembroke Dock flown by Flying Officer Donald A. Little. Six depth charges were dropped during an exchange of gunfire. These damaged the pressure hull and the U-boat eventually sank. Allied destroyers closed in and rescued seventy-one of the eighty-one men on board.

Ref: DEFE 3/734

```
ADM (2)

  TO I D 8 G                    ZIP/ZTPGU/29072
  FROM N S                                                          81

  9967 KC/S          T O O 1437      T O 1 332/5/8/44

  FROM: 1ST U/B FLOTILLA
  TO: CAPT (U/B) WEST

       B D U OPS

   MOST IMMEDIATE

   AFTERNOON 5/8 BOMBING ATTACK ON U-BOAT HARBOUR. SHELTER

   BERTH ROOF ((2 GROUPS)) AND DOCK 3 PIERCED RIGHT THROUGH. 2

   FURTHER ROOFS HIT. BOATS OF BOTH  FLOTILLAS ARE XX AFLOAT,

   SOME WITH BLAST DAMAGE. REPORT ON CONDITION AND SAILING

   READINESS TO FOLLOW. NO CASUALTIES AMONG PERSONNEL.

   CC:     T O I 1332/5/8/44

   0147/7/8/44 EGT/MW
```

On the night of 5/6 August 1944 fifteen Lancasters and two Mosquitos of 617 Squadron from Woodhall Spa in Lincolnshire attacked the U-boat pens at Brest. The Lancasters dropped Tallboy bombs of 12,000 lb, designed by Barnes Wallis to produce an 'earthquake effect'. Six of these were believed to have scored direct hits on the pens. According to this report, three of these bombs pierced the immensely thick concrete roofs of the bunkers and damaged two others. One Lancaster was shot down by flak.

Ref: DEFE 3/734

The effect of the bombing of the U-boat pens at Brest, photographed from the rear.

Ref: ADM 199/2061

```
ADM(1)

TO I D 8 G                    ZIP/ZTPGU/30042              51

FROM N S


8035 KC/S       T O O 2243        TOI: 2130/17/8/44


FROM: B.D.U. OPS.

TO:    10TH U/B FLOTILLA

       CAPTAIN (U/B) WEST


           SECRET 9061 A5

U 549 (KRANKENHAGEN) IS DECLARED MISSING WITH EFFECT FROM 4/8/44,

E STAR. BOAT LEFT LORIENT ON 14/5. LAST REPORT WAS PASSAGE

REPORT ON 22/5 FROM CG 17. FATE OF CREW UNKNOWN. DATE OF LOSS

VERY UNCERTAIN.

OR NECT OF KIN: BOAT OPERATED IN THE NORTH ATLANTIC. NO CLUE AS

TO CAUSE OF LOSS.

ADDITIONAL: NEXT OF KIN ARE BEING INFORMED BY ADMIRAL U/B.


CC LINE 2 READ 'LORIENT'
```

The Type IXC/40 *U-549* was built by Deutschewerft of Hamburg and commissioned on 14 July 1943. Under the command of Kapitänleutnant Detlef Krankenhagen, it left Kiel on 11 January 1944 and sank the escort carrier USS *Block Island* before arriving at Lorient on 26 March 1944. It left this port for its second war cruise on 14 May 1944 and when south-west of Madeira fifteen days later damaged the destroyer escort USS *Barr*. However, on the same day this destroyer together with three others depth-charged the U-boat, which was lost with all fifty-seven crew members.

Ref: DEFE 3/735

Opposite Top: The Type VIIC *U-981* was built by Blohm & Voss of Hamburg and commissioned on 3 June 1943. It made two war cruises and then left Lorient on 7 August 1944 under the command of Oberleutnant zur See Günther Keller, bound for the safer haven of La Pallice. After making contact with the Type VIIC *U-309* commanded by Oberleutnant zur See Hans-Gert Mahrholz, which had left Brest and was also on passage to La Pallice, it struck a mine near the mouth of the Gironde estuary in the early morning of 12 August. Then a Halifax II of 502 Squadron, flown from St Davids in Pembrokeshire by Flight Lieutenant J. Capey, homed in on the two vessels. Both U-boats fired on the Halifax, but five 600 lb bombs were dropped around *U-981*. The U-boat sank and forty of the crew were picked up by *U-309*.

Ref: DEFE 3/734

Opposite Bottom: The Type XIV *U-490* was built by Deutschewerke of Kiel and commissioned on 27 March 1943. It left Kiel for its first war cruise on 4 May 1944, under the command of Oberleutnant der Reserve Wilhelm Gerlach and bound for the Indian Ocean. On 11 June 1944, in the Central Atlantic, it was bombed by aircraft of VC-25 Squadron, US Navy, from the escort carrier USN *Croatan* and then depth-charged by three US destroyer escorts. It was blown to the surface, and all the crew of sixty were taken prisoner.

Ref: DEFE 3/735

```
     ADM   (3)                                                    798
   TO:  I D 8 G                           ZIP/ZTPGU/29705
   FROM:   N S


   5382 KC/S            T O O   1629         T O I  2146/13/8/44


   FROM:  3RD U/B FLOTILLA
   TO:   B.D.U. (OPS.)


   MOST SECRET 1302.

   SHORT REPORT OF U 981 (KELLER):

   LEFT LORIENT AT 2200/7/8. NO ESCORT FOUND AT POINT 1 AT
   0300/12/8. STEERED FOR U 309 (MAHRHOLZ), THEN ON COURSE 020
   DEGREES BACK TO POINT 1. MINED AT 0415, UNABLE TO DIVE,
   APPROACHED BY A HALIFAX THREE TIMES. ONLY 3 FLARES, DURING
   NEXT RUN-IN 6 BOMBS NEXT TO THE BOAT, SEVERE DAMAGE AND FIRES
   ON BOARD. THEN TWO ATTACKS BY A TWIN-ENGINED AIRCRAFT WHICH
   DROPPED BOMBS, SCORING A DIRECT HIT ON THE W/T ROOM. BETWEEN
   THE LAST 2 ATTACKS WAS MINED, LARGE INFLUX OF WATER. BOAT
   SANK QUICKLY. ONE WARRANT ENGINEER, 4 WARRANT OFFICERS AND 7
   MEN WENT DOWN WITH HER. THE REST ESCAPED IN RUBBER DINGHIES
   AND WERE PICKED UP BY MAHRHOLZ'S BOAT. DURING ALL A/C ATTACKS
   BOTH BOATS PUT UP ACCURATE FLAK FIRE.        0958·14·8·44· EGT·AH∨
```

```
   ADM(1)                                                       194
   TO I D 8 G                              ZIP/ZTPGU/30165
   FROM N S

   6290 KC/S       T O O 2359             TOI 2255/18/8/44

   FROM: B.D.U.
   TO:   ADMIRAL (U/B)
         12TH U/B FLOTILLA
         CAPT (U/B) WEST

   SECRET 9168

        U 490 (GERLACH) IS DECLARED MISSING WITH EFFECT FROM 28/7/44,
        ONE STAR. THE BOAT LEFT KIEL 4/5, LAST MESSAGE WEATHER FROM
        CD 23. FATE OF CREW UNKNOWN. DATE OF LOSS VERY UNCERTAIN.
        FOR NEXT OF KIN: BOAT WAS LOST X ON PASSAGE TO THE SOUTH
        ATLANTIC. NO INFORMATION ABOUT CAUSE OF LOSS. ADMIRAL (U/B)
        TO INFORM NEXT OF KIN

   2122/20/8/44+EGT/AM
```

This dramatic photograph was taken on 20 August 1944 by an aircraft of VC-42 Squadron from the escort carrier USS *Bogue*. It shows the Type IXC/40 U-boat *U-1229*, which was built by Deutschewerft of Hamburg and commissioned on 13 January 1944. The U-boat had left Trondheim on 26 July 1944, under the command of Korvettenkapitän Armin Zinke, bound for Long Island in order to land agents and saboteurs. Six Avengers and two Wildcats attacked with rockets and depth charges when it was south-east of Newfoundland. The U-boat crash-dived and raised its schnorkel but was unable to proceed underwater and was forced to surface. Eighteen of the crew were killed, including Zinke, but forty-one were rescued before it sank.

Ref: AIR 15/472

```
    ADM(5)

    TO I D 8 G                              ZIP/ZTPGU/30646        716
    FROM N S     :

    5705 KC/S              TOO 0857         TOI 0717/26/8/44

        BORDEAUX IS BEING AVXXXX EVACUATED. BOATS THAT HAVE TO TURN

    ABOUT FOR REPAIRS TO SMALL DEFECTS SHOULD NO LONGER CALL AT

    BORDEAUX BUT AT LA PALLICE OR ST. NAZAIRE. LA PALLICE REMAINS THE

    PORT FOR THE RETURNING CHANNEL BOATS — CONRAD, FIEDLER AND SIEDER.

    1050/26/8/44++ CEL/WAB++++
```

The end of Bordeaux as a U-boat base was signalled on 26 August 1944, following the advance of the Allied armies.

Ref: DEFE 3/733

The Type VIIC *U-247* was built by Germaniawerft of Kiel and commissioned on 23 October 1943. It made a war cruise in the North Atlantic, sinking one small ship, and then arrived at Brest. Under the command of Oberleutnant zur See Gerhard Matschulat, it left this port on 26 August 1944 bound for the Bristol Channel. On 1 September 1944 it was depth-charged by the frigates HMCS *St John* and *Swansea* 10 miles south-south-west of Lands End, and sunk with all fifty-two hands. This certificate commemmorating the 10,000,000th engine revolution was recovered by HMCS *St John* while looking for survivors.

Ref: ADM 199/2061

```
                                              27

ADM (3)

TO: I D 8 G                         ZIP/ZTPGU/31025

FROM: N S


8080 KC/S          TOO 1057         TOI 0945/5/9/44


FROM: DOENITZ, C.INC. OF THE NAVY AND B.D.U

TO:    U-BOAT BASE BREST


   DEAR WINTER,

   WITH THE DEPARTURE FROM BREST OF U 256 THE BASE'S LAST ACTUAL
   TASK IN THE U-BOAT WAR IS FULFILLED.   IN MY CAPACITY AS B.D.U
   I EXPRESS TO YOU AND YOUR MEN MY THANKS FOR THIS AND FOR THE
   SELFLESS AND UNSTINTED SERVICES RENDERED TO THE U-BOAT ARM
   DURING THE LAST FOUR YEARS.    THE WAR SITUATION NOW CALLS FOR
   THE USE OF THE HARBOUR TO BE DENIED TO THE ENEMY FOR AS LONG
   AS POSSIBLE.    I AM SURE THAT ALSO THOSE MEN NOT PREVIOUSLY
   EMPLOYED IN FIGHTING AT SEA OR ASHORE WILL PROVE THEIR WORTH.
   YOU KNOW HOW ATTACHED I AM TO YOU AND YOUR MEN.    I AM WITH
   YOU AND YOUR BRAVE MEN WITH ALL MY HEART.


LINE 2 'B.D.U'
```

The end of Brest as a German naval base was signalled in this message from Grossadmiral Karl Dönitz on 5 September 1944. It was invested by XIII Corps of the US Third Army and finally fell on 18 September, after stiff resistance from the garrison troops and naval personnel. Brest was required by the Allies as a port of entry for supplies and reinforcement but other bases on the west coast of France were simply invested and left to 'wither on the vine' rather than cause unnecessary loss of life.

Ref: DEFE 3/736

```
ADM(1)

TO 1D8G                          ZIP/ZTPGU/31278    304

FROM NS

4420 KC/S      T.O.O. 0312         T.O.I. 0225/11/9/44

FROM   MATUSCHKA

AM 2911 RETURN PASSAGE, ALL TORPEDOES EXPENDED. SUNK : ON 1/9

IN AM 56-XXXX 5612, ONE DESTROYER OUT OF A SEARCHING GROUP : OUT

OF INWARD - BOUND CONVOYS : ON 30/8 IN 5397, 7000 GRT TANKER,

ON 8/9 IN 5387, 5000  GRT FREIGHTER AND A 6000 GRT TANKER,

FIRED A T.5 ((CORRUPT GROUP)) AT A 5000 GRT FREIGHTER, EXPLOSION

AFTER 2 MINUTES 47 SECONDS. 95 CBM. SITUATION REPORT FOLLOWS.

0615/11/9/44   CEL/IH
```

This signal of 11 September 1944 was sent by Kapitänleutnant Hartmut Graf von Matuschka, the commander of the Type VIIC *U-482*. The U-boat had been built by Deutschewerft of Kiel and commissioned on 1 December 1943. It had left Horten in Norway on 14 August 1944 for its first war cruise, to operate off the north of Ireland. The report, sent early on its return passage, is broadly correct. It had sunk the American SS *Jacksonville* of 10,448 tons on 30 August, the corvette HMS *Hurst Castle* of 1,060 tons on 1 September, the Norwegian SS *Fjordheim* of 4,115 tons on 3 September, and then the British MV *Pinto* of 1,346 tons and the British SS *Empire Heritage* of 15,702 tons on 8 September. The U-boat arrived safely at Bergen on 26 September and left again on 18 November to operate in the same area. It damaged two more ships but was then hunted relentlessly by four sloops and a frigate of the Royal Navy. It was finally destroyed by depth charges on 16 January 1945 with the loss of all forty-eight crew members.

Ref: DEFE 3/736

```
ADM (2)                                              896

TO: I D 8 G              ZIP/ZTPGU/32787

FROM: N S

6675 KC/S      0918 /23/10/44   B

AM BEING ATTACKED BY AN AIRCRAFT IN SQUARE AN 2419.

JJE (U 1004)

1045/23/10/44+++++++ EGT+ MR
```

The Type VIIC/41 *U-1004* was built by Blohm & Voss of Hamburg and commissioned on 16 December 1943. It left Kristiansand on 22 August 1944 for its first war cruise and operated off the north of Ireland under the command of Oberleutnant zur See Hartmuth Schimmelpfenning. Having scored no sinkings it was attacked by an unknown aircraft when approaching Bergen on 23 October, but docked without damage on the same day. It made another war cruise under the command of Oberleutnant zur See Rudolf Hinz, sinking a merchant ship and a Canadian corvette before returning safely. It surrendered at Bergen at the end of the war.

Ref: DEFE 3/737

```
    ADM(1)                                              599

    TO I D 8 G                          ZIP/ZTPGU/31535

    FROM N S


    5900 KC/S          X 2107/18/9/44  B' 7 M O


        AM BEING ATTACKED BY AN A/C SQUARE AF 76 ((1 GROUP CORRUPT))

            BWE (U 867)


    0953/19/9/44+EGT/AM
```

The Type IXC/40 *U-867* was built by A.G. Weser of Bremen and commissioned on 12 December 1943. It left Kiel on 9 September 1944, under the command of Kapitän zur See Arved von Mühlendahl, but off Norway on 18 September was attacked with cannon and machine-guns by four Mosquito VIs and two Mosquito XVIIIs of 248 Squadron from Banff, led by Wing Commander D.G. 'Bill' Sise. Two of the Mosquito VIs, flown by Warrant Officer H.A. Corbin and Flying Officer R.G. Jefferson, also dropped depth charges which exploded near the stern. The U-boat did not sink but on the following day when west of Stadlandet was attacked by a Liberator VI of 224 Squadron flown from Milltown in Morayshire by Flying Officer H.J. Rayner. It was left in a crippled state surrounded by dinghies, but none of the men in the dinghies survived and all sixty crew members lost their lives.

Ref: DEFE 3/736

The Type IXC/40 *U-867* under attack by a Liberator VI of 224 Squadron on 19 September 1944.

Ref: ADM 199/2061

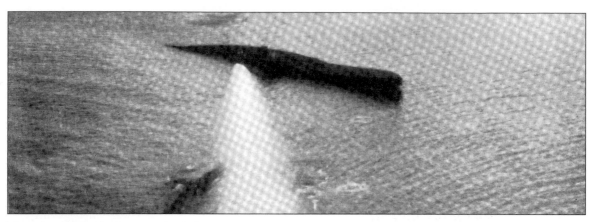

The Type VIIF *U-1060* was built by Germaniawerft of Kiel and commissioned on 15 May 1943, being employed initially on transport duties along the Norwegian coast. It left Bödö on 26 October 1944, bound for the Far East under the command of Oberleutnant zur See Herbert Brammer. Between Narvik and Bergen on the following day it was attacked with rockets by a Firefly of the FAA's 1771 Squadron from the carrier HMS *Implacable,* and ran aground on the island of Fleina, north-west of Namsos. On 29 October 1944 two Liberators of 311 (Czech) Squadron from Tain in Ross-shire and two Halifaxes of 502 Squadron from Stornaway in the Hebrides finished its destruction with rockets and bombs, as shown here. Twelve of the crew were killed in these operations, including Brammer, but forty-three were rescued.

Ref: AIR 15/472

```
      ADM(1)                                                         249
      TO: I D 8 G                              ZIP/ZTPGU/33211

      FROM: N S

      4075 KC/S            T O  O 2157         T O I 2329/8/11/44

      FROM: ACKERMANN

      8 ( OFFIZIER CYPHER )

      ORDINARY SEAMAN MOTYL WENT OVERBOARD IN NAVAL GRID SQUARE CC 1242

      ON 26/9 AND WAS NOT FOUND AGAIN . INQUIRY MAKES DESERTION SEEM

      PROBABLE .

      ( DEPT. NOTE: COMPLETE TEXT OF ZTPGU/33204).

      0728/9/11/44           CEL/UAK++
```

This signal was sent on 8 November 1944 by Oberleutnant zur See Paul Ackermann, the commander of the Type IXC/40 *U-1221.* The U-boat had been built by Deutschewerft of Hamburg and commissioned on 11 August 1943. It had left Bergen on 20 August bound for the Canadian coast near Halifax, but it was a long way from its destination when the crew member Motyl was lost overboard on 26 September. It seems unlikely that he could have survived. The U-boat docked at Marviken on 28 November, having sunk no vessels. It was destroyed on 3 April 1945 near Buoy A7 in Kiel Dockyard, during a massive raid on the port by 519 B-17 Flying Fortresses of the US Eighth Air Force, escorted by 157 P-51 Mustangs.

Ref: DEFE 3/738

```
ADM3                                                          601
TO  I D 8 G                            ZIP/ZTPGU/33486
FROM NS

7430 KC/S            TOO 1016         TOI 1306/20/11/44

FROM : U/BOAT BASE ST NAZAIRE

  TO : B D U

 (TO BE DECODED BY B D U ONLY)

    (OFFIZIER CYPHER)

 U.722 (REIMERS) ARRIVED ST NAZAIRE AT 0900. REQUEST

 ARRIVAL REPORT OF XXX BOTH BOATS BE PASSED TO GRUPPE WEST

    2153/21/11/44++CEL/JR
```

The Type VIIC *U-722*, commanded by Oberleutnant der Reserve Hans Reimers, left Marviken on 16 October 1944 and arrived at St-Nazaire on 20 November 1944, laden with stores for the beleaguered garrison. The U-boat was built by Stülcken Sohn of Hamburg and commissioned on 15 December 1943. This was its first cruise, employed as a supply vessel. (See also p. 229.)

Ref: DEFE 3/738

```
ADM (5)
 TO: I D 8 G                          ZIP/ZTPGU/33511 (N)      634
FROM: NS

2960 KC/S       T O O 1716          T O I 1829/21/11/444

FROM: U/BOAT BASE HARSTAD

TO:    CAPTAIN (U/B) NORTHERN WATERS

 U.668 AND U.310 WILL LEAVE HARSTAD ABOUT 0001/22/32 XXXX 0001/22/11

VIA ANDFJORD FOR AB 62.

 CC T.O I READ 1829/21/11/44

  2305/22/11/44+CEL/MH+
```

The Type VIIC *U-668* was built by Howaldtswerke of Hamburg and commissioned on 16 November 1942. It was on its sixth war cruise, under the command of Oberleutnant zur See Wolfgang von Eickstein, when leaving Harstad on 22 November 1944 for the Arctic. The Type VIIC *U-310* was built by Flenderwerft of Lübeck and commissioned on 24 February 1943. It was on its third war cruise, under the command of Oberleutnant zur See Wolfgang Ley, when it also left Harstad on 22 November 1944 for the Arctic. Both U-boats survived the war and surrendered in Norway in May 1945.

Ref: DEFE 3/738

```
ADM(1)                                                    788

  TO I D 8 G                    ZIP/ZTPGU/33634

FROM N S

  3800 KC/S       T O O 2347/26          TOI 0014/27/11/44

  1)  ON 2/11 FREIWALD SANK TANKER FORT LEA, 10000 GRT., 15 KNOTS,

      130 DEGREES IN NAVAL GRID SQUARE KU 49

  2)  IN NAVAL GRID SQUARE AE 4753 HEIN SANK A SMALLISH SHIP AND

      PROBABLY A 4000 TON STEAMSHIP

  0508/27/11/44+EE/AM
```

Fregattenkapitän Kurt Freiwald was the commander of the Type IXD2 *U-181*. This successful U-boat was on its fourth war cruise, having left Jakarta on 19 October 1944 to operate in the Indian Ocean. The American tanker SS *Fort Lee* of 10,198 tons was its twenty-seventh but final victim. It returned to Jakarta with a damaged propeller shaft on 5 January 1945 and was handed over to the Japanese.

Oberleutnant zur See Fritz Hein was the commander of the Type VIIC/41 *U-300*, built by Bremer Vulkan of Vegesack and commissioned on 29 December 1943. It was on its second war cruise, having left Trondheim on 4 October 1944 to operate off Iceland. It sank three merchant vessels before returning to Stavanger on 2 December 1944. It then left Bergen on 21 January 1945 to operate off Gibraltar but on 22 February 1945 was depth-charged and sunk by the minesweepers HMS *Pincher* and *Recruit*, as well as the armed yacht HMS *Invade*. Hein and eight of his crew were killed but forty-two men were rescued and became prisoners.

Ref: DEFE 3/738

```
ADM(2)                                                   1093

  TO I D 8 G                    ZIP/ZTPGU/33897(N)

FROM N S

  3750 KC/S       T O O 0015            TOI 0248/5/12/44

FROM:  HESS

     AC 8579. 3 STEAMSHIPS. 5 ESCORTING VESSELS. SEVERAL MOTOR-BOATS,

     PROCEEDING ALONG RYBATSCHI AT 8 KNOTS. 'FAT' HIT ON A 6,000

     TONNER, CURVE SHOT AT A LIBERTY. ONE 'T.5' REMAINS

  0556/5/12/44+CEL/AM
```

Oberleutnant der Reserve Hans-Georg Hess was the commander of the Type VIIC/41 *U-995*, built by Blohm & Voss of Hamburg and commissioned on 16 September 1943. It made five war cruises in the Arctic and then left Narvik again on 30 November 1944 and sent this report on 5 December. It was credited with damaging an unidentified merchant vessel of 6,000 tons on 4 December and then sinking this vessel of similar size the next day, possibly both Russian, before arriving at Bogenbucht on 9 December. It made three more war cruises in the Arctic and survived the war, surrendering at Trondheim in May 1945.

Ref: DEFE 3/738

```
        ADM(2)                                                    1047
        TO ID8G                              ZIP/ZTPGU/37917
        FROM NS

        4255 KC/S              T.O.O. 2210          T.O.I. 2217/7/12/44

        FROM     U-BOAT BASE ST. NAZAIRE

        TO       B.D.U.-

        SPECIAL CYPHER 161

        U 722 (REIMERS) AND U 773 (BALDUS) LEFT ST. NAZAIRE AT 2100.

        (DEPT. NOTE : COMPOSXXXX COMPLETE TEXT OF ZTPGU/33987)

        1550/8/4/45      EGT/IH
```

The Type VIICs *U-722* and *U-773* left St-Nazaire on 7 December 1944, according to this signal. The Allies had surrounded the port but did not pursue their attack. *U-722* had been built by Stülcken Sohn of Hamburg and commissioned on 15 December 1943; it had left Marviken on 16 October 1944 and arrived at St-Nazaire on 20 November 1944 laden with stores. *U-773* had been built by Kriegsmarinewerft of Wilhelmshaven and commissioned on 20 January 1944; it had left Marviken on 15 October 1944, laden with ammunition for the garrison, and arrived on 18 November 1944. Both arrived safely at Bergen, *U-722* on 29 December 1944 and *U-773* on 10 January 1945. *U-722* was sunk on its third war cruise, under the command of Oberleutnant der Reserve Hans Reimers, when it was depth-charged on 27 March 1945 by three frigates of the Royal Navy off Scotland and lost with all forty-four crew members. *U-773* survived the war and surrendered at Trondheim. It was towed out of Loch Ryan on 6 December 1945 and used for target practice by a British submarine.

Ref: DEFE 3/742

```
        ADMX2                                                     105
        TO ID8G                              ZIP/ZTPGU/34097 (N)
        FROM NS

        3750 KC/S              TOO 0553           TOI 0902/11/12/44

        FROM : TODENHAGEN

        SQUARE AC5763 'CURVE-HIT' ON DESTROYER 210 DEGREES, 14-16
        KNOTS, LOUD SINKING NOISES.   CONVOY PASSING NORTHWARD,
        TSIGNAL STRENGTH 4-5, 60 CUBIC METRES, ONE 'CURVE'((TORPEDO))

        1343/11/12/44+++++AND/JR
```

Oberleutnant zur See Diether Todenhagen was the commander of the Type VIIC *U-365*, built by Flensburger Schiffbau and commissioned on 8 June 1943. It made seven war cruises from Norway, two of which were special missions, and sank three Russian vessels. It then left Narvik on 22 November 1944 for another war cruise in the Arctic and, after sinking a small Russian vessel, damaged the destroyer HMS *Cassandra* on 11 December and sent this signal. However, when north-west of the Lofoten Islands on 13 December, it was bombed and sunk by two Swordfish of the Fleet Air Arm's 813 Squadron operating from the escort carrier HMS *Campania* and lost with all fifty crew members.

Ref: DEFE 3/739

```
ADM(2)                                                    011
TO  I D 8 G                              ZIP/ZTPGU/34562
FROM N S

3800 KC/S              TOO: 0721      TOI: 0705/21/12/44

FROM: GUDENUS' U-BOAT
TO:    CAPTAIN (U/B) WEST

       6TH COASTAL DEFENCE UNIT

EMERGENCY

  39 SURIVORS ON BOARD.  FURTHER SHIPWRECKED MEN ARE

  DRIFTING NEAR THE EXIT FROM FEIESTEIN CHANNEL.  AS THEY

  HAVE DRIFTED INTO SHALLOWS, RESCUE WORK BROKEN OFF.  AM

  PROCEEDING INTO STAVANGER.

  1440/22/12/44++TZ+DG
```

The Type VIIC *U-427* was built by Danzigerwerft and commissioned on 2 June 1943. It was commanded by Oberleutnant zur See Graf Karl Gabriel von Gudenus from 14 August 1944 and employed on escorting Norwegian coastal convoys. These came under frequent attacks by RAF Strike Wings based at Banff and Dallachy in Scotland, as well as from warships of the Royal Navy. This signal was sent on 21 December 1944 when *U-427* was unable to take on board any more survivors from sunken vessels. From 9 April 1945 it made two war cruises in the Arctic, without succeeding in sinking any vessels but coming under attack by Russian and Canadian warships. It surrendered at the end of the war. The end came when it was towed out from Loch Ryan on 20 December 1945 and destroyed by gunfire on the following day.

Ref: DEFE 3/739

```
ADM  (3)                                                 938
TO: I D 8 G
                          ZIP/ZTPGU/34831(N)
FROM: N S

403 KC/S       TOO : 0346     TOI : 0445/30/12/44

ON ARRIVAL IN PORT , BLAKE REPORTS SINKING A LIBERTY SHIP IN

NAVAL GRID SQUARE AM 8883. IN ADDITION, HE OBTAINED 2 HITS

ON A 14,000 TON TROOP TRANSPORT IN NAVAL GRID SQUARE BF 3525,

SINKING NOT OBSERVED BUT CONSIDERED PROAXXXX PROBABLE. THE BOAT

CARRIED OUT A CHANNEL OPERATION ALTHOUGH HER FORWARD HYDROPLANE

WENT OUT OF ORDER ON HER OUTWARDPASSAGE.

C GR 5:BALKE NOT AS SENT .

1323/30/12/44 CEL/JG
```

The Type VIIC *U-991* was built by Blohm & Voss of Hamburg and commissioned on 29 July 1943. It left Kristiansand on 15 October 1944, under the command of Oberleutnant zur See Diethelm Balke, to operate in the English Channel. It returned to Bergen on 26 December 1944. Despite these claims reported on 30 December 1944, there do not appear to be any sinkings in Allied records. The U-boat surrendered at Bergen in May 1945 and was sunk after being towed out from Loch Ryan on 9 December 1945, when it was used as target practice by the submarine HMS *Tantivy*.

Ref: DEFE 3/739

```
                                                              279
ADM   (3)

TO:   I D 8 G                        ZIP/ZTPGU/35251

FROM:   N S


ATLANTIC U/B SERVICES     TOO 2108/2256    TOI 1941/2226/9/1/45

OFFIZIER CYPHER

EXPERIENTIAL MESSAGE NO. 211.

THE ENEMY'S INTEREST IN THE NEW EQUIPMENT, CYPHER MACHINES AND

CYPHER KEYS CARRIED BY U-BOATS IS SO GREAT THAT HE MAKES EVERY

POSSIBLE EFFORT TO BOARD BOATS WHEN THEY ARE UNABLE TO DIVE,

  UNMANOEUVRABLE, AND EVEN SINKING.  MEN RETURNING FROM CAPTIVITY

REPORT THAT AS SOON AS A U-BOAT SURFACES THE ENEMY LAUNCHES A

BOAT WHICH ATTEMPTS TO COME ALONGSIDE UNDER THE PROTECTIVE FIRE    —   280

OF THE ENEMY'S LIGHT ARMS.  SEVERAL INSTANCES ARE KNOWN TO HAVE

OCCURRED OF THE ENEMY SUCCEEDING, EVEN IF ONLY FOR A SHORT TIME,

IN GETTING ABOARD SLOWLY SINKING BOATS THAT HAVE BEEN ABANDONED

BY THEIR CREWS.

MORAL:-  IF A U-BOAT IS COMPELLED TO SURFACE IN THE VICINITY OF

ENEMY FORCES, UNABLE TO FIGHT OR MANOEUVRE, TO ALLOW THE SHIP'S

COMPANY TO GET OUT, EVERYTHING MUST BE DONE TO ENSURE THAT UNDER

ALL CIRCUMSTANCES THE BOAT WILL SINK IMMEDIATELY.  THE COMMANDER

AND ENGINEER OFFICER, OR FAILING THEM THE SENIOR MEN ON BOARD,

MAY LEAVE THE BOAT ONLY IN THE LAST SECOND BEFORE IT SINKS.

REPEAT ON NORTHERN WATERS AND GULF OF FINLAND SERVICES.


1112/11/1/45   EE/AHM++++
```

This warning about the determination of the Allies to secure Enigma machines and code books was sent to U-boat commanders on 9 January 1945.

Ref: DEFE 3/740

```
ADM (1)                                                            972
   TO I D 8 G                        ZIP/ZTPGU/35876
   FROM N S
   3800 KC/S
              0007/30/1/45   B'NMA

   MY POSITION IS SQUARE AF 8775. HAVE SO FAR SUNK UP TO 20,000 TONS
   (NO MINE SUCCESSES).
                   RQN    (U.1055)

0815/31/1/45++AND/UC
```

The Type VIIC *U-1055* was built by Germaniawerft of Kiel and commissioned on 8 April 1944. It left Marviken for its first war cruise on 11 December 1944, under the command of Oberleutnant zur See Rudolf Meyer, to operate against Russian convoys. Between 9 and 16 January 1945 it sank two American and two British merchant ships, amounting to 19,416 tons, as well as another unidentified steamer. Two days after sending this signal on 30 January 1945 it arrived at Stavanger. It left Bergen on 5 April to operate off the South-West Approaches, but was sunk on 30 April by a Catalina of VPB-63 Squadron, US Navy, and went down with all forty-nine crew members.

Ref: DEFE 3/740

```
ADM(4)                                                            343
   TO I D 8 G                        ZIP/ZTPGU/36322 (N)
   FROM N S
   3750 KC/S           TOO 2037           TOI 2015/15/2/45

   FROM: CAPTAIN (U/B)
   TO:   FALKE

        YOU WERE EXPECTED TO PUT UP A GOOD SHOW.   WELL DONE!
   SERIAL NUMBERS UNIMPORTANT.  RETURN PASSAGE TO HARSTAD.

0752/16/2/45++EE/WAB+++
```

The Type VIIC/41 *U-1279* was built by Bremer Vulkan of Vegesack and commissioned on 5 July 1944. Under the command of Oberleutnant der Reserve Hans Falke, it left Horten for its first war cruise on 29 January 1945 to operate in the Shetlands area. This signal was sent to it on 15 February. However, some time after the following day it was lost, although the cause has not been fully established. There were no survivors from the crew of forty-eight.

Ref: DEFE 3/741

```
ADM  (4)                                                              496
   TO:  I D 8 G                    ZIP/ZTPGU/36449
   FROM:  N S

   5382 KC/S          T O O 1806        T O I 1752/17/2/45
   FROM:   5TH U/BFLOTILLA

   TO:      SCHNEIDEWIND FOR LT. (S.G.)BATH XXXBARTH(FRIEDRICH)

                                    U 1064

   BOY ARRIVED 12/2/45. MOTHER AND SON WELL.HEARTY CONGRATULATIONS.

   1110/19/2/45  EGT/IS++
```

This example of a morale-boosting message for crew members was sent to an officer in the Type VIIC/41 *U-1064* on 17 February 1945. This U-boat had been built by Germaniawerft of Kiel and was commissioned on 29 July 1944. It was on its first war cruise, having left Bergen on 7 February 1945 for the North Atlantic, under the command of Korvettenkapitän Karl-Hermann Schneidewind. After sinking one merchant vessel of 1,564 tons, it reached Trondheim on 9 April and was eventually taken over by the Russian Navy. Presumably Leutnant zur See Friedrich Barth was able to return to his wife and newly born son.

Ref: DEFE 3/741

```
ADM K(1)                                                     221
   TO: I D 8 G                    ZIP/ZTPGU/37190
   FROM:  N S

   3160 KC/S          T O O 0459        T O I 0452/15/3/45

   FROM: 11TH U/B FLOTILLA
   TO:    2ND NAVAL WAR STAFF,  B.D.U. OPS.
          ADMIRAL U/B

   U 774 (SAUSMIKAT), U 880 (SCHOETZAU) AND U 1235 (BARSCH) LEFT
   BERGEN AT 2000/14/3 TO CONTINUE 1ST OPERATION. DEPARTURE OF
   " 764 (VON BREMEN) POSTPONED ONE DAY OWING TO NON-ACHIEVEMENT
   OF FINAL PROGRAMME ('SCHLUSSPROGRAMM'). U 1235 (BARSCH) TOUCHED
   GROUND WHILE LEAVING. RETURN PASSAGE TO BERGEN. WAR READINESS
   WILL FOLLOW.

   1245/16/3/45 TZ/EB+
```

All three U-boats in this signal of 15 March sailed on their first war cruises to meet disaster. The Type VIIC *U-774*, built by Kriegsmarinewerft of Wilhelmshaven and commissioned on 17 February 1944, was under the command of Kapitänleutnant Werner Sausmikat; it was sunk on 8 April 1945 by the frigates HMS *Bentinck* and *Calder,* and was lost with all forty-four crew members. The Type IXC/40 *U-880*, built by A.G. Weser of Bremen and commissioned on 11 May 1944, was under the command of Kapitänleutnant Gerhard Schötzkau; it was sunk on 16 April 1945 by the destroyer escorts USS *Frost* and *Stanton,* and was lost with all forty-nine crew members. The Type IXC/40 *U-1235*, built by Deutschewerft of Hamburg and commissioned on 17 May 1944, was under the command of Kapitänleutnant Franz Barsch; it was sunk by the same two destroyer escorts on 15 April 1945 and went down with all fifty-seven crew members. None of these U-boats achieved any sinkings.

Ref: DEFE 3/742

```
ADM(4)                                              616
TO I D 8 G
FROM N S                        ZIP/ZTPGU/37540

5900 KC/S            TOO 1324           TOI 1253/24/3/45

FROM: KOCK

TO:    11TH U/B FLOTILLA

       HAVE BEEN ATTACKED BY MOSQUITO. AIRCRAFT SHOT DOWN, SLIGHT

DAMAGE, AM PROCEEDING INTO BERGEN. REQUEST ESCORT IMMEDIATELY.


   1929/25/3/45++EE/WAB++++
```

The Type VIIC *U-249* was built by Germaniawerft of Kiel and commissioned on 20 November 1943. It left Bergen on 7 March for its third war cruise, under the command of Kapitänleutnant der Reserve Uwe Kock, but returned defective nine days later. After repairs it left again on 21 March. Three days later it suffered damage and casualties when attacked by Mosquito VI letter Q of 235 Squadron, flown from Banff in Banffshire by Flight Lieutenant J.R. Williams. The Mosquito was shot down and *U-249* returned once more to Bergen. After further repairs it left Bergen for the third time on 4 April, heading for the West Channel of England. It surfaced and surrendered off the Lizard on 8 May, putting in to Portland the following day. It was towed out of Loch Ryan on 11 December 1945 and used as a torpedo target by a British submarine.

Ref: DEFE 2/742

```
ADM(1)                                              668
TO I D 8 G           ZIP/ZTPGU/37589
FROM N S

4020 KC/S      T O O 2035        TOI: 1226/24/3/45

FROM: JUERS

NO TRAFFIC ESTABLISHED IN THE MORAY FIRTH OPERATIONAL AREA AND ON

ROUTES TO PETERHEAD. CONSTANT PATROLS, INCLUDING AIR. SEARCHING

GROUPS IN 18926 AND 16737, INEXPERIENCED.  LOCATION BY

EXPLOSIVE SOUNDING, AND ASDIC. WHEN PURSUED, SHALLOW WATER. IN

INNER FIRTH DRIFTERS, CONSTANT DEPTH CHARGES. SCHNORCHELLING UNDISTURB
                                        NOISE
XXXX UNDISTURBED UNDER THE COAST. NOUSE FLOATS  IN 17336

AND 18616. LIGHTS  IN ACCORDANCE WITH PEACETIME PRACTICE. ALL

NAVAL GRID SQUARE AN. 11 DAYS IN OPERATIONAL AREA. RETURN  PASSAGE.

MULTI-UNIT HYDROPHONES OUT OF ACTION. NAVAL GRID SQUARE AN 4621.

0402/26/3/45+GFG+PG
```

The Type VIIC *U-778* was built by Kriegsmarine of Wilhelmshaven and commissioned on 7 July 1944. It left Horten on 4 March 1945 under the command of Kapitänleutnant Ralf Jürs, for a reconnaissance of the Moray Firth. This report was sent on 24 March and *U-778* reached Bergen four days later. It surrendered at the end of the war and then sailed to the UK. It was towed out from Loch Ryan on 3 December 1945 but sank on the following day while still under tow.

Ref: DEFE 3/742

```
ADM (3)                                                            351

TO:  I D 8 G                            ZIP/ZTPGU/38315 (N)

FROM:  N S

3750 KC/S         T O O 1901          T O I 2040/6/4/45

FROM:  THIMME

LARGE FREIGHTER INWARD-BOUND AT 1402/5/4 IN 858 (( SIC )) .

RAMMED BY A DESTROYER , MAIN TARGET PERISCOPE BENT BUT NO DAMAGE

APART FROM THIS . HAVE BEGUN RETURN PASSAGE AND AM 32 HOURS OFF THE

APPROACH POINT .


1601/15/4/45     CEL/UAK++
```

The Type VIIC *U-716* sent this signal on 6 April 1945, having left Bogenbucht on 12 March under the command of Oberleutnant zur See Jürgen Thimme for its ninth war cruise in the Arctic. This U-boat had been built by Stülcken Sohn of Hamburg and commissioned on 15 April 1943. After suffering minor damage on the day of this signal, it was forced to put into Narvik three days later. It made one more cruise and then surrendered at the end of the war. It was towed out of Loch Ryan on 9 December 1945 and used as a target by the RAF.

Ref: DEFE 3/743

```
ADM(1)                                                            667

TO I D 8 G                              ZIP/ZTPGU/38598 (N)

FROM N S

4985 KC/S         T O O 1040          TOI: 0915/23/4/45

    ON 4TH APRIL  IN NAVAL GRID SQUARE AN 1520  PULST SANK  OUT OF

CONVOY  A STEAMSHIP  OF 6000 GRT AND  ON 6TH APRIL TORPEDOED AN

'ILLUSTRIOUS' CLASS CARRIER.

1957/24/4/45+EGT+PG
```

The Type VIIC *U-978* was built by Blohm & Voss of Hamburg and commissioned on 12 May 1943. It left Bergen for its second war cruise on 25 February 1945, under the command of Kapitänleutnant Günter Pulst. This signal was sent on 23 April, after it had returned safely to Trondheim three days before. The merchant vessel was Russian but cannot be identified. The U-boat surrendered after the end of the war. It was towed out of Loch Ryan on 9 December 1945 and used as a target by a British submarine.

Ref: DEFE 3/743

```
ADM(1)                                                    1110

   TO I D 8 G                          ZIP/ZTPGU/38986

   FROM N S

   4200 KC/S            TOO 0201            TOI 0031/2/5/45

   TO: ALL U-BOATS

    ON 30/4 THE FUEHRER FELL AMONG HIS SOLDIERS IN THE HEROIC

   STRUGGLE FOR BERLIN. BY ⊠ HIS ORDER, GROSSADMIRAL DOENITZ

   HAS ASSUMED THE SUCCESSION. THE GROSSADMIRAL'S ORDER OF

   THE DAY FOLLOWS. THE FIGHT FOR OUR PEOPLE GOES ON.

   1136/4/5/45          CEL+++MPS+++
```

The announcement of the death of Adolf Hitler on 30 April 1944 and the appointment of Grossadmiral Dönitz as his successor. It implies that Hitler died in combat and does not mention that he committed suicide.

Ref: DEFE 3/743

On 2 May 1945 Squadron Leader A.G. Deck led thirty-five Mosquitos of 143, 235, 248, 333 (Norwegian) and 404 (RCAF) Squadrons from the Banff Strike Wing on an anti-shipping sweep over the Kattegat. They sank the Type XXIII *U-2359*, which had been built by Deutschewerft of Hamburg and commissioned on 16 January 1945. This new electro-boat had left Kiel and was on its way to Horten in Norway, under the command of Oberleutnant zur See Gustav Bischoff. Twelve of the crew were killed, including the commander.

Ref: AIR 26/597

```
TO:    I D 8 G                    ZIP/ZTPGU/38987
                                                          1113
FROM:  N S

5382 KC/S           T.O.O   1149      T.O.I  1100/2/5/45


1. HEADQUARTERS, 1ST MAY 1945.

   U-BOAT MEN, THE FIGHT AGAINST BOLSHEVISM GOES ON, TO SAVE

   HUNDREDS OF THOUSANDS OF GERMANS FROM DESTRUCTION AND

   ENSLAVEMENT. AS LONG AS THE BRITISH AND THE AMERICANS

   TOLERATE THE DESTRUCTION OF THE GERMAN PEOPLE BY BOLSHEVISM

   AND HINDER US IN OUR FIGHT AGAINST THE LATTER, YOUR FIGHT

   TOO GOES ON UNRESTRICTED. I DEMAND OF YOU THAT YOU CONTINUE

   THIS FIGHT WITH THE SAME TENACITY AS HITHERTO. AS THE

   FUEHRER'S SUCCESSOR I HAVE HAD TO GIVE UP COMMAND OF THE

   U-BOAT ARM AND HAVE APPOINTED GENERAL ADMIRAL VON FRIEDEBURG

   C. IN C. OF THE NAVY AND B.D.U. IN THIS HOUR I THANK YOU

   THE U-BOAT ARM, TO WHICH MY WHOLE HEART BELONGS, FOR ITS

   LOYALTY AND HEROISM WHICH SO MANY OF OUR COMRADES HAVE, SEALED

   WITH DEATH. I AM CERTAIN THAT YOU WILL SHOW YOURSELVES WORTHY

   OF THESE COMRADES. ((SIGNED)) DOENITZ, GROSSADMIRAL.

2. REPEAT ON ALL WAVES AND PASS TO SUBORDINATED AUTHORITIES.


1140/4/5/45   WE/AHM++++
```

A defiant message from Grossadmiral Karl Dönitz on 2 May 1945, confirming his appointment as the successor to Adolf Hitler and announcing the appointment of Generaladmiral Hans von Friedeburg as Commander-in-Chief of the German Navy and the B.D.U. (Befehlshaber der Unterseeboote, meaning Commander-in-Chief for Submarines).

Ref: DEFE 3/743

```
    ADM (5)                                                    172

    TO: I D 8 G                    ZIP/ZTPGU/39147

    FROM: NS


    XWR 4020 KC/S    T O O 0049       T O I 0220/4/5/45



    FROM: BDU OPS.

    TO:    ADMIRAL U-B

           ALL BOATS AND BASES IN THE HOMELAND


    1) THE U-BOAT WAR GOES ON

    2) BOATS COMING FROM KIEL ARE TO GO NOT TO FLENSBURG, BUT TO

    GELTINGER BAY. CDR. LIPPE OF B.D.U. OPS WILL SETTLE THERE AS

    FAR AS POSSIBLE WITH ADMIRAL U-B WHICH BOATS CAN BE MADE READY FOR

    FRONT LINE OPERATIONS AT THE COST OF OTHERS AND BE DESPATCHED TO

    NORWAY. SAME DECISIONS BY S.O. 33RD U-B FLOTILLA. ADMIRAL WILL

    TAKE OVER FURTHER DUTIES AS SOON AS POSSIBLE.

    3) ON KEYWORD 'REGENBOGEN', WHICH MAY ALSO BE GIVEN FOR SINGLE

    AREAS, U-BOATS ARE TO BE SCUTTLED OR DESTROYED OUTSIDE THE FAIRWAYS.

    4) OVER AND ABOVE THIS, THE ORDER IS: NO BOAT IS TO FALL INTO

    ENEMY ENEMY HANDS. EVERY MAN MUST SCUTTLE ON HIS OWN RESPONSIBILITY

    IN CASE OF DANGER.
```

This signal was sent on 4 May 1945, at a time when German defences in the ground war had crumbled and the Red Armies were sweeping in from the east. U-boats in the Baltic Sea or along its coastline had to be either prepared for sailing to Norway or scuttled.

Ref: DEFE 3/744

```
ADM(1)                                                    140

    TO I D 8 G                              ZIP/ZTPGU/39119
    FROM N S

    3160 KC/S          T O O 0134          TOI 0150/5/5/45

    MOST IMMEDIATE 'BLITZ'

    OKX I
    OFFIZIER CYPHER

    1)  NEW SITUATION.

    2)  IF POSSIBLE U-BOATS ARE TO GO TO NORWAY.

    1)  ALL U-BOATS WHICH AT 0800/5/5 ARE IN GERMAN OR DANISH PORTS,
        ROADS OR BAYS OR ARE SOUTH OF LATITUDE 5510 NORTH WILL CARRY OUT
        'REGENBOGEN', I.E. SCUTTLE IN AS DEEP WATER AS POSSIBLE, CREWS
        GOING ASHORE

    1249/17/5/45+TZ/AM
```

A surprising signal sent by Generaladmiral Hans von Friedeburg in the early morning of 5 May 1945, which must have caused some confusion and uncertainty in the minds of U-boat commanders.

Ref: DEFE 3/744

```
ADM(1)                                                    37

    TO I D 8 G                              ZIP/ZTPGU/39032
    FROM N S

    5382 KC/S          TOO 1528            TOI 1350/5/5/45

    FROM: NAVAL WAR STAFF (1ST DIVISION)

    MOST IMMEDIATE 'BLITZ'                  SECRET 1028

    CEASE ACTION FORTHWITH AGAINST THE BRITISH AND AMERICANS.

    ADDITIONAL FOR CAPTAIN (U/B) WEST:

    MAKE SURE THIS IS PASSED TO CAPTAIN (U/B) NORTHERN WATERS.

    1834/7/5/45        EE+++MPS+++
```

This dramatic signal of 5 May 1645 followed an instrument of surrender signed the day before by Generaladmiral Hans von Friedeburg, who had led a German delegation to the tactical headquarters of Field Marshal Sir Bernard Montgomery, Commander-in-Chief of the 21st Army Group, at Lüneburg Heath. This included all the German armed forces in north-west Germany, Schleswig-Holstein, the Netherlands and Denmark, as well as all the naval ships in those areas. The surrender took effect at 0800 hours on 5 May 1945.

Ref: DEFE 3/744

```
ADM(1)                                                    50

TO  I D 8 G                          ZIP/ZTPGU/39043

FROM N S


8075 KC/S              TOO 2158           TOI 2225/5/5/45


   MY MEN OF THE U-BOATS:

        SIX YEARS OF U-BOAT WARFARE LIE BEHIND US. YOU HAVE FOUGHT

   LIKE LIONS. AN OVER-WHELMING MATERIAL SUPERIORITY HAS SQUEEZED US

   INTO THE NARROWEST COMPASS. FROM THE FOOTING REMAINING TO US IT

   IS NO LONGER POSSIBLE TO CONTINUE OUR BATTLEM --- MEN OF THE U-

   BOATS, YOU LAY DOWN YOUR ARMS AFTER AN HEROIC STRUGGLE WITHOUT

   PARALLEL, UNBROKEN AND UNBLEMISHED. OUR THOUGHTS GO OUT REVERENT-

   LY TO OUR FALLEN COMRADES, WHO SEALED WITH THEIR LIVES THEIR

   LOYALTY TO THE FUEHRER AND TO THEIR FATHERLAND; COMRADES, IN THE

   FUTURE AS WELL, FOR THE BENEFIT OF OUR FATHERLAND, HOLD FAST TO

   YOUR U-BOAT SPIRIT, WITH WHICH YOU HAVE FOUGHT, BRAVELY, TOUGHLY

   AND UNSWERVINGLY, THROUGH THESE LONG YEARS.

            LONG LIVE GERMANY.

                    YOUR ADMIRAL OF THE FLEET.


   2306/7/5/45      EE+++MPS+++
```

A heartfelt message of gratitude sent to the surviving U-boat men on 5 May 1945 by their Commander-in-Chief, Generaladmiral Hans von Friedeburg.

Ref: DEFE 3/744

Opposite Top: The Type VIIC/41 *U-1008* was built by Blohm & Voss of Hamburg and commissioned on 1 February 1944. It made no war cruises but on 5 May 1945 was on passage to Norway under the command of Oberleutnant zur See Hans Gessner and near Hjelm in the Kattegat when it was attacked by an aircraft. There has been some doubt about the identity of this aircraft but it is now thought that it was Liberator letter T of 224 Squadron flown from Milltown in Morayshire by the commanding officer, Wing Commander Michael A. Ensor. The U-boat sank but forty-four of the crew were rescued, including the commander.

Ref: DEFE 3/344

Opposite Bottom: A further instruction given to all U-boats on 7 May 1945, on this occasion by Grosssadmiral Karl Dönitz. This included the Type XB *U-234*, built by Germaniawerft of Kiel and commissioned on 2 March 1944. This had left Kristiansand South on 17 April 1945 under the command of Kapitänleutnant Johann-Heinrich Fehler, headed for the Far East. It carried a crated Me262 jet fighter, 550 kg of uranium oxide, a quantity of mercury and various anti-tank weapons. When it surrendered on 14 May 1945 at Portsmouth, New Hampshire, there were twelve VIPs on boards, including Japanese (two of whom committed suicide). It became an experimental submarine for the US Navy before being sunk on 20 November 1947.

Ref: DEFE 3/344

```
        ADM   (1)
        TO:   I D 8 G                    ZIP/ZTPGU/39048         57
        FROM:   N S

        5710 KC/S           T O O   1138      T O I  1137/7/5/45

        FROM:  8TH DEFENCE DIVISION

        TO:    B.D.U.
               CAPTAIN (U/B) WEST

        A PETTY OFFICER OF U 1008 REPORTS BY TELEPHONE FROM HJELM

        ISLAND:   BOAT SEVERELY DAMAGED BY AIR ATTACK ON 5/5.  SHE

        TRIED TO REACH LAND, BUT SANK OFF HJELM.  20 MEN DRIFTED

        ASHORE.   C.O. WITH REMAINDER OF MEN, SOME WOUNDED, STILL

        ADRIFT.   SEARCH BY 2 R-BOATS FRUITLESS.

        0905/8/5/45   CEL/AHM++++
```

```
          M
        VETM
        ADM (3)                                                108
        TO: I D 8 G
        FROM: N S                         ZIP/ZTPGU/39091

        BX 5710 KC/S           TOO 1152         TOI 1147/7/5/45

        FROM: CAPTAIN (U/B) WEST

        TO BE DECODED BY BOATS AT SEA ONLY.
        (OFFIZIER CYPHER)

        THE FOLLOWING ORDER HAS BEEN PROMULGATED BY THE GROSSADMIRAL:
        ALL U/BOATS INCLUDING THE EAST ASIA BOATS ((AND FEHLER)) ARE TO
        CEASE OFFENSIVE ACTION FORTHWITH AND BEGIN RETURN PASSAGE UNSEEN.
        ENSURE ABSOLUTE SECRECY.   MANIFESTATION OF THIS STEP MUST NOT
        REACH THE OUTER WORLD FOR THE TIME BEING.
        ADDITION BY CAPTAIN (U/B) WEST:  WHEN ON RETURN PASSAGE, AVOID
        ALL POSSIBILITIES OF BEING ATTACKED BY HUNTING GROUPS.  NORWEGIAN
        PORTS OF ARRIVAL WILL BE GIVEN LATER.
                0253/13/5/45++++CEL/SMH
        (DEPT. NOTE:  COMPLETE TEXT OF ZTPGU/39067)
```

241

At 0748 hours on 10 May 1945 Liberator VIII serial KK294 of 59 Squadron flown from Ballykelly in Northern Ireland by Flight Lieutenant H.M. March encountered the Type VIIC/41 *U-293* on the surface off the Hebrides about 50 miles north of the island of St Kilda. This U-boat, built by Bremer Vulkan of Vegesack and commissioned on 8 September 1943, had left Narvik on 1 April 1945 under the command of Kapitänleutnant Leonhard Klingspor, for its fourth war cruise. It was flying the black flag of surrender, as ordered by Grossadmiral Karl Dönitz. March signalled visually in German and continued to circle the U-boat until 1300 hours, when relieved by Liberator VIII serial KK416 of 59 Squadron, flown by Flight Lieutenant R.C. Penning, on a photographic sortie.

Ref: AIR 15/142

This photograph was one of a series taken on 10 May 1945 from Liberator VIII serial KK416 of 59 Squadron, flown from Ballykelly in Northern Ireland by Flight Lieutenant R.C. Penning. It shows the Type VIIC/41 *U-293* flying the black flag of surrender, which had been photographed from Liberator VIII serial KK294 of 59 Squadron earlier in the day. This U-boat docked at Loch Ailsh in Scotland on the following day. It was used for target practice by the RAF and finally destroyed by naval gunfire on 13 December 1945.

Ref: AIR 15/142

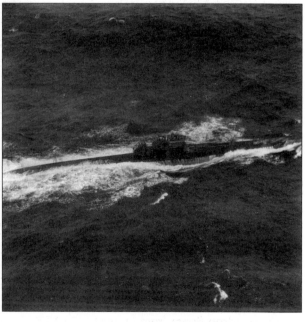

Opposite Top: The Type IXC *U-516*, flying a black surrender flag, was photographed about 275 miles west of St-Nazaire on 10 May 1945 from a Sunderland V of 461 (RAAF) Squadron flown from Pembroke Dock by Flight Lieutenant R.C. Allardice. This U-boat was built by Deutschewerft of Hamburg and commissioned on 10 March 1942. It was returning from its fifth war cruise, under the command of Oberleutnant zur See Friedrich Petran, having sunk sixteen vessels (including an anti-submarine tender) in its career, and damaged another vessel. On 2 January 1946 it was towed from Lisahilly in Northern Ireland to be used as target practice but sank in heavy seas.

Ref: AIR 15/743

This photograph of a surrendering U-boat was taken in the morning of 11 May 1945 by a Wellington XIV of 172 Squadron flown from Limavady in Northern Ireland by Pilot Officer J.N. Wilson. The position was about 150 miles west of the coast of Donegal and the U-boat was heading north. About twenty of the crew were on deck, wearing yellow life-jackets. They identified their U-boat by signal lamp as *U-825*. This was a Type VIIC, built by Schichau of Danzig and commissioned on 4 May 1944. It was on its second war cruise, having sunk one merchant vessel and damaged another in the Irish Sea on its first cruise, under the command of Oberleutnant der Reserve Gerhard Stölker. It had left Bergen on 1 April 1945 under the same command but had sunk no vessels. After its surrender it was towed out of Limavady on 3 January 1946 and sunk by gunfire.

Ref: AIR 15/743

```
ADM (5)                                                    157
    TO: I D 8 G                    ZIP/ZTPGU/39135
    FROM: NS


    8850 KC/S       T O O 1934        T O I 2030/16/5/45


    FROM: BDU OPS
    TO:    U 181, U 195, U 219, U 862


    1) ALLIED G.H.Q. PRESCRIBES THE FOLLOWING FOR U-BOATS LYING IN

    HARBOURS UNDER JAPANESE JURISDICTION:

    A) LEAVE PORT

    B ) AFTER OBTAINING AN OFFING OF MORE THAN 300 MILES REPORT ON

    600 METRE WAVE POSITION TO NEAREST ENGLISH, AMERICAN OR

    RUSSIAN COASTAL W/T STATION AND TO CALL SIGN GZZ  10 ON 16845

    OR 12685 OR 5970 KC/S.

    C) THEN HEAD FOR NEAREST ALLIED HARBOUR OR THE HARBOUR ALLOCATED

    BY THE ALLIED AUTHORITIES. HOIST BLACK FLAG OR PENDANT AND SET

    LIGHTS AT NIGHT. IN THE HARBOURS ORDERED AYXX WAIT FOR FURTHER

    INSTRUCTIONS.

    2) THE GRAND ADMIRAL EXPECTS YOU ALSO TO CARRY OUT, IF AT LLYXX _   158
    ALL POSSIBLE, EVERY INSTRUCTIONS OF THE ALLIES, HOWEVER

    DIFFICULT IT MAY BE FOR YOU. OUR THOUGHTS ARE WITH YOU.


    CC PENULT. LINE READ 'INSTRUCTION'



    1739/17/5/45+EGT/MH+
```

Another instruction issued to all U-boats on 16 May 1945, also from Grossadmiral Karl Dönitz, in order to comply with Allied demands.

Ref: DEFE 3/344

```
ADM (5)                                              191
TO: I D 8 G                ZIP/ ZTPGU/39162          END
FROM: N S

4020 KC/S       T.O.O 0402      T.O.I 0301/24/5/45

FROM: ADMIRAL WEST NORWEGIAN COAST, DUTY OFFICER

TO:   ALL U- BOAT COMMANDERS

MOST IMMEDIATE

    YOU ARE ACTING WRONGLY BY NOT SURRENDERING . YOUR REFUSAL

REPRESENTS A VIOLATION OF OUR SIGNATURE AND OF THE RULES OF WAR.

SERIOUS CONSEQUENCES CAN ARISE FOR YOU AND FOR GERMANY. SURFACE

FORTHWITH AND REPORT YOUR POSITION IN PLAIN LANGUAGE TO

GZZ 10 ON 5970 KC/S OR ON 500 KC/S TO ANY ALLIED COASTAL STATION.

REMAIN SURFACED AND AWAIT FURTHER ORDERS.

1042/24/5/45 EGT/MJU
```

An instruction issued on 24 May 1945 to any commanders of U-boats which had failed to surrender. This was the last signal concerning U-boats decrypted by the Government Code and Cipher School at Bletchley Park.

Ref: DEFE 3/344

Bibliography

Ashworth, Chris, *RAF Coastal Command 1936-1969* (Sparkford: Patrick Stephens, 1992)

Barnett, Correlli, *Engage the Enemy more closely* (London: Penguin, 1991)

Behrens, C.B.A., *Merchant Shipping and the Demands of War* (London: HMSO & Longmans, Green & Co., 1955)

Bohn, Roland, *Raids Aériens sur la Bretagne durant la Seconde Guerre Mondiale* (Tome 1, 1940–1942, Tome 2, 1942–1944) (Etudes et Recherches Thématiques en Finistère et en Bretagne, 1978)

Brown, David, *Warship Losses of World War Two* (London: Arms & Armour, 1990)

Cremer, Peter, *U333* (London: The Bodley Head, 1984)

Enever, Ted, *Britain's Best Kept Secret* (Stroud: Sutton, 1999)

Franks, Norman, *Search, Find and Kill* (London: Grub Street, 1995)

Freeman, Roger A., *The Mighty Eighth War Diary* (London: Arms & Armour, 1990)

Goss, Chris, *Bloody Biscay* (Manchester: Crécy, 1997)

Halley, James J., *The Squadrons of the Royal Air Force & Commonwealth 1918–1988* (Tonbridge: Air Britain, 1988)

Hinsley, F.H. et al., *British Intelligence in the Second World War* (6 vols) (HMSO, 1979–1990)

Hinsley, F.H. & Stripp, Alan, *Code Breakers* (Oxford University Press, 1993)

Hough, Richard, *The Longest Battle* (London: Pan Books, 1986)

Jones, R.V., *Most Secret War* (London: Hamish Hamilton, 1978)

Kaplan, Philip & Currie, Jack, *Convoy* (London: Arum Press, 1998)

Macintyre, Donald, *The Battle of the Atlantic* (London: Batsford, 1961)

Niestlé, Axel, *German U-boat Losses during World War II* (London: Greenhill, 1998)

Philpott, Bryan, *German Maritime Aircraft* (Cambridge: Patrick Stephens, 1981)

Price, Alfred, *Aircraft versus Submarine* (London: William Kimber, 1979)

Rawlings, John D.R., *Coastal, Support and Special Squadrons of the RAF and their aircraft* (London: Jane's, 1982)

Richards, Denis & Saunders, Hilary St G., *Royal Air Force 1939–45* (3 vols) (HMSO, 1953–1954)

Roskill, S.W., *The War at Sea* (3 vols) (HMSO, 1954–1961)

Schoenfeld, Max, *Stalking the U-boat* (Shrewsbury: Airlife, 1993)

Sharp, Peter, *U-boat Fact File* (Leicester: Midland, 1998)

Showell, Jak P. Mallmann, *U-boats under the Swastika* (Shepperton: Ian Allan, 1987)

—— *Enigma U-boats* (Shepperton: Ian Allan, 2000)

Spooner, Tony, *Coastal Ace* (London: William Kimber, 1986)

Stern, Robert C., *U-Boats in action* (Texas: Squadron/Signal Publications, 1977)

Sturtivant, Ray, *British Naval Aviation* (London: Arms & Armour, 1990)

Tarrant, V.E., *The Last Year of the Kriegsmarine* (London: Arms & Armour, 1994)

Terraine, John, *Business in Great Waters* (Ware: Wordsworth, 1999)

The National Archives, *German Naval Signals*, DEFE 3/1 – DEFE 3/744

Thetford, Owen, *Aircraft of the Royal Air Force since 1918* (London: Putnam, 1988)

Von Müllenheim-Rechburg, *Battleship Bismarck* (London: The Bodley Head, 1981)

Welchman, Gordon, *The Hut Six Story* (Cleobury Mortimer: Baldwin, 1998)

Index of U-boats